Police Management Today
Issues and Case Studies

Edited by
James J. Fyfe

International City Management Association

PRACTICAL MANAGEMENT SERIES
Barbara H. Moore, Editor

Police Management Today
Capital Financing Strategies for Local Governments
Creative Personnel Practices
The Entrepreneur in Local Government
Human Services on a Limited Budget
Microcomputers in Local Government
Practical Financial Management
Shaping the Local Economy
Telecommunications for Local Government

The Practical Management Series is devoted to the
presentation of information and ideas from diverse
sources. The views expressed in this book are those of
the contributors and are not necessarily those of the
International City Management Association.

Library of Congress Cataloging in Publication Data
Main entry under title:
Police management today.
   (Practical management series)
   Includes bibliographies.
   1. Police administration—United States—Addresses,
essays, lectures. I. Fyfe, James J. II. Series.
HV7935.P665   1985   352.2'0973   85-155
ISBN 0-87326-044-9

Printed in the United States of America.
91908988878685
54321

Foreword

Today's police administrator faces challenges on all fronts. Tax limitation measures and a decreased federal presence have reduced the funds available for local government services. Court decisions have increased fears that police officers and their employers will be subject to lawsuits. And all this occurs in a complex environment in which the chief must interact with many individuals and groups whose interests often conflict—a diverse population, the local administration and governing body, the press, departmental managers, and the officers and their labor organization.

Police Management Today provides administrators with information and ideas that can help them meet these challenges. It looks at long-term strategic responses to fiscal stress, provides background and examples for formulating policies governing citizens' complaints, false burglar alarms, high-speed chases, and other issues; looks at operational alternatives in patrol strategies, arrest, and crime prevention; and provides perspectives on such personnel questions as affirmative action, "problem" employees, labor-management relations, and sick time use.

This book is part of ICMA's continuing Practical Management Series, which is devoted to serving the needs of local government managers, department heads, and students for timely information on current issues and problems.

We wish to thank the organizations and individuals who granted ICMA permission to reprint their material and to James J. Fyfe, who organized and compiled the volume. Thanks also go to David S. Arnold, who was of great help in planning the entire Practical Management Series.

William H. Hansell, Jr.
Executive Director
International City
   Management Association

Police Management Today: Issues and Case Studies

The International City Management Association is the professional and educational organization for chief appointed management executives in local government. The purposes of ICMA are to strengthen the quality of local government through professional management and to develop and disseminate new approaches to management through training programs, information services, and publications.

Managers, carrying a wide range of titles, serve cities, towns, counties, and councils of governments in all parts of the United States and Canada. These managers serve at the direction of elected councils and governing boards. ICMA serves these managers and local governments through many programs that aim at improving the manager's professional competence and strengthening the quality of all local governments.

The International City Management Association was founded in 1914; adopted its City Management Code of Ethics in 1924; and established its Institute for Training in Municipal Administration in 1934. The Institute, now known as the ICMA Training Institute, provides the basis for the Municipal Management Series, generally termed the "ICMA Green Books."

ICMA's interests and activities include public management education, standards of ethics for members, the *Municipal Year Book* and other data services, urban research, newsletters, *Public Management* magazine, and other publications. ICMA's efforts for the improvement of local government management—as represented by this book—are offered for all local governments and educational institutions.

About the Editor and Authors

James J. Fyfe is an associate professor at The American University, College of Public and International Affairs, School of Justice, Washington, D.C., and a senior fellow of the Police Foundation. He was a New York City police officer for sixteen years, and left that agency with the rank of lieutenant. He holds a B.S. degree from the John Jay College of Criminal Justice, City University of New York, and earned his M.A. and Ph.D. degrees from the School of Criminal Justice, State University of New York at Albany.

Following are the affiliations of the contributors to *Police Management Today* at the time of writing.

Ralph A. Bailey, Personnel/Employee Relations Director, Monterey, California

Sandra Baxter, School of Justice, The American University, Washington, D.C.

Erik Beckman, Assistant Professor, School of Criminal Justice, Michigan State University, East Lansing, Michigan

Richard R. Bennett, School of Justice, The American University, Washington, D.C.

Richard A. Berk, Professor of Sociology, University of California, Santa Barbara, and Director, Social Process Research Institute

Gary E. Brown, Chief of Police, San Clemente, California

W. E. Eastman, Chief of Police, Pleasanton, California

Terrence L. Ellis, Assistant City Manager, Monterey, California

Paul G. Graupmann, Patrol Officer, Shelby Township Police Department; Chairman, Shelby Township Police Patrolmen's Association Bargaining Team; and Chairman, Shelby Township Police and Fire Pension Retirement Board, Utica, Michigan

Charles H. Levine, Senior Specialist in American National Government and Public Administration, Congressional Research Service, Washington, D.C.

Robert E. Lovell, Lieutenant, Danbury Police Department, Danbury, Connecticut

Candace McCoy, member of the Ohio bar and doctoral student in jurisprudence and social policy, University of California, Berkeley

Deborah D. Melancon, Lieutenant, Dallas Police Department, Dallas, Texas

Jack Pearson, Commission on Accreditation for Law Enforcement Agencies and senior labor relations officer, California Department of Personnel Administration

Steven D. Rittenmeyer, Associate Professor, Law Enforcement Administration Department, Western Illinois University, Macomb, Illinois

Hillary M. Robinette, Special Agent, Management Science Unit, FBI Academy, Quantico, Virginia

Lawrence W. Sherman, Vice President, Police Foundation, and Associate Professor of Criminology, University of Maryland, College Park, Maryland

Walt H. Sirene, Special Agent, Management Science Unit, FBI Academy, Quantico, Virginia

Contents

Introduction   1
James J. Fyfe

PART 1
Police Management Today

The Metamorphosis of a Police Executive   11
Gary E. Brown
Strategic Management   22
Charles H. Levine

PART 2
Emerging Standards of Police Performance

**National Accreditation: A Valuable Management
Tool**   45
Jack Pearson
**National Accreditation: A Costly, Unneeded Make-Work
Scheme**   49
W. E. Eastman
**Lawsuits Against Police: What Impact Do They Really
Have?**   55
Candace McCoy
Vicarious Liability: Legal Myth and Reality   65
Steven D. Rittenmeyer
Reviewing Citizens' Complaints Against Police   76
James J. Fyfe
**Police Agency Handling of Citizen Complaints: A Model
Policy Statement**   88
Police Executive Research Forum
High-Speed Chases: In Pursuit of a Balanced Policy   99
Erik Beckman

PART 3
Operational Considerations

**The Newark Foot Patrol Experiment: Executive
Summary**   109
Police Foundation
False Alarms: Do We Cope or Control?   113
Robert E. Lovell

The Minneapolis Domestic Violence Experiment 118
Lawrence W. Sherman and Richard A. Berk
**Police and Community Participation in Anti-Crime
Programs 132**
Richard R. Bennett and Sandra Baxter

PART 4
Personnel Management

Affirmative Action in Police Organizations 149
Candace McCoy
Management: Labor's Most Effective Organizer 162
Walt H. Sirene
Forced Arbitration: Why Cities Worry 171
The Police Problem Employee 181
Hillary M. Robinette
**Permanent Shifts vs. Rotation Shifts: Sick Time Use
Among Police Officers 194**
Paul G. Graupmann
**Healthy Police Officers Are Cost-Effective Police
Officers 201**
Terrence L. Ellis and Ralph A. Bailey
Quality Circles: The Shape of Things to Come? 207
Deborah D. Melancon
Quality Circles: Policy and Procedures 212
Orlando Police Department

Introduction

James J. Fyfe

Managing the police becomes more challenging with the passage of time, because new problems arise much more quickly than the old ones are solved. Many people are trying hard to address both old and new police problems, and this book is an attempt to provide administrators with information about their progress.

The book includes contributions from both scholars and practitioners. They generally report on successful innovations in police policy and practice, but they tell us also about failures. Both sets of information are important, because if we are to advance the state of the art of police management, we must know about new ideas or responses to new crises that have not worked.

Part 1 of this volume is given over to two issues of particular concern to municipal and police administrators during this period of tight budgets: leadership, and thinking about the future while we deal with the problems of today.

No individual is more vital to the success of a police agency than its chief. The chief's philosophies, policies, and priorities directly influence the actions of police field personnel, and the chief's ability to work with local officials and with the community determines the extent to which he or she is able to implement his or her ideas of what good policing is all about. The chief must be at once decisive and responsive; must balance the needs and demands of several constituencies—a diverse population, the local administration, the governing body, the press, departmental managers, officers and their labor organization—whose interests often conflict. If chiefs are to stay on the tightropes they walk, they must master a variety of skills and strategies.

Because these challenges are not easily met, it is appropriate that this volume's first reading offers the lessons of Gary E. Brown's experience as a successful chief executive in three police departments. Brown's observations are sure to be useful to those who hold or aspire to police chief positions, and to those whose work brings them into regular contact with chiefs.

The survival and success of police chiefs affects far more than their individual careers. Many observers have noted that police departments and communities suffer from an absence of systematic long-term planning. One of the major reasons is that traditionally police chiefs have enjoyed only brief tenures. Consequently, they have devoted most of their efforts to responding to immediate crises, and have tended to let their successors deal with developing problems that come to a head only after they leave office. There are encouraging signs that the short-term chief is becoming a thing of the past: at this writing, for example, the chiefs of Kansas City, Newark, Oakland, San Jose, Santa Ana, and Seattle have all thrived in their jobs for several years. Thus, it may be that the strategic police planning advocated and explained by Charles H. Levine may become the norm rather than the exception.

The issues addressed in Part 2 involve police conduct and accountability. The United States is unique among western societies in that responsibility for policing—and for criminal justice administration generally—is widely decentralized. By the best estimates, there are approximately 17,000 American law enforcement agencies. This dispersion of police power helps to assure that local police are accountable and responsive to the communities they serve, rather than to some remote, federal "Big Brother." But dispersion has also created great problems in assuring that there is some degree of consistency in police practices across the country and, in the extreme, that local police honor rights guaranteed by the U.S. Constitution.

One of the most significant recent attempts to strike a balance between national control of police and the potential chaos of 17,000 different sets of police philosophy and practice is the movement to accredit police departments that adhere to minimal standards of police conduct, as determined by representatives of the major national police management associations. At this writing, the Commission on Accreditation for Law Enforcement Agencies has certified that five agencies conform to the standards described by these organizations, is surveying 36 additional police departments, and has applications from another 130 departments seeking accreditation.

Thus, accreditation has become a reality. Some argue that this is a good thing, and that it will further police professionalism and result in a general improvement in the quality of local police service. Jack Pearson takes that position. Others, like W. E. Eastman, do not agree: he suggests that accreditation is a step in the wrong direction, and a threat to the independence of local jurisdictions and their police.

Other attempts to assure that police conduct conforms to constitutional standards have been undertaken by the federal judiciary. The Supreme Court's giant step along this line took place in 1978, when the Court extended liability for civil rights violations in *Monell* v. *Department of Social Services*. In that decision, the Court ruled that municipal employers could be held liable for constitutional violations committed by their employees if plaintiffs could demonstrate that the deprivations involved were a result of official custom and practice.[1] This case has opened the "deep pocket" of municipal treasuries to civil rights attorneys and their clients and, as the Court anticipated, has almost certainly increased the number of civil rights suits against police officers and their employers. It has also increased greatly the anxieties of mayors, city managers, city attorneys and comptrollers, and police chiefs.

Two articles discuss the effects on policing of *Monell* and the cases that have followed it. Candace McCoy suggests that court interventions have had a positive effect on police custom and practice, and Steven D. Rittenmeyer clears up some of the ambiguities and wrongful interpretations of these cases.

Civilian participation in review of complaints against police is another means of holding police accountable for their actions, which is proposed far more often than it is implemented. In an article on this subject, I discuss some of the reasons that civilian complaint review boards have not been widely adopted and suggest that taking administrative steps to ensure the integrity of the process of investigating and disposing of charges against officers is more important than simply changing the composition of the reviewing bodies. In the following chapter, the Police Executive Research Forum, a membership organization of police chiefs who serve populations of more than 100,000, presents its model policy for handling citizen complaints against officers.

As *Monell* and subsequent cases have made clear, however, it is not acceptable for police agencies to limit their attempts to control police conduct to after-the-fact investigations of charges brought by citizens who feel that they have been wronged. Those who manage police agencies are also obliged to do everything possible to *prevent* reckless or wrongful conduct by officers.

Certainly, state and local laws exert some influence on police field behavior. But most laws concerning police behavior are vague; they are not tailored to the needs of individual police jurisdictions; and they leave much to the discretion of individual officers. Police must exercise discretion, but the nature of their work demands that they make critical decisions in hurried and emotional circum-

stances. Since hasty decisions are often repented at leisure, both police and public are best served by meaningful guidelines that give
officers as much help as possible in their street judgments.

Erik Beckman's contribution illustrates that point. Few, if any,
state laws provide meaningful instructions to officers for dealing
with motorists who have committed traffic infractions or other violations and who flee from police attempts to stop them. These are
trying situations for officers. They know that they are obliged to
enforce the law and apprehend violators; but should they do so at
any cost? We have learned from hard experience that many high-
speed police pursuits begin when a young traffic violator panics at
the sight of a revolving police light in the rearview mirror. On too
many occasions these youths—who are often unskilled and unli-
censed drivers—lead officers on reckless chases that endanger everybody in the vicinity, and that sometimes result in tragedy.
Beckman discusses the need for internal police administrative policies to guide officers' conduct in such situations.

Current issues of concern to police field commanders are examined in Part 3. During the last several decades, we have generally
provided the "cop on the beat" with a patrol car. Consequently, the
officer has been able to cover more ground and to respond more
promptly to calls for service. But there is a downside to this mobility. Officers in cars usually meet the people they serve only when
they are in crisis—when they have been victimized, have had vehicle
accidents, or have committed traffic violations. Because these officers do not interact with citizens under more "normal" circumstances, they sometimes view them only as complainers and violators and become estranged from them. The citizens, on the other
hand, often view officers as individuals who are never around when
needed, but who invariably appear on the spot at the wrong time.
Every experienced police officer has often heard two refrains:
"Where were you when the burglars were in my house?" and "But I
was only double-parked for a few seconds."

In recent years, several police departments have taken steps to
improve the relationship between patrol officers and their constituencies by putting officers "back on the beat" rather than assign
them to car patrol. In Newark, New Jersey, the results of such an
effort were formally evaluated by the Police Foundation, and the
executive summary of the foundation's report is presented here.

Like the technology of the patrol car and the police radio, other
scientific advances have helped crime control efforts, but have created some headaches. One of the most severe of these is caused by
the burgeoning electronic alarm industry, which is largely unregu-
lated, and which frequently produces systems of inferior quality. As
a result, false alarms of burglary and robbery have become a major
drain on the police. David Johnston of the *Los Angeles Times*, for
example, recently calculated that his city's police department spent

more money on responding to faulty alarms than on homicide investigations.[2]

The dilemma of Los Angeles is not unique. In city after city, electronic burglar alarms are needlessly activated and send recorded messages to police emergency communications systems requesting immediate response. Worse, these telephone messages are often repeated every few minutes until the alarm systems are deactivated. Thus, when property owners cannot be easily located (e.g., when alarms in commercial premises are triggered on long weekends when owners and all their employees are away), police emergency lines may be tied up for days while these cheap marvels of the electronic age redial police headquarters and repeat their taped messages.

Robert E. Lovell recounts the manner in which the Danbury, Connecticut, Police Department documented its alarm problem and proposed and drafted a city ordinance designed to control the electronic chaos that plagued his department. His experience is worthwhile reading for any administrator faced with this problem.

A longer-term nightmare for police has been domestic violence. This form of criminality is, obviously, a far greater problem for its victims than it is for police; but the assignment most dreaded by almost every police officer is a command to respond to a report of a fight in a home. For generations, police—with much public encouragement—have treated such calls as special cases, and have generally attempted to mediate differences between combative family members rather than to effect arrests, even when criminal assaults have been committed. This approach has generally been based on the theory that what goes on in the home is a private matter, to which police intervention provides no solution.

This theory has recently been challenged by those concerned with the alarming incidence of wife-battering and other forms of family violence. They point out that the *laissez-faire* approach to domestic assaults deprives victims of the protection to which they are entitled, and may even encourage further violence on the part of those who learn that the police are reluctant to take formal action against them.

Lawrence W. Sherman and Richard A. Berk report on a study in which police responses to domestic violence were experimentally manipulated by the Minneapolis Police Department and the Police Foundation. Their results are provocative, suggesting that the best police response to domestic violence may be the most formal: to arrest and prosecute those who assault their families in the same manner that they arrest those who commit criminal assaults outside the home.

Another important aspect of the relationship between police and community involves citizen participation in crime prevention efforts. We have recently come to see that it is more advisable for the police to enlist the aid of citizens in this effort than to go it alone; crime is a community problem, and all quarters of the community should be encouraged to take part in crime prevention. Richard R. Bennett and Sandra Baxter discuss police attempts to obtain community participation in crime prevention programs. As their work indicates, few systematic evaluations of these programs have been undertaken. The studies that do exist, however, suggest that we must take care to determine whether citizens' fear of crime is grounded in fact; often, those who are least likely to be victimized are the most fearful. As a result, they alter their lifestyles, and, consequently, the quality of life in the communities in which they live and work declines.

Part 4 treats issues concerned with the management of police departments' most valuable and most expensive resource: people.

Candace McCoy discusses problems encountered in determining whether affirmative action plans will be regarded by the courts as reasonable and legal. The questions she takes on are not easy and, in an addendum, she considers also the probable effects on affirmative action programs of a major recent Supreme Court decision.

How to provide equal job opportunity and how to structure police agencies so that their personnel are reasonably representative of the populations they serve are not the only dilemmas facing police personnel managers. Walt H. Sirene tells us that the most single-mindedly militant police employee organizations are likely to develop in a management void. Using actual experience to illustrate his points, he describes management philosophies, strategies, and skills useful in avoiding confrontational police management-labor relations.

One of the major goals of many police labor organizations is contract resolution through forced arbitration. From a management perspective, forced arbitration should be avoided at all costs because it involves the surrender of "a major portion of a city's budget . . . to a non-elected third party." An article on this subject details the experiences of six California cities whose charters oblige them to engage in forced arbitration with police and/or fire departments.

If it is true that "there is one in every crowd," it follows that there is *somebody* the chief would love to lay off in almost every police agency. Hillary M. Robinette defines the police problem employee: the marginal performer who is capable, but who does only enough to get by. There really is no place in public agencies for such employees, and it is tempting simply to fire them. This solution, however, is often made impossible by civil service law. Further, when it is possible, it may be (to use a very bad pun) merely a cop-out that does not address the causes of marginal police performance. What is accomplished when a poor performer is dismissed and replaced by another capable individual who, perhaps because of poor management practices, quickly loses enthusiasm for police work? Robinette suggest that we are better advised to identify the reasons for marginal performance and attempt to ameliorate them. Those reasons, he acknowledges, may well be peculiar to individual employees, in which case dismissal may be appropriate. In other cases, we may have to look carefully at the organization rather than at the individual to locate the causes of officers' loss of enthusiasm.

For nearly ten years, I worked "around the clock" and rotated tours of duty every week. Because this irregular schedule left my colleagues and me in something akin to a state of chronic jetlag, and because it was very disruptive to our family and social lives, I read Paul Graupmann's study of shift rotation with interest. He reports that permanent shifts may be easier than rotating shifts on officers' health and, consequently, on municipal finances and on those who are required to assure the presence of adequate numbers of officers on the street. Because he analyzed the experiences of only one relatively small police department, his report cannot be considered definitive; but its implications should be of interest to police administrators.

Policing has other negative effects on officers' health. It is a job characterized by long periods of relative inactivity interrupted by unpredictable situations in which officers may suddenly be called upon to use every bit of physical and psychological strength they can muster. Consequently, most police departments make every effort to assure that *new* officers are in excellent condition; but most departments do little or nothing to assure that officers remain fit after they have completed their probationary periods. That may be a disservice to the public and to officers. Officers who have fallen out of physical shape may simply be unable to do their jobs, and may consequently suffer an inordinate number of injuries and illnesses. Terrence L. Ellis and Ralph A. Bailey report on a Monterey, California, program that established mandatory physical fitness standards for in-service officers.

The last two chapters treat an emerging issue in American management. In their quest to increase the quality of their products and services and the satisfaction of their employees, many private corporations have adapted the Japanese "quality circle" to their needs. As Deborah D. Melancon reports, this method of increasing worker self-esteem and participation in organizational decisions has also been successfully adopted by her employer, the Dallas Police Department. Her contribution to this book is important because it details the process by which quality circles became a part of her department's managerial ambience. This method has also been introduced in the Orlando Police Department, and a statement of that department's quality circle policy demonstrates how it can be put into a format suitable for police department manuals.

This volume is not encyclopedic, but its contributors do address some of the most pressing concerns of those responsible for providing police service. In some cases, these concerns are of recent vintage and have arisen because of new technology, shrinking budgets, or changing views about how police personnel should be selected. Other issues discussed in the book have existed for generations; we have long fretted and conjectured about the *best* ways to handle family violence, management–labor relations, citizen participation in crime prevention programs, and issues of police accountability for their conduct, for example.

This volume offers no hard and fast solutions to any of these issues; where police problems, new or old, are concerned, panaceas simply do not exist. Instead, the book is offered as a compendium of some of the best recent thinking and research about some tough police issues. Hopefully, its contributors' work will be useful to others who confront these issues.

1.   436 U.S. 658 (1978).
2.   David Johnston, "Burglar Alarms—False Reports Drain Police Resources," *Los Angeles Times*, August 9, 1982, pp. 1–3, pt. 2.

PART 1

Police Management Today

The Metamorphosis of a Police Executive

Gary E. Brown

This article is intended to provide newly appointed and "would be" police executives with an overview regarding the challenges and problems associated with managing contemporary law enforcement organizations. It focuses on the administrator's relationships with various people and events that may contribute to either his success or demise as a manager. Keep in mind, however, that there are no absolutes; that the same approach won't work in all situations, and that the focus is on political realities rather than academic theory.

What's a metamorphosis?

The title "police executive," of course, refers to the top echelon of a law enforcement agency, whether it be a police chief, public safety director or sheriff. The dictionary defines metamorphosis as "a change of form, structure, or substance; figuratively a noticeable or complete change in appearance, character, circumstances or condition." When someone is promoted from the number two slot in an organization to number one, a significant change does take place. Generally, it's not that noticeable at first, but circumstances change, and if one is uncomfortable in the new role, there may even be a "change in appearance, character, circumstances or condition."

Preparing to become a police chief requires taking a look at the role of the police executive. Unfortunately, existing administrative law offers few, if any, legal definitions as to what a police chief is supposed to do. California Government Code 38630 states, "a police department of a city is under the control of the chief of police." Section 31611 indicates only that "he shall perform such other services as general law and city ordinances require." In essence, the question, "What is a police chief supposed to do?" could be answered, "Whatever the city manager (or mayor) tells him to do."

It's probably more revealing to examine the characteristics of the "ideal" chief of police as highlighted in a recent announcement bulletin for a chief's position in a medium-size California city: "A high-energy self-starter with a work ethic orientation who can delegate, but maintain overall management control; intellectually curious, progressive and open to new ideas; participatory management style, able to share decision-making, but still decisive; proactive, stays ahead of problems and goal-oriented; comfortable in involving himself with the community, and able to use its resources and address its concerns without being political; team player with the city manager and other city administrators; a working knowledge of and skill in line operations and ability to understand the needs of the rank-and-file officers." Analysis of the above characteristics ˅ ill provide a potential candidate insight as to what appointed authorities are looking for in a new police administrator.

Becoming a police chief

The various job announcements for police chief throughout the nation reflect a prevailing educational requirement of a bachelor's degree. A review of resumes for a police chief appointment today reveals a high number of those with master's degrees, and even some with Ph.D.'s. Whether a degree better prepares a person for the position of police chief is not the point; it's sometimes necessary to be "lettered" in order to get through the resume screening.

"Experience required" varies, but generally the notice may read, "three to five years' command experience." Another might require command experience in "a city of similar size." This prerequisite is subject to much debate, as some believe a successful administrator can manage almost any size city, since the "span of control" is generally similar regardless of size. Those who support it feel there is considerable difference in managing a 50-member agency, compared to one of 500.

Internal/external candidates

Often, there's a debate as to whether the appointing authority should stay within the agency or appoint a chief from outside. Generally speaking, the larger the department, the less likely it is to go outside. If it does so, it is generally for one of three reasons: there isn't a sufficient number of "qualified" candidates from which to choose; to obtain a person not constrained by prior agency relations (internal IOUs); or to alleviate the potential for adverse institutional conformity. Philosophically speaking, the community deserves the best person possible for the job, whether he is an internal or external candidate.

The application/resume process

The first obstacle to overcome in the quest for a police administrator's position is the resume review process. Sorting large numbers of resumes often leads to the "three-pile" theory of review. If a person meets the minimum qualifications and appears to be an average candidate, he'll probably be placed in the middle pile. A "borderline" candidate or one who doesn't meet the minimum requirements will probably be placed in pile number three. Those who have advanced degrees, attended reputable colleges, and come from well-known agencies will probably be placed in the first pile. Though this system may not be too objective, and a top-notch candidate may often be overlooked, that's the way it's usually handled in one form or another.

As an aside, when a police chief considers leaving for another chief's position, he should be concerned about confidentiality. When information that the chief is looking for another job comes back to the department, it can have a significant impact on his ability to manage.

Due to the subjective nature of the resume-screening process, the most effective resume is one that is brief, neat and identifies relevant education, work experience and personal data. Also, due to the vast number of resumes received, it might be important to complete a synopsis of your resume and attach it as the cover for the expanded version. An introductory letter that catches their eye, indicates a personal insight to their needs, and highlights "meat and potatoes" is also important.

Match yourself with the city/department

In looking for a police chief position, there are many resources available to help you determine whether you are the right person for the job. Questions to be answered include: What happened to the previous chief? Am I the type they need? Is the process wired? What are the major concerns? How solvent is the city financially? It is also important to let your immediate supervisor know you are being considered for a particular position before he hears it second-hand.

There are three schools of thought when considering employment as a police chief of another agency:

1. If you take over a thoroughly out-of-date organization, whatever contemporary changes you make should make you look good.
2. If the agency is too far gone, with insurmountable problems, you could sink with it if you're not careful.
3. A "living legend" who has the department in tip-top shape and on a continual high will be a hard act to follow.

Executive search

More and more agencies are using executive search as a means for selecting police chiefs. Executive search firms essentially pre-screen the candidates to ensure that only viable applicants are invited for testing. Generally, they develop a list of resource persons whose opinions they value and who, in turn, identify potential candidates. If the same candidate is mentioned several times, it is a good indication that the person is capable of handling the task. The primary reasons for employing executive search firms appear to be: the city manager doesn't have time to conduct an extensive search, and/or there may be political pressure to promote from within. This affords him an alternative by referring to the "experts" in identifying the best candidates available.

Other considerations

Before throwing your hat in the ring, there are certain things you should consider, such as the answer to the question, "What is your management style?" There has been considerable dialogue regarding autocratic and participative styles (X or Y theory), but the real world suggests that the best style is "situational," in which you adapt your management style to the particular organizational environment. Also determine how visible you want to be in the community. Try to determine in advance whether you will fit in with the community.

The new police executive

You can never fully appreciate what it's like to be the head of a police department until you've been one. Newly appointed police executives finally begin to realize the enormous responsibilities they've assumed. As an assistant chief or captain, there was always someone else to accept the final responsibility for the department's action or inaction. The following are only a few of the changing conditions you'll experience upon being appointed chief.

There will be all kinds of rumors about you circulating in the department prior to your arrival. It's important to minimize such apprehension. It's also extremely important, prior to accepting the job, to have a preliminary meeting with the city manager to discuss the rules of the game. Be up-front as to the issues you consider non-negotiable, *e.g.*, ethical standards, organizational authority, etc. Likewise, it's important to identify all the city manager's concerns with the organization; don't let him off the hook by saying, "You assume the position, then advise me." You're going to be evaluated—if not consciously, then subconsciously—on your ability to deal with the problems *he* perceives in the department.

If you're appointed from the outside, another concern may be that you competed against an internal candidate. If that's the case, you'll have to deal immediately with potential conflict in your relationship with the individual, as he is usually in the number two or three slot within the organization. Hopefully, he will be honest enough with himself to recognize that you had no more control over the final decision than he did. To start off on the right foot, express your need for his assistance in making a smooth transition, and let him know that you want to be able to trust him and to rely on his expertise and knowledge of the community/organization.

Department members are going to be concerned as to who you are, so try to minimize their fears of the unknown by advising them of your management style and what your "absolutes" are. Be careful not to build up any unrealistic expectations on their part; if you promise something you can't deliver, it will damage your credibility. Also, be leery of saying too often, "we did it this way" in your former department.

There are two schools of thought about when to implement change. One is to move slowly, as people are not receptive to rapid change. The second theory is that if the problem is significant, make the change now, as your power to effect change may lessen in time. In general, a new police chief should spend the first few months identifying the organization's strengths and weaknesses. However, the most "power" you may ever have will be during your first month or two in office. Initially, people will probably yield to your expertise, based upon the favorable reputation that generally precedes you. However, after you've been there for some time and have alienated a few people, both internally and externally, you may find that even though your authority is the same, the power to implement change has eroded.

Recognize that during your first year in office, you'll probably be constrained by someone else's budget. This gives you the option of throwing up your hands and saying, "I wouldn't have done it that way, but I'm saddled with a budget I didn't prepare." However, after the first year, you'll have to accept the responsibility for your own budget. If your first budget is submitted during the honeymoon period, it will probably be better received than any subsequent one, so use it to your advantage as long as your intentions are noble.

The honeymoon period

The duration of the honeymoon period varies, depending upon the individual and the city he works for. If you are faced with a major problem immediately after being appointed that may result in a conflict with a council member or institute a major discipline, the honeymoon period may be very short.

Initially, you were probably highly received in both the community and the department, especially after you effected your first major cost savings, *e.g.*, reduced overtime by 20 percent. However, when you've had to deal head-on with a city council member, and/or discipline the association president, the perception of you may change dramatically.

Use the first six months to conduct an in-depth analysis of the existing organization. This analysis may help to support future budget justifications, facilitate a needed reorganization, and serve to identify strengths and weaknesses in the department, complete with a list of recommendations for needed change. An inexpensive but time-consuming way to do this would be to interview a cross-section of personnel from the lowest entry-level position to the highest-ranking staff member. In a smaller city, you may want to interview everyone within the organization.

Begin the interview by asking about their personal life, as it is important for them to know someone in authority cares about them as individuals. Then, pose a rhetorical question, such as "With what you know about the organization, if you were appointed police chief today, what would you do?" Quite often, they'll say, "Well, I have a minor concern, but it's really not that important." Always encourage them to share this concern with you; if three or four others mention the same "minor" problem, it's no longer minor. With this simple method, you can quickly identify, categorize and prioritize the most pressing issues.

Depending on the size of the organization, you may want to use an outside consultant to conduct an in-depth management survey. Some of the reasons for using an outside consultant are: a lack of expertise in the organization; not enough time to complete the study; a third party opinion is needed; you want someone else to do the "dirty work"; or you want someone to support your opinion.

Key individuals, groups and events

The following is a partial list of individuals and groups with whom you'll come in contact during your administration. You must know how to deal with them effectively—how to gain their support and avoid their wrath. They can help you look very good or very bad, depending on your interaction with them.

City manager   The most important person affecting the success or failure of a police chief is the city manager. In "strong mayor" cities, it would be the mayor. As mentioned previously, it's important to establish a mutual understanding before your appointment, as you'll never be in a better bargaining position. The city manager probably received very favorable information from the oral board and was told that he should hire you whatever the cost. However, after a few months, perhaps after you've had a disagreement with him or mishandled a problem, he might start wondering if he made the right choice. Your bargaining position has declined considerably.

The city manager can be your most trusted ally or your most feared enemy. Politically speaking, the police chief and the city manager are probably the most sensitive of the municipal executive positions. In some recorded cases, city managers have fired their police chiefs and subsequently seen the chiefs reinstated while they were fired themselves. City managers are justifiably very cautious about who they appoint as police chief.

Above all else, remember to keep the city manager informed. It is embarrassing for the city manager to receive a call from a city council member inquiring about a problem supposedly occurring in the police department when he isn't aware such a problem exists. Unfortunately, some police chiefs feel they can't share all information with the city manager. There may be reasons in some cities, but this should be the exception, not the rule. If you feel concerned about sharing "supersensitive" information with your boss, you probably should be working for someone else.

On occasion, you're going to disagree with the city manager; if it's important enough to argue your position, do so in private. Once the decision is made, accept it. If you take it personally, it will be very apparent.

Utilize the city manager as a political buffer, allowing him to deal with the "politicos." If you make a mistake, be candid about it. It's very difficult to chastise someone after he's already said, "Yeah, I goofed, it's my fault, it won't happen again." The city manager is also concerned about people who bypass him and go directly to an elected official to try to lobby for a particular program. The chain of command principle doesn't end at the police chief.

City council   Good elected officials are highly appreciated. But remember that they are political in nature and have various goals and interests. Police executives should establish an ongoing business relationship with the council; it's more difficult to fire someone you know than someone you don't know. If they know you're married, they've met your wife, and know that your four children go to the orthodontist, they may be less apt to encourage the city manager to dismiss you upon a whim. The primary contact with them should be through the city manager.

Treat all council members equally. If you have information to share with them, do so through the city manager and make sure that each council member gets a copy. If you become politically ambitious, they may see you as a potential threat. As with the city manager, you may debate with them in a professional manner, but don't embarrass them in public. If things are going well, let them take the credit; if things are faltering, accept the blame yourself.

Some of them may remember how you helped prevent them from looking politically foolish.

Department heads   The old saying, "it's lonely at the top," is finally realized when you get there. As police chief, you have few, if any, peers. It's difficult for a police executive to share his self-doubts and inner conflict with the city manager or police captains. The only real peers we have in city hall are other department heads. Sometimes, there are natural barriers between departments—some may resent the police department getting the "lion's share" of the budget and being the last to be cut in lean economic times. It's important to establish a good working relationship with other department heads and not be viewed as a threat to their security.

Your management staff   It is extremely important to establish a mutual feeling of trust and admiration between you and your key staff. Recognize that they may be interested in becoming chiefs themselves and help develop them to perform at that level of responsibility. You must be willing to give them a lot of responsibility and commensurate authority in the operation of the organization. Sometimes you may have to let them do what they want, within reason, even though you may prefer to do it another way. Delegate and hold them accountable.

First line supervisors   The key to a successfully managed police organization appears to depend on whether the sergeants have a management orientation. If we lose management control over the department to police unions, we'll do so in the trenches at the sergeant's level. Sergeants are entry-level managers and should be treated as such by bringing them into the management arena. Include them in staff meetings, listen to them, prepare them to take over the organization when it's their turn. If they are neglected by management, they will naturally remain more oriented to the line.

POA   It is important to establish a positive relationship with the police officer organization, guild or union. You would prefer they deal with any operational problems first through the chain of command, and come to you only if they are unable to resolve the conflict. With this process, you might be able to avoid some formal grievances. Try to obtain their support without establishing any IOUs. They have a vested interest in how the organization is run, but until they are held equally accountable for its success or failure, the police chief still has the final say.

News media   The power of the press is beyond comprehension. Consequently, police chiefs shouldn't enter into a battle with the press unless they can afford to lose. However, the news media can be very supportive of the goals of your administration if you get off on the right foot. The primary objective in dealing with the media is to project an image that you've nothing to hide, that the department is not a "sacred cow," and that you're open to inspection.

Service clubs   Once you've become police chief, everyone will want you to speak to and/or join their particular service club (Kiwanis, Lions, Rotary, etc.). You may want to hold off for a while before you decide which, if any, to join. Some police chiefs won't join any, because they don't want to belong to one group and exclude another. Participation in a service club can be rewarding, both politically and personally, but be sure you pick one that has a luncheon or breakfast meeting, as your uncommitted nights will become very precious to you. Service clubs can serve as a forum to acquaint the community with your programs and gain their moral and financial support.

The budget process   The budget process is hard to identify and difficult to put your finger on, but it is extremely important to be knowledgeable about. First, identify the players and determine their agendas. City managers often feel their performance is judged based upon how much money they can save. The reality is that elected officials tend to look at only one year at a time, focusing on the next election; they tend not to be concerned with long-range planning.

Meet-and-confer   On occasion, a new police chief has difficulty feeling comfortable in the "management" role when it comes time for the meet-and-confer process. When it's time for negotiations involving give-and-take with line officers, a police chief may discover it's difficult to completely cut the cord with the rank and file. It is important for the police chief to keep in tune with the negotiation process to ensure that his management prerogatives aren't traded off during a period in which there is not enough money to go around. More important than anything else, remember that if labor strife takes place between the POA and the city, the police chief is *management.*

Emergency operations   When you become a police chief, it is sometimes difficult to let go of all your involvement in managing operations, especially at a major event or disaster. You must not take over your staff's responsibilities. The police executive in an emergency operation should show up, size up, and ship off.

Promotions/assignments   There are few rewards a police executive can hand out, especially since the rank and file now represent themselves at the bargaining table for "bread and butter" issues. Police chiefs used to champion for these items, but the responsibility now rests with the police associations. Under the circumstances, making promotions and reassignments assumes greater importance. One thing to remember is to reward only team players. People in the organization must realize that if they are to get ahead, they have to be supportive in carrying out the organization's objectives. In essence, your ability as a manager is judged more on who you promote than anything else you do.

The choice of a prince's ministers is a matter of no little importance; they are either good or not according to the prudence of the prince. The first impression that one gets of a ruler and his (intelligence) is from seeing the men he has about him. When they are competent and faithful, one can always consider him wise, as he has been able to recognize their ability and keep them faithful. But when they are the reverse, one can always form an unfavorable opinion of him, because the first mistake he makes is in making this choice (*The Prince*, Machiavelli).

Votes of no confidence   While votes of no confidence have been around for several years, for the most part they seem to be on the wane. The consequences of a "vote of no confidence" depend upon the rapport you have with your city manager. If you have a good relationship, the city manager is more likely to support your position; if, on the other hand, he doesn't like the way you've been handling matters within the department and has lost faith in your ability, he'll probably use the vote to rid himself of an undesirable police executive.

Occupational hazards   There are many reasons for the turnover rate among police chiefs. There are many obstacles facing police executives today. For example, when Proposition 13 (the "tax revolt") occurred, California police chiefs were encouraged to "consider it a challenge." After five years of "cutback management," it is difficult to remain enthusiastic. Likewise, civil liability concerns continue to heighten. A single split-second act of one police officer working the graveyard shift while you're 500 miles away at a police chiefs' conference may result in punitive damages being assessed against *you*.

Another pitfall for police executives relates to decision-making: if you make the wrong decision too many times, it's fatal. If you *don't* make a decision, you're damned as indecisive. You also are caught between liberals and conservatives who both want to influence police operations.

The trend for the future seems to be toward employment contracts for police chiefs to avoid an improper dismissal. However, if city managers are to have the flexibility to remove an incompetent chief, a fair compromise would be to develop severance agreements providing for a six-month notice and/or severance pay during the period in which one is looking for another job.

Another problem lies in becoming a police chief too early in one's career. Young, would-be police executives who are in their early to mid-thirties and who want to be police chiefs "now" should be content with being number two (or three) for the present and waiting until they're in their mid-forties or older before "taking the plunge." A police executive is expected to be an innovative, dynamic, problem-solving leader, and it's difficult to remain in a high-pressure position such as this over a 20-year period.

Conclusions

The successful police executive of the future must remember the following:

1. Be a stronger leader, but at the same time become more sensitive to the needs of people both inside and outside the organization.
2. Be willing to take a close look at your own organization and the way you presently do things, especially when confronted with scarce fiscal resources.
3. Rely on your ability to "sell" your policies, instead of force-feeding them. No longer can you afford to say, "This is the way we're going to do things, and don't ask why."
4. Be an open, effective communicator with the ability to listen.
5. Set aside the pure models of theory Y/theory X and be willing to adjust your management style to suit your situation.
6. Foster a "team player" image in city hall, letting others know you are not interested solely in the needs of the police to the exclusion of the city's other needs.
7. Be able to use the news media to your advantage.
8. Become a successful negotiator (broker/arbitrator), able to leave a bargaining session with both sides believing they have won without weakening your power and authority.

Strategic Management

————————————————— Charles H. Levine

If the early 1980s was not an easy time for local governments, it was an especially sobering time for their police and sheriff's departments. After a decade or more of unprecedented federal aid and budgetary growth, funding growth came to a halt and in many places actually declined. In the mid 1980s, the growing gap between demand for service and scarce resources has forced many top police managers to rethink their role and the role of their departments in local affairs.

This article is intended to address many of the problems that fiscal stress has posed for police managers and their departments. It presents models for understanding the typical choices most police departments have made to cope with the "resource-demand gap," the consequences of these choices, and what some departments are doing (and more could do) to overcome the most negative effects. In doing so, it argues that problems stemming from fiscal stress require creative and innovative solutions and advocates a "strategic management approach" to revitalization. Such strategic responses require: (1) a multiyear time frame (usually three to five years); (2) a significant reallocation and reconfiguration of resources; (3) substantial changes in organizational structure and work force activity; and (4) a comprehensive as opposed to an *ad hoc* reexamination of the organization's problems, mission, and structure. Changes of this scope suggest that strategic management involves political as well as financial and technical considerations.

To partially substantiate this argument, several data sources

This article is from "Law and Public Affairs," edited by Charles Wise and David O'Brien, a special issue of *Public Administration Review,* © 1985 by the American Society for Public Administration. Forthcoming.

will be used, including the results of a national mail survey to which 92 cities with populations over 50,000 responded. In addition, several of the cities were examined in greater depth through field interviews.[1]

Fiscal stress, police services and "decrementalism"

Police departments in the United States have undergone many changes as a result of fiscal stress. For example:

1. Of the 92 police departments surveyed, 73 indicated that there was a perception of fiscal stress within their cities.
2. Thirty-eight percent of the departments reported having made budget cuts and 72 percent indicated that they had made other changes due to fiscal stress during the 1976–1981 period.
3. About one-quarter of the departments laid off employees, decreased overtime use, or slowed promotion rates.
4. Fifty-two percent of the departments terminated programs in the 1976–1981 period. Most of these terminations were in new services whose funding came largely from federal sources.
5. About one-third of the departments decreased in size.
6. Thirty percent of the departments made major changes in their budget formats and processes.
7. Eighty-eight percent of the departments reported that in 1981 they used call prioritization procedures to ration immediate dispatch as a response to calls for service, up from 56 percent in 1976.
8. Fifty-six percent of the departments reported that they used vehicles that exceeded their "ideal" replacement point and 53 percent reported having other equipment that needed replacement.

While not all of the items were exclusively results of, nor responses to, fiscal stress, taken together they present a picture of agencies grappling with serious resource and cutback problems.

Decremental responses   There is a marked pattern in the way police departments have been coping with fiscal stress. For the most part, they have been balancing their budgets by making marginal adjustments in their operating procedures and expenditures. In doing so, they have been essentially pursuing a strategy of "decrementalism"; i.e., they have made small, short-term adjustments in their operating arrangements that have yielded some cost savings without a corresponding loss of visible operating effectiveness. Examples of such tactics include stretching the use of patrol cars an extra year, marginally thinning out manpower on patrol, and targeting patrol activity more carefully through the use of patrol allocation models.

But many departments have arrived at the point where any additional revenue cuts likely will produce a more than proportional decline in services. The problem now for many police managers is how to live with long-term resource scarcity while protecting their department's capacity to fulfill its core mission. This is no easy problem because there is a strong preference among policymakers for familiar, short-run, incremental, and piecemeal problem-solving methods and an aversion toward viewing retrenchment as a long-term problem requiring large-scale strategic choices.

Furthermore, although decremental strategies usually include some productivity improvements that have potential long-term value to a department, other tactics for stretching resources (such as across-the-board budget reductions, hiring freezes, reduction by attrition, deferred maintenance, and freezing and rationing operating expenses) cause problems that may eventually catch up with the organization if funding is not restored or increased. Over time these problems may become compounded, producing long-run costs that eventually may cause the need for additional expenditures to improve services or prevent serious erosion in the level and quality of services. These problems occur especially when the length and depth of fiscal stress is underestimated or when policymakers act as if resources can be stretched indefinitely. These consequences include:

1. *Human resource erosion*—a decline in the aggregate skill levels of an agency's work force, a decline in its energy, commitment, and physical and mental health, and a concomitant decline in its performance and responsiveness.
2. *Overcentralization*—increased control and clearances at higher and higher levels for smaller and smaller expenditures. If in place too long, such overhead control discourages initiative and stifles innovation throughout the organization.
3. *Allocation shifts*—resources gradually shift to the more powerful service-delivering units in the department (e.g., patrol) and away from the less powerful staff units (e.g., planning and analysis) irrespective of their importance to the long-term effectiveness of the organization.
4. *Decisional paralysis*—the inability of policymakers to make hard decisions about the long-term mission and priorities of the agency because of their disinclination to confront public employees and interest groups with new work rules, service cutbacks, or organizational arrangements. Decisional paralysis is marked by across-the-board cuts and "delay and denial" strategies—i.e., denying that there is a crisis and delaying any major changes.[2]

In the most fiscally stressed jurisdictions, these problems tend to cluster together, threatening to produce a condition called "general service default," when the government is no longer capable of delivering services that either enhance or protect the quality of life of its residents. Such a condition is a particularly critical concern for law enforcement agencies because if they are no longer seen as an effective and benign institution of government that provides security and safety, then alienation, with all its attendant problems of grudging compliance, vigilantism, and middle class flight, is likely to result.

The purpose of describing these consequences of decremental adjustments to long-term fiscal stress is to underscore the point that shortsighted responses eventually will produce departments that are not only smaller and cheaper but also weaker and less vital, and, as a consequence, less able to cope with problems of crime and public disorder. The next section will describe "strategic management," an attractive alternative to decrementalism, that is beginning to be used by some police departments. It is an approach to managing resource scarcity that is fundamentally different from decrementalism but is within the reach of most law enforcement agencies. Above all, a strategic management perspective recognizes that decrementalism at the margins of units and programs does not reflect a realistic assessment of public needs and preferences for services. Instead, a strategic perspective requires top law enforcement managers to develop a clear understanding of what their department's mission and core services are, to prioritize accordingly, and to create administrative arrangements to finance and deliver these services.

The strategic management of police services

Example: The city of Oakland, California, was confronted with the triple bind of an increasing dependent population, rising crime rates, and Proposition 13, which limited the revenues that could be derived from taxes on property built before 1978. But hope is literally in sight as several large, new buildings have been constructed to reshape Oakland's skyline. The problem the city faced was how to provide the perception of a secure environment in the area of new construction within the constraints of a declining budget for the police department. The answer came in the form of a ten-year agreement with developers to provide a fund to pay for a highly visible horse patrol in the downtown area, a stable, trained police dogs, and additional officers. The initial contribution was for $400,000; in the second year they provided $350,000 to continue these activities. The program calls for the fund to rise to approximately one-half million dollars in 1986 and then decrease to zero in 1990. The assumption behind this funding scheme is that by the end of the decade the new economic activity will have increased the tax base enough to absorb program costs.

Example: Unemployment and unpaid property taxes (about 16 percent of the total owed the city) forced the city of Eugene, Oregon, to cope with fiscal stress in two ways: enhance economic development and cut expenditures by laying off city employees. In the police department actual layoffs were minimal, but unfilled vacancies meant that the complement of sworn officers had declined significantly. To make up for this shrinkage, the department recruited, trained, and extensively used (up to 80 hours per month) reserve police officers in a wide variety of roles including patrol work. The result was the maintenance of departmental effectiveness while allowing the city to capture appreciable savings.

Example: The city of South Bend, Indiana, was experiencing extreme economic hardship. The population declined from 130,000 to around 100,000 during the 1970s and unemployment exceeded 15 percent. To facilitate the active involvement of neighborhood groups in crime prevention, the police department decentralized into a "neighborhood team policing" mode, thereby cutting central administrative staff and strengthening the effectiveness of the neighborhood watch program.

These jurisdictions were among the nation's most hard hit by the deep recession of the late 1970s and early 1980s. But in coping with fiscal scarcity their responses and those of their police departments moved beyond simply balancing budgets through short-term decremental means. Instead, they made strategic management choices affecting what services they deliver and the way they are organized to deliver them. In each case, fundamental tradeoffs in police management were considered and eventually made. To date, the result of these changes has been to maintain and enhance the capacity of these departments to serve their constituents despite resource declines.

These examples have been characterized as "strategic" because they involve realigning an organization's resources and skills with the environmental opportunities and risks it faces and the purposes it wishes to accomplish.[3] By encouraging the examination of linkages between governmental and nongovernmental actors, a strategic management perspective encourages police managers to look beyond the police department as their focus of analysis and to view the *direct provision* of police services by the department and its sworn officers as only one of several options for designing law enforcement and crime prevention service delivery systems.

Key assumptions behind strategic management

The idea of a strategic approach to managing fiscal stress in policing depends on four key assumptions:

1. The effectiveness of a management plan depends on "contingency relationships" between the strategy and the situation. For example, deep, long-term resource declines must be met by extensive restructuring of police operations, while short-run, shallow declines can be managed by decremental tactics.
2. Strategic choices require that a department have an appropriate "strategic capacity." For example, a police department cannot develop long-term plans for reallocating its budget without financial forecasting and cost accounting systems.
3. Strategic choices require an examination of a full array of alternative service delivery options. Major cost adjustments are likely to require significant changes in the way police departments deliver services. Options such as shifting service responsibility, contracting for services, user fees, and service co-production need to be given full consideration in designing long-term departmental strategies.
4. Fiscal stress will close some "windows of opportunity" for innovative ideas, but will open others. For example, proposals that promise to save money or generate revenue are likely more feasible than proposals that promise to improve service but may cost more.

Each of these ideas has direct applicability to the management of police departments under conditions of fiscal stress, especially to the effectiveness of strategies that departments choose. To illustrate this point further, the remainder of this section will explore each of the four assumptions in greater detail.

Contingency relationships   In the cities studied, fiscal stress created a crisis for local government and its departments or was managed like a routine budgeting problem. The difference was in whether coping with fiscal stress required radical changes in a department's decision-making processes—and eventually in its operations—or whether the problems that arose from fiscal stress were well within the existing decision-making and operational capacity of the department.

The cutting edge of what constituted a fiscal crisis differed somewhat from city to city and from agency to agency. A number of factors intervened in the relationship between revenue shortfalls and the perception of crisis. Of these, several were especially significant: (1) the authority and will of the top administrative and political officials to cut expenditures; (2) the power of interest groups to protect agencies and services against cuts; and (3) the ability of departments to absorb budget cuts without having to make major downward adjustments in services delivered.[4] In addition to these political and administrative factors, the size of the cut and the time available for planning and adjustment were key factors in determining whether or not fiscal stress produced a fiscal crisis. For example, one-year budget cuts of 7 percent or less (in noninflated dollars) were much less likely to produce a crisis than a cut of greater magnitude. Likewise, the longer the duration of fiscal stress, the more time and experience managers had to create appropriate responses to it. For example, fiscal stress episodes of three years or longer allowed police managers to install new techniques for improving operations such as improved budgeting and cost accounting procedures, prioritization arrangements to screen calls for service, and beat and shift realignments to improve resource targeting. In addition, there was time to change technologies (downscaling the vehicle fleet, for example) and to adjust the size of the work force through attrition. More important, in many communities, long periods of fiscal stress provided evidence to all the political forces in the community that a serious problem had arisen and that no outside

| | Duration of fiscal stress | |
	Short term	Long term
Low	**I. Fiscal crunch** Absorb attrition Hiring and expenditure freezes Defer maintenance Stall payments	**III. Fiscal squeeze** Improve operations management Target overtime Trade off raises and benefits for staff reductions Downscale fleet and contract out peripheral programs
High	**II. Fiscal crisis** Lay off civilians Cancel equipment replacement Close some peripheral programs Reorganize "desk to field ratio"	**IV. Fiscal crush** Use more reserves and volunteers Shed functions Use citizen watches and patrols Extensive contracting out and cooperation with the business community and civic associations

(Severity of fiscal stress)

Figure 1. Types of fiscal stress situations and tactics for coping with them.

"bailout" was likely. As a consequence, a consensus was built about the objective characteristics of the problem and the appropriate means for dealing with it.

The duration of the fiscal stress combines with its severity to create four general types of problems, presented in the typology in Figure 1.[5] The four types are simplifications of many possible combinations. They are presented as "ideal types" so that the range of crisis types and responses can be categorized and narrowed to a few common properties. Of the four types, the situation of low fiscal stress and short duration is the most familiar and the most easily dealt with by police managers. It occurred when a reduction in revenues relative to demands and costs was not especially severe, but happened with little forewarning. Such a "fiscal crunch" may have been caused when a jurisdiction changed its program priorities; or when revenues dropped more than expected because of a sudden change in tax laws (e.g., taxing and spending limits); or when tax revenues declined because of factors such as slumping retail sales, payrolls, or simply because of large amounts of unpaid taxes. In most cases revenue reductions were less than 7 percent over one fiscal year and were often met with budget balancing mechanisms such as the issuing of short-term revenue anticipation notes or with decremental strategies such as freezing unfilled vacancies, reducing overtime, deferring maintenance, and other cost control devices, for instance, increased clearances for equipment replacement that stalled expenditures until the next fiscal year.

The second type of fiscal stress—high severity but short duration—usually was preceded by danger signals (e.g., falling tax collection, inflation, rising short-term debt, year-end budget deficits, etc.) that were either ignored or met by delaying tactics for at least one or two fiscal years so that when the fiscal situation had to be dealt with, the situation had become very severe, requiring cuts in excess of 7 percent or more in one fiscal year.

In these cases the inability of political leaders to come to terms with a growing "fiscal crisis" eventually forced their successors to take drastic action to restore fiscal solvency. In addition to all the tactics employed in minor stress situations, in these cases, short-term fiscal stress required police departments to lay off employees, both sworn and civilian, but especially civilian; cancel equipment replacement; eliminate overtime; terminate some peripheral programs; renegotiate work rules; and reassign headquarters personnel to patrol work (i.e., reorganize the "desk to field ratio").

The third type of stress—low severity but long duration—evolved over a period of at least three to five years. This type of situation occurred in slowly declining communities and also in slow-growing communities where budgets did not keep up with the rate of inflation or increases in demand for service. The effect was a slow "fiscal squeeze" on agency budgets.

In communities that experienced this type of fiscal stress, the opportunity existed to anticipate budget cuts and to plan some appropriate action. For the most part this involved changes in operations and management systems; but some changes also occurred in the size and mission of the local government and its agencies. In police departments, slow squeezes prompted a more "managerial approach" to administering the department at all levels. This involved training, upgrading records management and fleet management, and improving budgeting, financial management, and cost accounting systems. Finally, time allowed "factor substitution" and other innovations to be implemented. For example, the number of police employees frequently was reduced in order to provide raises that at least approximated increases in the cost of living; some user fees for copying reports or for answering false burglar alarms were initiated; vehicle fleets were reduced and downscaled (4- and 6-cylinder engines instead of 6- and 8-cylinder vehicles); overtime was allocated with greater care; and some minor functions were contracted out or reorganized on a regional basis. In short, the long time frame and relatively minor level of stress at any one time allowed many departments to adjust gradually to lower levels of resource consumption without causing a decision-making crisis or major declines in service.

Finally, the fourth type of fiscal stress—deep cuts over a long period of time—was the most difficult to cope with and required the greatest change in organization and services. It occurred in cities which experienced a series of major economic shocks such as the closing of a large plant (with a deep drop in jobs, sales, or population and therefore the tax base), or to the contrary, a rapid rise in demand for services without a concomitant rise in tax revenues (as in the case of some Sunbelt cities or some jurisdictions with restrictive taxing ceilings). In these cases of "fiscal crush," cuts of more than 15 percent of revenue relative to inflation or rising demand over three to five years created the need for police departments to: (1) redefine their mission; (2) realign their service mix; (3) reallocate resources internally; (4) reorganize their internal structure; and (5) redesign means for delivering services (including the creation of new service delivery arrangements with other organizations in the community).

Under these conditions, law enforcement services were significantly affected. Changes included: police encouragement of greater citizen involvement in crime prevention through such means as increasing the responsibilities of neighborhood watches and patrols and crimestopper programs; greater use of reserves and auxiliaries; shedding functions to the private sector ("privatization") and to other units of government (e.g., jails and courts from cities to counties and from counties to states); the use of business and civic groups to fund some services and purchase equipment; and the regional consolidation of some functions. Clearly, extended fiscal stress episodes required major changes in police services and the way they were organized.

The contingency relationships outlined in Figure 1 suggest that some tactics "fit" some situations better than others. It should be recognized, however, that fiscally troubled departments used tactics that were appropriate to more than one of the four situations simultaneously. In general, however, departments chose tactics that were more extreme in impact as their fiscal problems deepened. In other words, departments moved their choice of tactics from the upper left-hand corner of the typology in Figure 1 toward the lower right-hand corner in order to meet the full range of contingencies produced by deep and extended episodes of fiscal stress.[6]

It is important to note that as fiscal stress deepened, many possible solutions to long-term fiscal stress which at first appeared to officials to be too radical later proved to be workable. For example, local governments and police departments began to give greater attention to the mix of services they delivered. Such analysis increased the possibility of finding services that were amenable to termination or "load shedding" onto the private and nonprofit sectors or other units of government. The consequence of these changes has been to create governments of narrower scope that perhaps will be more fiscally solvent in the future.

Strategic capacity   One of the most significant issues confronting police departments trying to cope with fiscal stress is the capacity of their management systems to design and implement strategies. The strategic capacity of a department also has a contingency quality; i.e., departments do not build sophisticated management systems unless they expect to confront complex problems. It makes little sense to set up an exhaustive checklist of ideal management tools for a department with few problems, where citizens demand little in the way of services, or where resources are ample. The tools must fit the task. If a rather rudimentary set of management systems serves a community now and in the foreseeable future, then spending time, money, energy and political capital upgrading them simply may not pay off. If, however, problems arise that cannot be handled by the old machinery, then a reassessment and redesign of the department's problem-solving capacity is in order. In short, the key question for determining the appropriate strategic capacity for a police department is: What is the ability of this department to meet its current problems and what additional capacity will it require to meet probable future contingencies?[7]

This definition of "appropriate strategic capacity" relates directly to the problem of coping with fiscal stress and, if need be, retrenchment. Earlier research found that given equal levels of fiscal stress, some cities and agencies managed their stress and retrenchment far better than others.[8] Those cities and agencies which adjusted best to deep and protracted levels of fiscal stress were able to:

1. Formulate and stick to a strategic plan with a multiyear time frame of three to five years (in other words, had a "strategic management capacity")
2. Develop a political and administrative climate conducive to the creation of an "experimenting polity" (that is, they created a governmental situation where citizens, clients, public employees and political officials were willing to try new methods for delivering traditional services).

Without the capacity to plan and implement strategic responses and engage in experiments and innovations in methods of service delivery, cities and police departments are likely to fall victim to all the short-term hazards and pitfalls of decrementalism, and consequently service quality and quantity are bound to deteriorate as budgets contract.

What are the attributes—functional components—of a strategic management capacity that police departments will need to meet the problems of fiscal stress successfully? Based on recent empirical studies of cities confronting fiscal stress, the following nine functions appear to be preconditions for managing fiscal stress successfully:

1. Forecasting and planning capacity
2. Decision-making authority
3. A management philosophy to define the department's future
4. Rapid and accurate feedback
5. Budgetary flexibility
6. Performance incentives
7. Ability to identify core services
8. Ability to target resources to high-priority programs and cuts to low-priority programs
9. Ability to link service and expenditure decisions to economic development strategies.[9]

Without these elements, the process of adaptation to problems of fiscal stress will likely be both confused and painful. To underscore this point, two of these preconditions will be explored in greater depth: management philosophy and the linkage between services and expenditures and economic development.

Management philosophy   A management philosophy is an indispensable aspect of strategic management. In the case of law enforcement this involves a way of thinking about *local* crime problems, citizen expectations, and the future development of the community. Such a philosophy supports consistency and multiyear strategies so a retrenchment plan can unfold over several budget cycles without confusion, backtracking, and changes of direction. Lack of such a philosophy, in contrast, breeds uncertainty among middle managers and employees who are needed to carry out the strategy. When there is rapid turnover in police chiefs, elected officials, or other top managers, or vacillation in management philosophy, there is always the possibility that subordinates will delay implementing the plan in order to be sure the new managers support both the intent and the content of the strategy. These delays can accumulate into a period of general immobility, creating a financial or service delivery crisis of major proportions.

Linking services and expenditures to economic development
Some services have a greater effect on attracting and retaining taxpayers than others, and some levels of taxation will have different effects for encouraging or discouraging the inward and outward mobility of taxpayers from a community.[10] All agencies of local government must have at least a rough idea of these relationships in order to protect and enhance their community's economic base. Without an understanding of these linkages, a local government may make policy choices that are self-defeating, whose net effect is to worsen the fiscal situation of the community.

One clear example of this linkage has already been cited in the case of the Oakland Police Department working with local developers to provide a highly visible mounted patrol in a downtown redevelopment area. By providing such a patrol, the department *directly* increased the likelihood that the redevelopment project will be successful or at least will not fail because potential patrons fear for their safety.

This example shows that some cities and police departments have been able to develop their strategic capacity well enough to allow the planning of integrated strategic responses to fiscal stress on a multiyear basis.

Service delivery alternatives   From a strategic perspective, the main task of police management is thinking through the mission of the police department and designing an organizational system to accomplish that mission. Part of this strategic planning activity is the systematic identification of opportunities and risks that lie in the future as well as the tools to exploit these opportunities and avoid these risks. What strategic management means in this context is the activity of designing a desirable future for a community and identifying methods for bringing it about.

In police management there has been a tendency to put too much emphasis on daily operations by maximizing patrol and investigations and not to devote nearly enough concern to defining the appropriate scope, quality and levels of police services. In short, too much attention has been devoted to tactics and the fine tuning of police operations within the traditional framework of police management and the questions of grand strategy—mission, design and service delivery options—have largely been ignored.

Perhaps the most important message to be derived from a strategic management perspective on policing is that *a variety of institutional arrangements can be used for providing police services.* This is the case even though in most cities law enforcement functions are commonly provided by a municipal police department organized into a closed system of complex rules, procedures, and positions. This form of organization, called "direct service provision," is taken as a given in most jurisdictions. It implicitly accepts as fact that: (1) the advantages of a bureaucratic form of organization (i.e., reliability, political neutrality, fiscal integrity, and technical rationality) outweigh the advantage of alternative arrangements; and (2) the "proper" way to organize public services is for public employees to be seen as the *producers* of public services and the citizens to be viewed as *consumers* of these services. However, in the past few years local government officials have begun to question both of these assumptions. As a consequence, changes in the way services are organized and delivered are taking place in many localities and others have begun the process of reassessing their service delivery arrangements.[11]

These activities recognize that outside of the decision of whether to provide a service at all, the most important strategic choice in urban management involves methods of service provision. Shulman observes: "To *provide* service is to decide that a service shall be made available and to arrange for its delivery. . . . To *deliver* a service, on the other hand, is to actually produce the service. Although a local government may decide to provide a service, it does not necessarily have to be directly involved in its delivery."[12] Furthermore, services can be provided in communities in several other ways even if the local government does not provide it. A particular service may be provided by another local government (a special district or a county), by a nonprofit agency (United Way), or simply by the private sector, thus eliminating the need for the local government to get involved at all. Even though these choices may have significant political and equity implications, it is appropriate for now to point out that the major alternatives to direct service provision used by police departments in the United States (shedding service responsibility to other service providers, contracting for service, franchising, intergovernmental agreements, voluntary service, and individual and neighborhood self-help) are gaining increasing popularity as solutions to some of the problems caused by scarce resources.

It is important to note that most police services are unlikely to be totally shed. Their long tradition, strong constituency, and the legal monopoly of police departments in law enforcement assure that most police services will continue to be considered central to city government.[13] This helps to explain why the services that police departments have shed or privatized so far can generally be classified as peripheral to the department's core mission.

Innovation opportunities   The final key attribute of a strategic management approach concerns the feasibility of innovation. The previous sections have argued that when confronting fiscal stress most public managers—including police chiefs—have been either passive or reactive, preferring decremental tactics to large-scale innovative solutions. But if fiscal stress deepens, passive or reactive responses and decremental tactics eventually lead to decline in service levels and quality. In order to avoid this outcome, managers must search beyond *conventional* policy options (i.e., methods of stretching resources) to explore nontraditional service delivery approaches. Such a search forces managers to view service delivery in a new light because relying on traditional methods is no longer possible without incurring a loss of service. Managers searching for new ways to provide services are likely to be cross-pressured by the demand from citizens and elected officials to *do something* and the high risks (e.g., job, career, lost opportunities, etc.) of carving out very scarce resources to try something new. At a minimum the search for a resolution to these pressures is likely to push police managers toward innovations that strengthen the management system. In their review of the effects of fiscal contraction on innovation in the public sector, Walker and Chaiken identify five types of management innovations that appear likely to succeed in time of fiscal constraint.[14] They include:

1. Low-cost innovations—innovations with high initial costs are unlikely to be tried no matter how persuasive advocates of cost saving projects might be. "Innovations that have low continuing cost and yield substantial improvements in efficiency will . . . be likely to gain sufficient support for implementation."
2. Revenue generation—innovations that promise to generate revenue are likely to gain ready acceptance. Such innovations include computer software packages that facilitate collecting revenue such as fines, parking tickets and user fees as well as

"imaginative legal or institutional restructuring that allows for collection of new fees."

3.   Effective budgeting tools—innovations likely to be implemented give clear answers to such questions as: How much will be saved by a specific budget cut? Who will be affected? What will the consequences be? Such budgetary tools will likely conform more or less to the principles of zero-base budgeting.

4.   Resource allocation packages—innovations that rationally allocate resources by need or demand such as patrol allocation models and call screening schemes are likely to be found attractive during periods of resource contraction. Such models are especially attractive to departments and jurisdictions attempting to minimize the negative consequences of budget cuts. Such departments and jurisdictions want to have scientific-looking documentation (i.e., computer printouts) showing that they did the best they could under the circumstances.

5.   Innovations that confer relative advantage on an agency— innovations that are likely to be accepted because they convey advantage to an agency in budget battles and other turf struggles. Such innovations provide meaningful management information about productivity, workloads, and priorities that allow a department with well-documented charts and graphs to fare better in relative budget allocations than agencies whose demands are undocumented.

Clearly, the opportunity available for innovation during fiscal contraction is not great, but it does not disappear altogether. The need to stabilize funding and staffing levels; remove position and promotion freezes; replace equipment and reward good performance in order to improve morale, productivity and effectiveness induces top managers to search for innovations in organizational and management structures suitable for both smaller size and re-vitalization.

Conclusion
The main challenge confronting police managers who must cope with the squeeze between rising demand and costs and stable or declining budget and work force is how to maintain organizational effectiveness. As we have seen in the preceding sections, in the long run their response likely will have to include changing the way things are done—including the way they *think* about problems and solutions.

Another way to illustrate this point is presented in Figure 2. The structure of police departments is broken into four levels of

Levels of analysis	Traditional approaches	Nontraditional approaches
Operations	Case management (tighten productivity)	Case prioritization (differential response)
Programs	Program prioritization (core vs. periphery)	Alternative service delivery arrangements (contracts, interjurisdictional agreements, volunteers, cooperation)
Intraorganizational structure	Emphasize cost control (audits and clearances)	Emphasize capacity building (financial analysis and human resource development)
Organization–environment relations	Minimize interdependencies (reduce cooperative arrangements)	Network leadership (arrange combinations of interorganizational agreements)

Figure 2. Traditional and nontraditional approaches to managing fiscal stress.

analysis—operations, programs, intraorganizational structure, and organization–environment relations. Traditional, primarily internal approaches to managing fiscal stress are categorized in the center column and nontraditional, primarily external responses are listed in the right-hand column. Throughout, it has been argued that as episodes of fiscal stress deepen, strategies must shift from the traditional to the nontraditional and from operational tactics to realignment of the organization's relationship to its environment.

The movement of strategies from traditional (primarily internal) to nontraditional (primarily external) responses is hardly automatic.[15] It depends on a combination of leadership and political factors, and most important, learning how to ask the "right" questions about the department's environment, its mission and its administrative capacity (see the example on pages 38 and 39).

The central task for many police chiefs in the 1980s will be to make their departments adapt to diminishing resources and to revitalize them once the initial shock of cutbacks has ended. To do that, it is necessary to develop a new "strategic image" of the organization that defines what it will look like in the near-term future, what it will be doing, and how it will be doing it. Such an image specifies the department's purposes, plans, programs, size and resources. It fixes the balance between resources and programs into the future and describes how to reach this new arrangement. Thus, the strategic management process will involve an iterative analysis; that is, a series of comparisons between the resources required to operate proposed programs and a realistic assessment of what political and managerial actions will be necessary to fund and implement them.[16] In doing so, top managers are bound to address one of

---

Asking the right questions in Alexandria, Virginia

The city of Alexandria, Virginia, police department does not do comprehensive strategic planning, but has developed a set of attitudes and the administrative capacity to ask—and answer—questions that indicate a sensitivity to issues of strategic importance.

Alexandria is a wealthy city of approximately 100,000 which has undergone an extensive renewal and revitalization in the last 20 years. The average home in its downtown renewal area sells for around $175,000 and its minority and low income populations have decreased as the city has become "gentrified" by white upper middle class residents. In 1983, Alexandria's crime rates reached their lowest point in ten years, with crime against property continuing to decline (because of "target hardening" by property owners and a campaign against career criminals) and violent crimes rising only slightly.

In this kind of environment one might think that there is little need to think strategically about crime prevention and law enforcement services. But the Alexandria city council and some taxpayers groups remain vigilant about the cost of police services. As a consequence, the police department has taken the initiative in addressing several major questions about the department's operations and future activities. For example:

What will be the impact of economic development on the criminal justice system? How are crime rates likely to change as land in the city is converted to new uses?

- In 1979 and 1980, the city participated with neighboring jurisdictions in Northern Virginia in a "Criminal Justice Impact Assessment" (CJIA) project sponsored by the Law Enforcement Assistance Administration (LEAA).
- The police department reviews special use permits so that people with training in crime resistance work can advise developers in methods of "target hardening" to minimize the potential for criminal activity.

How can police activities be related to overall city government initiatives?

- Alexandria is in the process of consolidating the administration of its public safety functions (i.e., police, fire, administrative services, sheriff, etc.) under a public safety director who will become part of the city manager's cabinet: the first time public safety functions have been represented there.

---

the key questions of strategic management: *Is there another way of delivering this service that is better or costs less than the way we have been doing it?*

In those communities that have grappled with this question, new ideas have come forward that have resulted in entirely new

---

What do services cost to deliver and what level of service is cost effective?

- Alexandria has developed an effective computerized cost analysis technique that can be used to cost services. Among the uses of this scheme are: (1) to price services that are or might be fee reimbursable (e.g., false burglar alarms); (2) to identify the cost of new development projects so that the additional costs of policing can be returned to the city through taxes and fees paid by the developer and residents; and (3) to show city officials graphically and defensibly what changes in service levels and directions actually will cost.

How does the department identify and develop its human resources capacity?

- Alexandria contracts with a professional assessment testing agency to conduct an assessment center to identify and select officers for promotion from the rank of corporal to police captain.
- The department developed an extensive program in leadership development and supervisory training with heavy emphasis on dealing with real life problems supervisors routinely face on the job (e.g., a poorly performing employee, pilferage, terminating an employee, etc.).
- The department will soon have a personnel performance and evaluation system in which managers and officers will receive pay raises on the basis of their setting goals and objectives and accomplishing them. In this system there will be no automatic pay raises. Managers will be evaluated on their performance, officers on the accomplishment of their unit's objectives.

How do we get citizens involved in the crime prevention and law enforcement process?

- Alexandria has developed and actively maintains an extensive and effective system of neighborhood watch and crime prevention activities.

These are but a few of the questions and answers that the police department in Alexandria is addressing. While not specifically related to the issue of managing fiscal stress, they do point in the direction of strategic management and suggest steps that might be taken by other departments. Furthermore, in the unlikely event that Alexandria faces the need to retrench, it will already have all the pieces in place to carry out cutbacks with the least damage to the department's capabilities.

public and private linkages requiring a substantial modification of relationships between line command arrangements *within* the department and the service delivery *outside* the department. As this process has developed, the structure of public organizations—including police departments—has begun to be transformed from a tightly controlled *hierarchy* into a much more complex structure of *networks* of cooperative relationships.[17] Examples of such networks in policing are numerous. In addition to neighborhood and block watch groups, police departments are increasingly involved in working with other government agencies and nonprofit organizations in arranging for services such as victim assistance and rape crisis centers, spouse abuse programs and shelters, and so on. Also, many departments are moving toward better and more integrated relationships with private security firms that routinely provide guard, patrol, and burglar alarm services in their jurisdictions.

This cooperative approach is a departure from the past when many police managers chose either to ignore other agencies and private firms, to regard them as peripheral, or to try to control them by legally circumscribing their activities. In many places these responses will no longer suffice. Departmental effectiveness will increasingly come to depend on the ability of top managers to build networks that link service provision and delivery functions. In such a system, police chiefs, sheriffs, and other top managers will have to build cooperative relationships with public and private organizations all across their communities and regions. In doing so their role will have to change from that of a "commander" of a closed hierarchy to that of an "arranger" of interorganizational networks.

1. These data will be presented in greater detail in: Charles H. Levine, *Fiscal Stress and Police Services: A Strategic Perspective* (Washington, D.C.: National Institute of Justice, U.S. Department of Justice, forthcoming 1985). Because police departments have only recently begun to experiment with the idea of strategic management, some of the points made in this article are admittedly impressionistic and may seem somewhat at odds with the way police chiefs, sheriffs, and other police managers have traditionally thought about their jobs, but they should be more persuasive when considered within the framework of the trends of the past decade.

2. These "hidden" costs of retrenchment are explained at greater length in: Charles H. Levine, "Retrenchment, Human Resource Erosion and the Role of the Personnel Manager," *Public Personnel Management*, Fall 1984, pp. 249–264.

3. See: Robert W. Backoff and Barton Wechler, "Integrating Tools and Networks: A Strategic Management Approach," prepared for the Annual Meeting of the American Political Science Association, Denver, Colorado, September 2-6, 1982, pp. 15–16.

4. For similar findings, see: Charles H. Levine, Irene S. Rubin, and George G. Wolohojian, *The Politics of Retrenchment* (Beverly Hills, Calif.: Sage Publications, 1981).

5. For a similar approach, see: Todd D. Jick and Victor V. Murray, "The Management of Hard Times: Budget Cutbacks in Public Sector Orga-

nizations," prepared for the Annual Meeting of the Academy of Management, San Diego, California, August 15-17, 1980, pp. 15-16.

6. The process involved in changing strategies as fiscal stress episodes deepen and extend over time suggests that the choice of strategies followed a *developmental sequence*; that is, old strategies were abandoned (but not necessarily *all* the old tactics) and new strategies were formed to better deal with the new, more difficult situation. In general, each new set of decision rules and strategies built upon the previous set and allowed for consequences that were broader and more extensive in scope than the previous set.

7. See: John Gargan, "Consideration of Local Government Capacity," *Public Administration Review*, November/December 1981, p. 652.

8. Levine, Rubin, and Wolohojian, *The Politics of Retrenchment*.

9. Ibid., chapter 8.

10. See: Paul E. Peterson, *City Limits* (Chicago, University of Chicago Press, 1981), p. 34; Stephen L. Garman, "The Terminal City," *State and Local Government Review* 15, no. 1 (winter 1983): 32-37.

11. See, for example: Harry P. Hatry, *A Review of Private Approaches for Delivery of Public Services* (Washington, D.C.: Urban Institute Press, 1983); E. S. Savas, *Privatizing the Public Sector* (Chatham, N.J.: Chatham House, 1982); and Robert W. Poole, Jr., *Cutting Back City Hall*, (New York: Universe Books, 1980).

12. Martha A. Shulman, *Alternative Approaches for Delivering Public Services*, Urban Data Service Reports, vol. 14, no. 10 (Washington, D.C.: International City Management Association, October 1982), p. 1.

13. See: Mark H. Moore and George L. Kelling, "To Serve and Protect: Learning from Police History," *The Public Interest* 70 (winter 1983): 64.

14. Warren E. Walker and Jan M. Chaiken, "The Effects of Fiscal Contraction on Innovation in the Public Sector," *Policy Sciences* 15 (1982): 157-60.

15. For more on this problem, see: Robert P. McGowan and John M. Stevens, "Local Government Initiatives in a Climate of Uncertainty," *Public Administration Review* 43, no. 2 (March/April 1983): 134.

16. See: Robert D. Behn, "Leadership for Cutback Management: The Use of Corporate Strategy," *Public Administration Review*, November/December 1980, pp. 613-620.

17. See: Ted Kolderie, "Rethinking Public Service Delivery," *Public Management*, October 1982, pp. 7-9.

PART 2

Emerging Standards of Police Performance

National Accreditation: A Valuable Management Tool

Jack Pearson

Editor's note: This article and the one that follows summarize two views of national police accreditation. In the months since they were written, the standards have been formalized and five police departments have received accreditation.

Every book on police administration written in the last 20 years, in discussing management or administrative techniques, includes such activities as planning, organizing, staffing, budgeting, directing, and controlling. To be effective, these processes must be mastered by anyone who assumes the mantle of law enforcement authority.

Over the last few years, the International Association of Chiefs of Police (IACP), National Organization of Black Law Enforcement Executives (NOBLE), National Sheriffs' Association (NSA), and Police Executive Research Forum (PERF), have been working on a voluntary accreditation program for law enforcement agencies to serve as a management tool for American law enforcement chief executives for every phase of their responsibilities.

It is not a simple task to develop standards for a law enforcement community as diverse as that found in the United States. According to census data, there are at least 19,600 law enforcement agencies of various kinds throughout the country. More than 10,000 have fewer than nine employees.

One strength in this decentralization and diversity is that local law enforcement agencies can be responsive to citizen demands and expectations. Local governments can determine the role of the agency within the community it serves.

Reprinted with permission from the July 1983 issue of *Western City* magazine, the monthly publication of the League of California Cities.

However, such diversity in law enforcement agency size and functions presents many challenges to any uniform approach to upgrading the effectiveness and professionalization of law enforcement.

History

The accreditation program for law enforcement agencies began in 1979 with a grant from the Law Enforcement Assistance Administration (LEAA), and included active participation from staff of IACP, NOBLE, NSA and PERF. Some discussions on the program took place as early as 1970, when one of the four associations solicited LEAA for funding. It was not until September, 1979, however, that the relationships between the four associations were formalized and a concept for accreditation drawn up and approved.

These four associations created a governing commission with 21 members; 11 law enforcement practitioners and 10 representatives from local, county and state governments, and academia. The four associations incorporated the commission as a private, nonprofit independent corporation in October 1980.

In 1980, commission and association staffs identified 46 topic areas which the standards should address. These areas covered role and authority, administration, operations and auxiliary and technical services of law enforcement agencies.

In May 1982, a "discussion draft" standards manual of 1,012 standards was tentatively approved by the commission for field review and comment. The commission approved key components of the accreditation process and public information policy for field testing.

The commission contemplated using qualified individuals, primarily from other law enforcement agencies (out-of-state) as on-site representatives to verify compliance with appropriate standards by agencies. All assessors will go through specialized commission training.

The standards

Each of the four associations identified a staff manager as responsible for program development for the association. Each employed staff to research and draft specific chapters of standards. Every draft standard ultimately was reviewed and commented on by all four associations. Some used committees of their membership, some used selected law enforcement agencies for input and others used in-house conferences to discuss each standard.

Recognizing the diversity of law enforcement, the commission established levels of compliance for each standard, based on the number of personnel in an agency according to these sizes: 1 to 9 officers, 10 to 24, 25 to 49, 50 to 199, 200 to 999, and departments with over 1,000 officers.

Certain standards are mandatory (M), some "other than mandatory" (O), and some are not applicable (N/A). Once final levels are established, an agency will comply with all mandatory standards for its size, and at least 80 percent of the designated "O" standards that apply.

The commission met in April 1983 to consider the recommendation of the four participating associations and the field review agencies. Duplicative standards were combined into single standards; commentaries were clarified in some cases, as were levels of compliance.

In March 1983, the commission announced the selection of five law enforcement agencies to serve as pilot test sites for the accreditation program. The pilot test agencies were police departments in Hayward, California; Mt. Dora, Florida; Elgin, Illinois; Baltimore County, Maryland; and the Elkhart County Sheriff's Department in Goshen, Indiana. These volunteer agencies implemented the entire program and represented five of the size categories the commission uses in applying standards.

The process

The accreditation process begins when an agency applies. A questionnaire will be sent to the applicant agency to profile its size, legal responsibilities and functions. From the agency's response, commission staff will identify specific standards with which the agency must comply. Once the agency completes its self-assessment and identifies proof of compliance, the commission selects a team for an on-site assessment. Once the assessment is completed and reported, the commission determines whether the agency is accredited or, if not, what actions are necessary to achieve accreditation.

Accreditation is for a five year period; agencies must apply for reaccreditation before the end of the fifth year. An on-site assessment is required as part of the reaccreditation process.

The commission recognizes that waivers of standards may be necessary in some circumstances. An appeal process for commission decisions also is being developed.

The hope is to structure a process through a single coordinator and conduct the assessment with a minimum number of assessors in a minimum amount of time. A committee of the commission has the important responsibility to develop a fee structure that is fair, reasonable and attainable by an interested agency, regardless of size.

Concerns

Although the concept isn't new, the fact that a program of national impact and scope nears completion causes concern to some law enforcement executives.

Some chiefs are concerned that voluntary programs too often become mandated programs. The process of accreditation will begin with the *voluntary application* by a law enforcement agency. Applications will not be accepted unless the chief executive officer of the agency initiates the request.

Some chiefs are concerned about a "federal" program. From its inception, the commission has strived to become autonomous, independent, and a nonprofit, tax-exempt corporation. The commission now is expanding its efforts to become self-sufficient through private foundation and private industry grants. When the accreditation program is implemented, participating agencies will be asked to support the effort through a fee structure. No one wants a continuing dependence on federal funding, yet support from the government was essential during these initial stages and is much appreciated.

The process does not usurp the rights of any locale or individual. The standards indicate "what to," if an agency has responsibility for certain functions. The "how to's" are the prerogative of the chief executive. It was never the intention of the commission to disturb this authority or the sovereign rights of any state, county or city.

Some chiefs contend the commission's goals and objectives are duplicative of existing programs. This is *not* just another report by a blue-ribbon panel suggesting procedures to be applied by some and ignored by others.

For the law enforcement administrator, accreditation will offer a means of monitoring performance and correcting deficiencies, and access to a wealth of knowledge and experience gathered by commission staff. Accreditation guidelines will help justify budget requests, and will reduce the likelihood of liability suits and liability insurance rates. It will improve relations with the other components of the criminal justice system—the courts, prosecutors, correctional agencies, state and local government officials—and with the community.

For neighboring law enforcement agencies, it offers cooperative agreements and fewer jurisdictional disputes.

For city, county, or state officials accreditation offers an independent evaluation of department policies, useful for attracting qualified officers, justifying budget and personnel policies, and building community support.

To the citizens in an agency's service area, accreditation offers an understanding of law enforcement roles and authority, and greater confidence in the local department's effectiveness and commitment.

National Accreditation: A Costly, Unneeded Make-Work Scheme

W. E. Eastman

Editor's note: This article and the one that precedes it summarize two views of national police accreditation. In the months since they were written, the standards have been formalized and five police departments have received accreditation.

Local police departments faced a dilemma when the federally funded Commission on Accreditation for Law Enforcement Agencies (CALEA) began to carry out its planned program for officially accrediting America's police departments.

The California Police Chiefs, in an annual conference, passed a strongly worded resolution against the accreditation scheme and the CALEA. The vote was very nearly unanimous. Many police chiefs feel the accreditation program is a federally funded pie-in-the-sky project, based on objectives born from naivete, that is simply too ambitious an undertaking to be effective in the final accounting.

The Commission on Accreditation for Law Enforcement Agencies came into being as a result of a 1979 grant from the federal Law Enforcement Assistance Administration (LEAA). The International Association of Chiefs of Police (IACP), the National Organization of Black Law Enforcement Executives (NOBLE), the National Sheriffs' Association (NSA), and the Police Executive Research Forum (PERF) are the catalyst organizations. The managers of the accreditation program were selected by and from these four organizations. They drafted standards for "the full range of administrative and operational procedures" conducted by a law enforcement agency.

Reprinted with permission from the July 1983 issue of *Western City* magazine, the monthly publication of the League of California Cities.

The standards developed are to evolve into a process where agencies will apply for accreditation, which would either be awarded or denied. The standards are, according to the commission's literature, measurable and each standard is to be answered by a "yes" or "no" when applied to an agency.

The approval of the standards was the responsibility of a 21-member commission. Each commissioner was appointed by the executive directors and presidents of the four participating associations. Of the 21 commissioners, 11 are "practitioners" from law enforcement and ten "non-practitioners" are selected from outside of law enforcement from both the public and private sectors.

Hazards of disagreement

The first steps taken in the project could be of use to police administrators. In the discussion drafts and selection of standards a compendium of information was established from past writings. References and footnotes of publications preceding the commission's work fill the draft standards. The list is quite recognizable: the National Advisory Commission on Criminal Justice Standards and Goals, the President's Commission on Law Enforcement and Administration of Justice, the American Bar Association Standards Relating to the Urban Police Function, *Local Government Police Management, Municipal Police Administration, Police Administration* (Wilson). . . .

What was created, to this point, was a list of readings, assembled by topic, of materials readily available to police administrators who care to look. There was really nothing new, and the only surprise was that the Law Enforcement Assistance Administration had come such a short distance from the President's Commission on Law Enforcement to the Commission on Accreditation for Law Enforcement Agencies. Nonetheless, the topical compendium might be handy to some police executives and that is where the "commission" would be well advised to stop.

But has the commission really done its homework? Is it realistic to hope that accreditation will accomplish its objectives? And is there a need to be concerned whether these objectives are actually met? Today, more than ever, police departments must exercise both practicality and political awareness before we either buy into a program or tacitly accede to it.

Unfortunately, disagreeing with this national accreditation exercise has its hazards. Those who have openly criticized it are considered to be philistine in some small, but vocal, circles. Speaking against something as high sounding as a "Commission on Accreditation for Law Enforcement Agencies" is akin to attacking motherhood, lobbying against apple pie, and flying in the face of all that is decent. Those seven words when strung together imply great credibility: it's nothing short of an ad man's dream. But this is a far more expensive and lasting proposition than the purchase of a bar of soap based upon an advertising impression.

Insurmountable problems

There are seven significant—cumulatively insurmountable—problems with this accreditation scheme that should influence practical thinking law enforcement leaders to respond to the commission and its adherents with a resounding, "No, thank you."

Is it voluntary?   In their writings and coast-to-coast promotional tours, the program's salespeople insist accreditation would be completely voluntary. But it is voluntary in name only, and without a united stand by law enforcement executives this ruse will sweep the country. Once a department jumps aboard, for whatever motivation, pressure will be brought to bear on neighboring departments. City councils and politicians will not be aware of what accreditation really means. Special interest groups are certain to use the program for the advancement of their own peculiar causes.

The Executive Director for the "commission" was asked why the standards and other information compiled couldn't simply be shared with the law enforcement community. This way they could use what they needed and save unnecessary expense, process, and bureaucracy. He replied that this would not be done, because voluntary compliance does not work.

Public meetings   Another shoe was dropped. The "commission" plans—and this is no more negotiable than the program is voluntary—to hold public meetings in every jurisdiction when its police agency undergoes accreditation. This will be done to avoid giving the appearance that the commission is sneaking in and out of town.

The commission wants to hear public dialog about the agency's compliance or non-compliance with the standards. This, they assure us, will take a lot of pressure off of the police agency!

Federal program   Advocates of this plan take pride and care in telling us they are pushing a national rather than a federal program. Hence, no strings are now attached, nor will any be added in the future. Yet, they were initially funded in 1979 by a $1.3 million grant from the Law Enforcement Assistance Administration. In 1981 an additional $1.2 million was anted up by the Department of Justice.

Their next announced money move is to go after private grants and funding in order to get out from under the yoke of federalism.

Cost   The commission informed us that handsome fees would be charged to police agencies seeking accreditation. An estimate of around $5,600 cash outlay would cover accreditation for an agency of about 100 sworn personnel.

This was based on four assessors being on site for four days ($4,000) and additional CALEA administrative costs. A few minutes later that figure was re-guessed at about $8,000. But, nobody really knew. This did not include in-house administrative costs, which would be considerable. Whatever fees the commission decides on are recurring. Reaccreditation is required every five years and the same fee is recharged to the agency.

Commission staffing   The commission sprang into being as the dying gasp of the Law Enforcement Assistance Administration. Soon the IACP, NSA, NOBLE and PERF jumped on the bandwagon, naming their people as program managers and helping their executive directors in appointing a 21-member commission. This process is certainly suspect and police departments may be well advised to accredit commissions, rather than to annoint commissioners whose function is the accreditation of law enforcement agencies.

The organizations at the forefront do not have a history of speaking or acting in the best interests of local police departments. For example, IACP's Operation Identification Program moved into communities without so much as the courtesy of discussion with local police executives, and it perpetrated what many consider to be a "bunco scheme" on the public.

The second glaring incident of separate interest was brought to light by the recent statements of a NOBLE director on the nationally syndicated "Donahue" show. He painted a picture of white police officers routinely gunning down minority, primarily black, victims. And now police departments are expected to apply for accreditation from organizations whose high ranking representatives run scams on the public and are racist in both title and espoused ideology, to the detriment of the police profession.

Police departments have been assured they will be fairly represented on the commission, since it takes all four of the law enforcement groups to bestow commissioner status on an individual. However, the commission will change by one-third every three years as seven new appointments are made. Six of these positions have already turned over for a variety of reasons—including not attending any meetings. Next year will mark the first scheduled turnover. Thus, by 1984 we will see a shift of at least 13 of the original 21 positions established in 1979.

Local rule   The concept of CALEA chips away at the very cornerstone of local rule and community desires in the provision of safety services. Chief Daryl Gates of the Los Angeles police department said it best in a recently published interview.

The wonderful thing about policing in the United States is that we have community policing, policing that is done in step with what the community wants. This present effort toward accreditation, to develop a national standard, is something that I think we should be very cautious of because it smacks of nationalizing the police, getting away from the community to what people on a national scale think is right for policing in America. I think that's wrong. I'm opposed to this whole accreditation program. I'm not opposed to professionalism and I am not opposed to developing good standards. We do that in California. But even in California, where we have a state commission imposing standards, it takes away some of the individual community's ability to decide what is right for them. We don't have a national police in this country and we should never have a national police.

The "trust me" mentality   Whenever questions are put to the commission and their spokespersons, the responses are, alarmingly, "Trust me, it'll be all right!" Police administrators should be more skeptical of these soothing replies to well-grounded concerns. This most unsatisfactory response has followed such questions as:

1. What vicarious liability does a non-accredited police agency face?
2. What vicarious liability does an accredited police agency face when the standards apply nationwide yet the *Peterson* decision[1] applies to California, not Nevada, Illinois, Texas, Michigan, Georgia . . .
3. With the Commission on Peace Officer Standards and Training working in California, why do we need CALEA?
4. Why is an assessor from another state more qualified than a police chief, a city manager, a city council, or a community to judge the police department?
5. With a liberal high court, an adversary press with a predominant "60-Minutes" journalistic mentality, and lawyer unions who perceive their role as sitting in review of police to further their own causes, why do police agencies need yet another non-representative body to sit in judgment of their day-to-day efforts?
6. Isn't this just a national police review board by another name?

The Commission on Accreditation has nothing to offer: the only gains that will result, should the plan come to fruition, will be the self-serving benefits to the commission and its members.

Editor's note: In the closing portion of this article, which was shortened somewhat, the author noted that "California appears to be the last stop in CALEA's campaign to win acceptance for the concept of accreditation of local police departments" by presenting accreditation as a fait accompli. *He then urged the state's law enforcement leaders to actively counter CALEA's efforts. Subsequently, he reports, police chiefs in the state took a major role in opposing accreditation nationwide.*

1. *Editor's note:* The "Peterson decision" to which Chief Eastman refers is *Peterson* v. *City of Long Beach,* 24 Cal. 3rd 238, 594 P.2d 447 (1979). In this case, the California Supreme Court ruled that police administrative manuals and regulations carried the force of law in court determinations of negligence, and that violations of police administrative regulations carry a rebuttable presumption of negligence.

James Wright's observations about *Peterson's* effects on California police may clarify Chief Eastman's concerns about accreditation:

"First, *Peterson* labeled the police manual to be regulations with the force of law; the practical result is that the police manual has the same effect as *legislative* rules under administrative rulemaking. They both have the force of law and both have civil liability.... Second, the effect of viewing the manual as having force of law is to impose tort liability. By imposing tort liability *Peterson* discourages the use of police rulemaking to guide police activities...."

From: James Wright, "Police Shootings—Administrative Law as a Method of Control over Police: *Peterson* v. *Long Beach,*" 8 *Pepperdine Law Review,* 419, 445 (1981).

Lawsuits Against Police: What Impact Do They Really Have?

Deterrence is a concept much maligned by criminologists and much endorsed by law enforcement professionals. That vigorous law enforcement can deter criminal acts is generally conceded; opinions split, though, on how much and what kind of criminality can be deterred. Accepted criminological wisdom holds that the threat of punishment will deter instrumental criminal activity (i.e., planned, rational lawbreaking, such as burglary or income tax evasion) but will not appreciably reduce expressive crimes (e.g., "heat-of-passion" murder or terrorism by juvenile gangs).[1] Some prosecutors and police, on the other hand, maintain that a tough-guy image of law enforcement in any given community can serve significantly to dampen criminality of all types.[2]

Testing the concept of deterrence

We may never know which approach to deterrence is more plausible because testing the concept with objective empirical indicators is quite difficult. Simply put, successful deterrence means that crime has not happened, but we can't easily measure what isn't there. Assessing the impact of vigorous law enforcement on crime rates, then, must be accomplished by a combination of indirect, occasionally subjective methods.

The same considerations apply to deterring unlawful actions of police. It is almost impossible to count how many illegal searches and seizures have been prevented by the existence of the exclusionary rule, for instance. At any given time, unconstitutional police activity may be common or uncommon for a variety of reasons. But we

Reprinted with permission from *Criminal Law Bulletin*, copyright 1984, Warren, Gorham & Lamont, 210 South Street, Boston, Massachusetts 02111.

assume that an officer contemplating an apartment search, for example, will be deterred from conducting the search in an unconstitutional manner partly because his thought processes are rational; he is planning purposive action and will therefore take into account the unpleasant consequences his illegal actions could engender should he be held accountable for them in court.

Objective indicators of deterrence

Although we cannot measure directly the officer's subjective thoughts and perceptions, certain objective indicators do support the argument that he and his fellow officers are often deterred from conducting illegal searches. For example, although one commentator doubts that exclusionary rules have as powerful a deterrent effect as their proponents would wish, another has countered by noting that some deterrent effect seems evident because so very few cases actually result in evidence suppression.[3] For the most part, police must be acting legally—and by inference, they must have been deterred from acting illegally—or there would be many more successful motions to suppress than can be counted today. Further, Murphy[4] points to the great numbers and depth of training courses instituted in police academies after *Mapp* v. *Ohio*[5] was decided; the increased emphasis on constitutionality demonstrates that police are now well educated to avoid illegal actions in daily law enforcement work. (This presumes, of course, that such training can indeed have a measurable deterrent effect in the decisionmaking of the patrol officer.)

Threat of civil lawsuits

The same considerations apply when attempting to assess whether the threat of civil lawsuits deters police from unlawful behavior. A movement to scrutinize and control police misconduct has sprouted and become firmly rooted in mainstream litigation over the past decade,[6] and its supporters presume it has a significant deterrent effect. Police misconduct litigation, like any civil litigation, aims both to compensate victims and to deter future wrongdoing.

The case law under 42 U.S.C. § 1983 has evolved sufficiently so that a seamless web of liability (or at least a liability scheme as seamless as abstract legal principles are likely to provide) may be applied to defendants on each level of a police department's hierarchy. Because deterrence is strongest when punishment is certain, current case law developments should please those who would "police the police." Furthermore, certain nonlegal indicators such as higher insurance rates and increased media coverage of police misconduct issues indicate that these cases are probably becoming increasingly important to police administrators. Thus, administrative actions within police departments themselves taken in response to litigation can significantly aid deterrence. Whether all this will result in meaningful deterrence of unlawful behavior by patrol officers remains problematic,[7] but this article will offer a few suggestions for attorneys and police administrators who may want to ensure that it does.

Case law: from *Monroe* to *Monell*

In a sense, civil litigation against the police elicited the sort of response from police administrators in the 1970s that the Warren Court's due process rulings had in the 1960s. Naysayers were convinced that court inquiry into policing would so dishearten the "troops" that no officer would bother to fight crime for fear of being sued by any citizen who would pay the cost of a court filing fee. Surely the quality of law enforcement has not declined because of police misconduct litigation any more than it has under *Mapp* or *Miranda*. But the question is: Has court oversight *improved* policing? Furthermore, how can litigation most fully encourage improvement?

Probably, the reason that discussion became so heated in the 1970s was that a series of Supreme Court rulings had successively tightened the liability structure for the entire range of police defendants. In the 1960s, the only police personnel generally susceptible to suit were patrol officers, and that in itself had been considered a major innovation. Under *Monroe* v. *Pape*,[8] individual line officers were held to be proper subjects of legal attack under 42 U.S.C. § 1983,[9] the federal statute designed to prevent abuse of constitutional rights by officers who "under color of state law" deny defendants those rights. Insofar as *Monroe* said that officers did not enjoy immunity from suit, it was a sharp break from tradition. But it also said that police would not be liable if they could prove a good-faith defense.

A claim that he was acting "in good faith," even though his actions later were shown to be illegal, allowed a patrol officer to duck liability by passing the blame onto his superiors. If he neglected to adhere to constitutional standards in his arrest methods, for example, he could claim that he believed in good faith that his actions were legal; if he had been mistaken, the fault lay with his superiors in the police department whose lack of supervision and/or training led him to believe that his actions had simply been good policing.

But the supervisors at that time were immune from suit because of a misapplication of tort doctrine to constitutional adjudication. Courts consistently held that the doctrine of respondeat superior (responsibility for an employee's sins must be shared by his employer) did not apply in police cases, on the theory that supervisors were not the employers of the patrol officers. In the 1970s, however, federal courts slowly recognized that the issue did not involve the nature of the employment relationship, but rather that "the question ought to be whether there was a sufficient degree of involvement in the illegal actions by the supervisory personnel to serve as a basis for liability."[10] Failure to train patrol officers properly, or failure to supervise them so that they adhere to constitutional standards, are independent activities sufficiently negligent in themselves to bring supervisory personnel into the web of liability, and respondeat analysis is therefore inapplicable. The result was that, in the 1970s, citizens harmed by unconstitutional police activity that was ultimately traceable to departmental policy and callous neglect of what line officers did on the street could successfully recover damages in federal court.[11]

Finally, in the 1980s, the web-spinning was completed. Even though the case law of the 1970s had abandoned supervisory immunity, personnel who had failed to train or to supervise patrol officers could nevertheless claim a good-faith defense, as line personnel could under *Monroe*. Supervisory personnel would often point to a city or departmental policy that they had faithfully followed but that was later found to have been unconstitutional. In Nuremburg-style buck-passing, police "brass" could claim that, although their acts were indeed unconstitutional, they had believed that they had been acting correctly because the city's written policies or traditional bureaucratic customs had approved the acts. Traditionally, a municipality had not been considered a "person" amenable to suit under the language of Section 1983, and therefore police personnel at all levels would pass liability onto the immune city.

At each level of the departmental hierarchy, then, "I was only following orders" was the good-faith response; yet when responsibility finally rested on the city, tradition held it immune. But in 1978, the Supreme Court held that municipalities that violated constitutional rights under local "custom, policy, or practice" were also proper defendants in Section 1983 suits. *Monell* v. *Department of Social Services*[12] thus provided plaintiffs with the opportunity to challenge governmental misconduct directly by challenging the city's policies, and it also prevented a constitutional claim against the police from vanishing if police personnel had made a cognizable claim that their actions were simply conforming to municipal custom. The liability web was completed in *Owen* v. *City of Independence*,[13] which held that municipalities could not claim good-faith defenses to constitutional violations.

The result, reformers hope, is that police activities (and governmental policies and practices generally) will be more carefully controlled at all levels of hierarchically arranged public service departments. If no particular component can escape constitutional scrutiny, trying to duck responsibility by blaming other city workers would be fruitless. Perhaps all decisionmakers will then work together to prevent unconstitutionality at all levels of municipal policing.

The impact of police misconduct litigation

In theory, then, the case law on police liability for unconstitutional acts has developed so as to provide compensation for victims (they no longer meet with a shrug of the shoulders from courts mewing "governmental immunity") and deterrence of future conduct (if everyone is responsible and must pay the price for unconstitutionality, together they should plan to avoid it).

Compensation has increased dramatically over the past decade, an impact easily measured by the phenomenal increase in the size and number of monetary awards given to aggrieved plaintiffs. A recent compilation of the most spectacular of such awards reveals that of the twenty-nine cases of wrongful death discussed, the average amount awarded in damages was $657,864; the average amount awarded in the thirty-eight cases of excessive use of force not resulting in death was $565,859.[14] Or consider the Richmond, California, case. There, the city, its police chief, and two officers were ordered to pay $3 million to the families of two black men whom the officers had shot and killed.[15]

Cost of insurance coverage

Another calculable result of police misconduct litigation has been a steep increase in the costs of providing insurance coverage for police departments and municipalities. In 1975, prior to *Monell,* insurance premiums for Dade County, Florida, had increased from $60,000 to $150,000 in one year,[16] apparently as a response to the police officers' and supervisors' greater susceptibility to suit. Today, cities are also liable, so "local governments currently are facing an insurance crisis"[17] that is particularly acute for smaller cities that do not have access to a broad endowment of municipal property from which to pay large judgments. Commentators have noted:

Quite clearly, absent insurance, a substantial judgment or series of judgments could monetarily cripple a municipality and force it to forgo or reduce services in vital areas. Yet insurance is unavailable to some municipalities and for many others it has become prohibitively expensive. Due to the expanding liability of local governments and concomitant disappearing [legal] defenses, insurers are facing greater underwriting costs and will not significantly lower municipal premiums.[18]

Alternatives for insurers

From the insurer's point of view, the only alternative to charging astronomical rates for civil rights "police professional malpractice insurance" is for the municipality and its police department to take decisive action to reduce the risk of adverse judgments. Police administrators must prove that they have reviewed departmental policies and that line officers are trained and supervised to keep within constitutional bounds; such "loss prevention" vigilance may persuade an insurer to provide liability coverage at comparatively affordable rates. In noninsurance terms, this means that police administrators must deter departmental and officer misconduct.

Yet the question remains: What impact do these court judgments and sizable insurance premiums have on actual police practices? Do they deter? Again, statistics offer little information; one cannot count cases of abuse that do not happen, and even when reformers point to lower rates of use of deadly force or illegal arrests or the like, it is almost impossible to isolate litigation as the factor that sparked concern for constitutionality. However, if the opinions offered by police themselves faithfully mirror their subjective assessments of whether litigation affects their actions, the legal reform is indeed deterring abuse. Speaking of restriction of deadly force, one chief of police outlined the common response to stricter civil liability and increased public awareness of abusive practices:

What many chiefs have done is set up more restrictive policies within their own departments and enforce compliance by regulations ... and every time an officer goes to the range, he or she should be reindoctrinated on both the shooting policy and skills. ... Each department should have a review process, and as chief, you should indicate to the officer how very seriously you take the firing of that weapon. ... I believe that as a direct result of such enforced policies, we have had no shootings of police or citizens in my jurisdiction.[19]

Internal police review

Other chiefs of police, city attorneys, and patrol officers echo these sentiments, although many are disgruntled at what they perceive to be overly strict monitoring. In any event, if opinion evidence from police themselves is taken as an objective indicator of the impact of civil rights litigation, the greatest impact is felt in those communities where police departments have thoroughly reviewed their written procedures and on-duty standard operating procedures to assure that they pass constitutional muster. Even more important, police supervisory personnel in those cities have carefully encouraged compliance by straightforward and resolute internal departmental review of alleged rights violations.[20] Undoubtedly these activities are prompted partly by the knowledge that if police departments themselves do not hold their employees accountable to constitutional standards, the courts will do it for them—at a considerably higher cost.

From a practical, commonsensical viewpoint, of course, the most obvious result of Section 1983 litigation should be that police departments would review their policies and procedures, assure adequate internal enforcement, and carefully maintain a good training program to teach and remind officers of constitutional standards. This is a huge undertaking, but it is necessary and clearly well underway nationwide. Yet it is such a vague prescription that police administrators may understandably search for some specific indicator to help them assess whether the lessons of litigation are spreading through their departments.

Two points to watch in any department would be the quality of internal discipline and the quality of communication between city attorneys and police administrators.

Quality of internal discipline

Internal police review of patrol officers' actions is crucial. Departments will vary in their internal investigation of and discipline for unconstitutional activity, and each department will have different political constraints acting upon it in these matters. But one fairly objective indicator cuts across these variations: Does the department have meaningful recordkeeping of each officer's "rights rap sheet"? Police departments must maintain records of each officer's questionable behavior. The officer who often exhibits brutal tendencies, who habitually makes bad arrests, who conveniently and consistently forgets proper booking or interrogation guidelines is the officer who must be disciplined and deterred. Civil rights cases constantly recite damaging facts unearthed by plaintiff's attorneys: Officer Doe has been the object of several citizens' complaints. (As complaints become more numerous, even if the officer is "exonerated" of each by an internal review board, the weight of complaints renders the officer's defenses less convincing in a jury's eyes.) Officer Doe's partners have frequently recounted horror stories and informal expressions of dismay about Doe's street performance to their supervising sergeant or other superiors. Perhaps Doe has been reprimanded off the record by judges or prosecutors. Yet he has not been disciplined by the department. Sloppy recordkeeping and poor disciplinary methods will surely result in court judgments for plaintiffs; the adverse impact of Section 1983 litigation is only as powerful as a department's supervision and internal investigative machinery allow it to be.

Communication with city attorneys

Similarly, police cannot learn from constitutional litigation if city attorneys are lax in reporting what happens in court. The police departments that successfully deter misconduct are those in which administrators demand full explanations of legal actions taken by city attorneys. A measure of impact is whether city attorneys report frequently and fully to police administrators (who, after all, are their "clients") about the issues raised when the city and the department are sued, why the cases were won or lost, and what police procedures can be redesigned or better enforced so as to prevent liability. There is an unfortunate tendency for attorneys to discuss fully with police administrators and patrol officer defendants only those cases that go to trial or that receive wide publicity. While such cases are important for policymaking, deterrence is not most effectively accomplished in such a crisis atmosphere. Regular reports by city attorneys of the character of *all* police misconduct cases filed—including those that are settled or dismissed—are essential. We will know that police misconduct litigation is having a real impact on policing when we observe a regular flow of information and policy review between police administrators and city attorneys.

Conclusion

Thus, increased procedural review and adequate recordkeeping, disciplinary actions, careful policy training, and a steady exchange of information between city attorneys and police are all good indicators that police departments indeed take deterrence seriously. The presence of one other interesting phenomenon may also be an objective indicator that civil rights litigation *is* serving to check unconstitutionality: No police department in the United States has ever been placed in its entirety under court administration to force it to function constitutionally.[21]

When abuse of constitutional rights by a public agency becomes so systematic and so deepseated that reform from within is improbable, courts have been willing to place the offending organization under judicial administration. Judges will monitor compliance with constitutional norms in virtually all areas of agency functioning until the organization performs legally. This has been a common approach in prison and public hospital reform and, to a more limited degree, it has been used to desegregate public schools. If police disregarded constitutional standards to the same degree that other public agencies have, we would expect them to be operating under court orders, too. The fact that there is no police equivalent to the prison system's *Holt* v. *Sarver*[22] indicates that the case-by-case litigation strategy of individual civil-rights plaintiffs has indeed deterred widespread police abuse.

1. Chambliss, "Types of Deviance and the Effectiveness of Legal Sanctions," 1967 Wis. L. Rev. 703; see also Andenaes, "Deterrence and Specific Offenses," 38 U. Chi. L. Rev. 537 (1971).
2. P. Utz, *Settling the Facts: Discretion and Negotiation in Criminal Court* 65 (1978), profiling the history of

law enforcement attitudes in San Diego.
3. Oaks, "Studying the Exclusionary Rule in Search and Seizure," 37 U. Chi. L. Rev. 665 (1970). Cf. Cannon, "Is the Exclusionary Rule in Failing Health? Some New Data and a Plea Against a Precipitous Conclusion," 62 Ky. L.J. 681 (1974). An update and

overview of the arguments are found in Kamisar, "Is the Exclusionary Rule an Illogical or Unnatural Interpretation of the Fourth Amendment?" 62 Judicature 67 (1978); Canon, "The Exclusionary Rule: Have Critics Proven That It Doesn't Deter Police?" 62 Judicature 398 (1979).

4. Murphy, "Judicial Review of Police Methods in Law Enforcement: The Problem of Compliance by Police Departments," 44 Tex. L. Rev. 939 (1966).

5. 367 U.S. 643 (1961).

6. See the compilation of cases in C. Antieau, *The Federal Civil Rights Acts* (1971 & yearly supplements).

7. The most complete study of whether Section 1983 lawsuits have a deterrent impact was conducted by *Yale Law Journal* student editors. They examined 149 misconduct cases filed from 1970-1977 and interviewed many attorneys, judges, and police officials. The data indicated that few of the cases were won, in large part because juries were unsympathetic to plaintiffs who, although victims of police abuse, were nevertheless "involved in a criminal lifestyle." The authors therefore inferred that there would be little deterrent effect from the litigation, and they bolstered this argument by noting that "both the individual [line officer] defendants and the police departments were insulated from the financial burden consequent to a [successful] section 1983 suit." Few officers ever personally paid their adverse judgments; insurance companies or self-insured municipalities would indemnify them. "Project: Suing the Police in Federal Court," 88 Yale L.J. 781, 814 (1979).

For reasons stated in the text, the deterrent effect of misconduct litigation may have been considerably strengthened since the Yale study. After a decade of litigation, juries and the civil rights bar are considerably more sophisticated than they were when misconduct cases first appeared in federal courtrooms. Perhaps most important, the study covered cases decided before municipalities themselves were declared proper subject of suits under Monell v. Department of Social Servs., 436 U.S. 658 (1978). Closing the municipal immunity loophole has made city administrators and attorneys much more aware of the costs of police litigation, and therefore much more willing to review departmental policies and practices in order to deter costly misconduct. See notes 12-13 *infra* and accompanying text.

However, the researchers' admonition that police officers should be required personally to pay judgments against them if deterrence is to be effective still rings true.

8. 365 U.S. 167 (1961).

9. 42 U.S.C. § 1983 reads:
Every person who, under color of any statute, ordinance, regulation, custom, or usage, of any State or Territory, subjects, or causes to be subjected, any citizen of the United States or other person within the jurisdiction thereof to the deprivation of any rights, privileges, or immunities secured by the Constitution and laws, shall be liable to the party injured in an action at law, suit in equity, or other proper proceeding for redress.

10. *Police Misconduct Litigation Manual* 22 (M. Avery & D. Rudovsky eds. 1978).

11. See, e.g., Sims v. Adams, 537 F.2d 829 (5th Cir. 1976); and others discussed in *Police Misconduct Litigation Manual*, note 10 *supra*; Hampton v. City of Chicago, 484 F.2d 602 (7th Cir. 1973); Roberts v. Williams, 456 F.2d 819 (5th Cir. 1971); Carter v. Carlson, 447 F.2d 358 (D.C. Cir. 1971).

12. 436 U.S. 658 (1978). An overview of civil rights cases from *Monroe* through *Monell* is provided by Schapper, "Civil Rights Litigation After *Monell*," 79 Colum. L. Rev. 213 (1979). For a discussion of how *Monell* changes the legal framework of municipal liability, see Kushnir, "The Impact of Section 1983 after

Monell on Municipal Policy Formulation and Implementation," 12 Urb. Law. 466 (1980) (does not cover the question of what demonstrable behavioral impact *Monell* may have on the actions of city workers); see also Einhorn, "*Monell* and *Owen* in the Police Injury Context," 16 U.S.F. L. Rev. 517 (1982), for a discussion of the nexus between police supervisory fault and municipal liability.

13. 455 U.S. 622 (1980).

14. *Money Damages in Police Misconduct Cases: A Compilation of Jury Awards and Settlements* (A. Lloyd ed. 1983).

15. Linda Roman & Edna Minor v. City of Richmond, et al., No. C-80-4702, and Juanita Guillory v. City of Richmond, et al., No. C-80-0142 (N.D. Cal. June 1983) (unpublished). The cases involved a group of white officers called "cowboys" who were well-known in the department and city for using racist enforcement techniques.

16. Takagi, "Death by Police Intervention," in U.S. Dep't of Justice, Law Enforcement Assistance Administration, *A Community Concern: Police Use of Deadly Force* 37 (1979) (hereinafter cited as *Community Concern*), (quoting N.Y. Times, Feb. 2, 1975). Takagi believes that reforming police practices through civil rights litigation is inappropriate, because it requires juries to set dollar amounts for loss of life or rights—thus reinforcing the capitalist notion that anything, even rights, is simply property to be bought or sold.

17. Vitullo & Peters, "Intergovernmental Cooperation and the Municipal Insurance Crisis," 30 De Paul L. Rev. 325, 336 (1981); see also Hagerty, "Insurance Coverage and Civil Rights Litigation," 27 Fed'n Ins. Couns. Q. 3 (1976).

18. Vitullo & Peters, note 17 *supra*, at 335. The authors opine that cities should cooperate to pool their insurance risks and liabilities in "risk management agencies." In addition to providing insurance, such an agency would take responsibility for reviewing the insured municipalities' civil rights policies and procedures and recommending improvements. The aim, of course, is to prevent litigation (and thus insurance) losses; the result could be one more organizational actor working for deterrence.

19. Van Blaricom, "A Chief's View of Deadly Force," in *Community Concern*, note 16 *supra*, at 21.

20. Of course, departments in cities with strong police unions will encounter particular adversarial jostling in internal investigations disciplinary hearings. But whether or not an officer is disciplined, if he has had a number of complaints lodged against him, administrators should become aware that he is a "civil rights violation waiting to happen."

21. Some departments have been placed under judicial supervision to force them to comply with constitutional provisions in specific areas of endeavor; recruit hiring in New Orleans and Boston, for example, has been accomplished under court orders to integrate the departmental work forces. Courts may have been willing to order and oversee compliance in a particular departmental practice such as hiring but no court has yet ordered systemwide reform of virtually all fundamental organizational functions as has been true in prison litigation. One case attempted to accomplish this in the Philadelphia Police Department while Frank Rizzo was mayor, but the district court declined to do so. The history of that issue and others is in Rizzo v. Goode, 423 U.S. 362 (1976). An early proposal to consider police departments as proper subjects of court monitoring is discussed at 5 Harv. C.R.-C.L. L. Rev. 104 (1970).

22. 309 F. Supp. 362 (E.D. Ark. 1970), *aff'd*, 442 F.2d 304 (8th Cir. 1971); attorneys' fees and other compliance problems in this lengthy litigation are discussed in Hutto v. Finney, 98 S. Ct. 2565 (1978).

Vicarious Liability: Legal Myth and Reality

Steven D. Rittenmeyer

Since the United States Supreme Court revived the Civil Rights Act of 1871[1] with its decision in *Monroe* v. *Pape*,[2] public officials in general and police officials in particular have experienced an unprecedented challenge of their action. Increasingly, private citizens have petitioned courts for redress in cases alleging personal injury and property damage resulting from unconstitutional acts on the part of state and local authorities.[3] Such suits arise from a myriad of factual circumstances from the gross[4] to the trivial[5] and are based on a variety of legal theories. One of these is a concept of liability often termed "vicarious liability." What is usually meant when the term is used is that supervisory level personnel, along with the employing governmental agency, are held personally responsible for the torts of subordinate employees. From the beginning, there has been much confusion and consternation among courts and public officials regarding the applicability of the doctrine in "1983 suits." The situation has been exploited from time to time by some with monetary interests but little of an objective nature has been written. This article, primarily using case law analysis, points out misinterpretations and clarifies the vicarious liability doctrine, also termed *respondeat superior*, as it applies, or fails to apply, in police administration contexts.

A representative fact situation

On October 5, 1982, the U.S. Court of Appeals for the Seventh Circuit decided the case of *Iskander* v. *Village of Park Forest and Zayre Inc.*[6] Factually, the case arose when the plaintiff was detained by

"Vicarious Liability in Suits Pursuant to 42 USC 1983: Legal Myth and Reality," reproduced from *Journal of Police Science and Administration*, volume 12, no. 3 (1984), with permission of the International Association of Chiefs of Police, P.O. Box 6010, 13 Firstfield Road, Gaithersburg, Maryland 20878.

store security personnel for alleged shoplifting as she exited defendant's department store in Park Forest, Illinois. Following standard procedure, police were notified and an officer dispatched. Defendant was taken into custody for misdemeanor theft, transported to the Park Forest Police Department, booked, strip searched, and held until her husband posted bond. As a result of these actions, a suit pursuant to 42 U.S.C. Section 1983[7] was filed on behalf of Mrs. Iskander naming the store detective who made the initial arrest, the police officer who took her into custody, the police matron who performed the strip search, and their corporate employers as responsible parties in violations of plaintiff's right to be free from deprivations of liberty without due process of law guaranteed by the Fourteenth Amendment.[8]

The pertinent question before the jury at trial, and later before the appellate court, was the scope of liability among the named defendants. Specifically, were the employing agencies liable for the alleged constitutional torts of their employees? A second pertinent question for present purposes involves the choice of defendants— defendants who had no direct involvement in the allegedly illegal acts but who could theoretically be held "vicariously" liable. Specifically, why were the police chief and other supervisory personnel employed by the Park Forest Police Department spared the entanglement of this action?

Respondeat superior and the "affirmative link" standard

Before embarking on an analysis of the applicable precedent, some definitions and general background information will aid both the answering of the above questions and the accomplishment of the overall purpose of this article.

The word "vicarious," in its purest sense, describes a situation which involves someone or something functioning as a substitute; serving instead of someone or something else, or taking the place of someone or something else.[9] The term "vicarious liability" is often simplistically defined as indirect legal responsibility or "legal responsibility for the acts of another person because of some relationship with that person."[10] Commentators have, however, expended great effort in explaining the concept:

The growth of doctrines of responsibility in the law of torts gradually developed theories of liability in which *an actor was not personally at fault* in the causation of another's injury ... [L]ittle by little, in the evolution of the law, one person became liable for another's wrongdoing, where the other had acted on behalf of the one as agent or servant ... Liability is predicated on the broad ground that he who would manage his affairs through others is obligated to third persons damaged by such others acting in the course of their employment [emphasis added].[11]

There are many reasons why a party seeking redress for damages caused by police officers is anxious to extend the liability to supervisors and to the employing government body. First, with the inclusion of these additional defendants, the likelihood of obtaining and satisfying a judgment of damages is increased. Additionally, there is perceived deterrent and policy making value in including the policy makers and those responsible for immediate control of the actual tort feasor. Finally, and usually for social policy or political reasons, such inclusion can potentially reveal systematic problems, thus negating the "one bad apple in the barrel" response.[12]

Still the application of the traditional vicarious liability rules to police supervisors and employing agencies under Section 1983 has been problematic and some have concluded that "[d]octrinal confusion has resulted from misapplication or misunderstanding of basic tort principles."[13] There is, however, some measure of consensus on a number of points.

The first point of agreement is that in civil suits alleging violation of civil rights under Section 1983 the doctrine of *respondeat superior* does not apply.[14] Thus, one who is without personal fault cannot be held answerable in a Section 1983 action on the basis of his supervisory relationship with the person whose act, or lack thereof, actually caused the harm. The rationale for this proposition is twofold. First, the *respondeat superior* doctrine imposes liability on an employer or a master primarily because he draws direct, usually economic, benefit from the efforts of his employees while maintaining that power to hire, control, and dismiss offenders. Such is not the case in public employment. There is generally thought to be no master-servant relationship between supervisors and subordinates. They are seen as different grades of employees in the service of the public, thus negating any application of traditional vicarious liability.[15] Employing municipalities and governmental entities also benefit from this logic thanks to the decision by the U.S. Supreme Court in *Monell* v. *New York Department of Social Services*[16] to require more than a showing by the plaintiff of more than an employer-employee relationship.[17] On the other hand, there is equal agreement that the rejection of the *respondeat superior* doctrine does not totally immunize supervisors and municipalities from Section 1983 accountability.

In deciding *Scheuer* v. *Rhodes*,[18] a suit by the survivors of the victims in the Kent State shootings against, among others, the governor of Ohio, the U.S. Supreme Court found that

... the common law[19] has never granted police officers an absolute and unqualified immunity.... In the case of higher officers ... the inquiry is ... complex since the range of budget decisions and choices—whether the formulation of policy, ... of budgets, or of day-to-day decisions is virtually infinite.

These considerations suggest that, in varying scope, a qualified immunity is available to officers of the executive branch of government, the variation being dependent upon the scope of discretion and responsibilities of the office and all the circumstances as they reasonably appeared at the time of the action on which liability is sought to be based.[20]

To this point it is clear that supervisory officers and municipalities will not be liable in Section 1983 suits simply due to the relationship between them and the actual offender. However, they are still held to a standard of reasonable conduct within the context of specific job descriptions and the surrounding circumstances. If the standard of responsible conduct is not met, there may be a justified conclusion that the supervisor was at fault. The same rule applies to municipalities. They are not liable just because they employ a person who perpetrates a constitutional tort while acting in an official capacity. The Supreme Court was clear, in *Monell*, that a governmental body is liable only if the constitutional tort results from the promulgation or administration of an ordinance regulation, policy, or custom.[21] Consequently, the New York Department of Social Services policy requiring female employees to take unpaid maternity leaves while male employees did not suffer the same deprivation was found to be an unconstitutional violation of the former group's right to equal protection of the laws.

Returning to individual supervisors and executives, the issue of fault must be addressed. If fault is required, in what sort of conduct must policy management engage to breach the duty to take responsible action? This is the area of greatest misunderstanding.

Several cases have held that supervisors are not accountable without a showing that they actually directed, ordered, participated in, or approved the tortious acts.[22] A good example of this thinking exists in the *Kostka* v. *Hogg*[23] decision of the U.S. Court of Appeals for the First Circuit.

There the administrators of the estate of a man killed by a police officer during an arrest sued the officer, the police chief, and the town of Westford, Massachusetts, alleging violations of, among others, the decedent's Fourteenth Amendment right to be free from deprivation of life without due process of law. The plaintiff's theory for holding the chief and city answerable was that they failed to act responsibly in instructing, training, educating, and controlling the offending officer. The appellate court affirmed the dismissal of the claim against the chief (the allegations against the city had been dropped previously) saying:

To negate [the chief's] official immunity, plaintiffs would have to establish active, bad faith participation in the wrongdoing. For example, if the police chief ordered the constitutional violations or possibly, if he deployed or hired the officer under conditions which he should have known would create a threat to the constitutional rights of the citizenry.[24]

Continuing in a footnote the court opined:

Indeed this theory strikes us as a transparent attempt to hold [the chief] vicariously liable under the guise of his having breached a duty owed plaintiff's decedent. Plaintiffs seemingly have taken one of the modern justifications for the doctrine of *respondeat superior*, the master's opportunity to select, train and control his servants ... and converted it into a constitutional duty on the part of all police chiefs. If there is a practical difference between this theory and a vicarious liability theory, we fail to perceive it.[25]

The authority for this and the other decisions requiring actual personal participation by supervisory people stems from the language used by Justice William Rehnquist in *Rizzo* v. *Goode*.[26] In finding that the Philadelphia mayor and police commissioner could not be enjoined to submit to the Federal District Court a comprehensive program for improving the handling of citizen complaints regarding police mistreatment, Justice Rehnquist concluded that there had been no showing of an

affirmative link between the occurrence of the various incidents of police misconduct and the adoption of any plan or policy ... showing ... authorization or approval of such misconduct.[27]

In a later action by the residents of Philadelphia's Youth Study Center (YSC) against Mayor Rizzo, the judges of the family court, the staff of the YSC, the Philadelphia school district and the Pennsylvania Department of Education, the U.S. district court issued an instructive opinion.[28] The class of plaintiffs, juvenile offenders sent to the YSC as a result of court action, made broad based claims concerning the constitutional deprivations stemming from the conditions of their confinement. The court, in its treatment of the allegations against the executive and supervisory defendants, concluded that the weight of authority indeed demanded a showing of participation but went on to include knowledge of an acquiescence in the official misconduct.[29] However, applying the broadened standard was a problem. The court, looking to several factors which had been applied historically in other contexts, decided that to determine if knowledge was present a trier of fact must do the following: first, decide whether the defendant supervisor possessed actual knowledge of the misconduct or, given his duties, should have possessed such knowledge; second, scrutinize the degree of authority and control over the conduct of the offending subordinate; third, determine the existence of policies and procedures which relate to the particular type of conduct; and fourth, assess the extent to which the supervisor has actually encouraged such behavior and/or allowed the alleged misbehavior to go on through a lack of appropriate action.[30] To these factors three principles are to be applied. First, where there is a greater duty and opportunity to control the subordinate there is a lesser degree of actual knowledge of the specific misconduct required. Thus, as one moves up the supervisory ladder, higher officials, to be liable, must be shown to have possessed a greater degree of specific knowledge. General knowledge of misconduct by subordinates will not suffice to hold executive level personnel. The same applies to acquiescence and ratification. Second, the existence and acceptance of general policies and procedures which deal with the actions can create a constructive knowledge of and acquiescence in the alleged misconduct. Such evidence can substitute for proof of actual supervisory complicity or ratification. In such cases courts may conclude that the constitutional deprivations are proximately caused by the implementation and endorsement of the policies and practices by the supervisors.[31] Third, the *Santiago* court concluded that the degree of participation required is less if the plaintiff is seeking injunctive or declaratory relief over monetary damages.[32]

A reading of the language of Section 1983 not only supports that broader view of the "participation" standard applied in *Santiago*, it also lays the groundwork for a still more liberal interpretation. The statute speaks in terms of "subjects, or *causes* to be subjected . . ." (emphasis added).[33] This, together with the bulk of case authority, reveals that the necessary "affirmative link" between the rights deprivation and official action or policy may be established pursuant to a showing that the civil rights violation resulted as a natural and foreseeable consequence of supervisory action, or more probably, inaction where a duty exists.[34] Examples abound where supervisory personnel have been found liable without actual personal participation in the misconduct.

In *Byrd* v. *Brishke*,[35] the Seventh Circuit reversed a directed verdict in favor of defendants and held that a police sergeant could well be accountable for injuries resulting from a beating administered by officers under his command during an arrest while the sergeant was in a different room but within hearing range of plaintiff's screams. Reading the case against the background of general tort law, the court found that where there is an affirmative duty to act and a negligent failure to do so liability may flow.[36] Specifically, in the words of Chief Judge Swygert, the court concluded:

. . . that one who is given the badge of authority of a police officer may not ignore the duty imposed by his office and fail to stop other officers who summarily punish a third person in his presence or otherwise within his knowledge. That responsibility obviously obtains when the nonfeasor is supervisory officer to whose direction misfeasor officers are committed.[37]

Likewise, a man who was arrested by a New Mexico state patrolman for speeding, held incommunicado in the Farmington, New Mexico, jail and illegally interrogated and beaten, sued not only the arresting officer and the jail personnel who allegedly battered him, but also the chiefs of the New Mexico State Patrol and the Farmington Police Department. Neither was present during the incidents.[38] Adopting the rationale of the *Hogg* decision,[39] the defendants argued that plaintiff's claims of negligent training and supervision plus failure to act to prevent misconduct despite knowledge of past acts of abuse were disguised *respondeat superior* claims due to the fact that neither chief had personal knowledge of the misconduct, did not participate, and did not acquiesce in the acts of the subordinates.[40]

Underscoring the lack of fault on the part of a master premise of vicarious liability and distinguishing it from the proximate cause theory of section 1983 liability, the Tenth Circuit found clear legal foundation for such a suit "as long as a sufficient causal connection is present."[41] In a review of the evidence, affidavits and documents showed that the chiefs had met their statutory duties to train the offenders and the departmental policies were such as to be adequate in preventing such acts. The court commented:

Showing that individual officers violated a person's constitutional rights on an isolated occasion is not sufficient to raise an issue of fact whether adequate training and procedures were provided.... To extend the general duty ... to prudently select, educate and supervise police department employees to an isolated, spontaneous incident ... would be beyond reason.[42]

Regarding the allegation of negligent retention, Judge Logan wrote that a person in a position of responsibility who fails to take preventive action once he knows or reasonably should have known of misconduct breaches a duty and is negligently liable to a damaged plaintiff[43] (see also *Carter* v. *Carlson*,[44] *Thomas* v. *Johnson*,[45] and *Moon* v. *Winfield*[46]).

Finally, in *Bruner* v. *Dunaway*,[47] a recent case which at this writing is before the United States Supreme Court,[48] the Sixth Circuit reaffirmed the rule stated in *Byrd* v. *Brishke*.[49] In *Bruner*, the plaintiff sought to hold six regular Knoxville, Tennessee, police officers plus a reserve officer and a police explorer scout liable for a skull fracture, permanent diminished intellectual capacity, and "post traumatic epilepsy"[50] sustained after a beating received during an arrest process. Four of the officers testified that they had not arrived at the scene until after the plaintiff had been arrested and did not assist in the subduing of the arrestee. The others, with the exception of the officer who made the initial contact and the explorer scout, while admitting being at the scene, flatly denied ever striking the plaintiff.[51] The initial trial resulted in a jury verdict against all defendants, save the City of Knoxville, which had been previously dismissed. After an appeal and reversal, a subsequent trial found in favor of the four officers who were not present during the actual confrontation and the officer who had made the initial contact and from whom the plaintiff ran after a brief scuffle. The jury, however, held against the explorer scout and the two remaining officers who aided in the subduing process.[52] In the subsequent appeal the Sixth Circuit, in a per curiam opinion, restated that rule of *Byrd*[53] and added that

a law enforcement officer can be liable under Section 1983 when by his inaction he fails to perform a statutorily imposed duty to enforce the laws equally and fairly, and thereby denies equal protection to persons legitimately exercising rights guaranteed them under state or federal law. Acts of omission are actionable in this context to the same extent as are acts of commission.[54]

Summary and application

In the treatment of the representative fact situation at the outset several things were deliberately left unanswered, specifically the fates of the named defendants and the question regarding the theoretical vicarious liability of the unnamed supervisors, including the police chief.

Briefly, the representative fact situation involved the arrest by store security of a suspected female shoplifter and the subsequent custodial detention and strip search by public authorities. Named in the Section 1983 suit were the store and its employee, the arresting officer, police matron, and employing municipality. Applying the *Monell* standard, the Seventh Circuit ruled that neither the store nor the municipality was liable to the plaintiff for any illegal action surrounding the initial arrest and the taking into custody. As has been discussed, vicarious liability in the sense of holding a master, or one with the authority to control a subordinate, legally responsible for the actions of that subordinate simply because of the employment relationship does not exist in Section 1983 causes of action.[55] The *Monell* doctrine operated differently when it came to the strip search which followed the detention. There were included in the complaint allegations that the search was conducted in a room open to public view and indeed that an unknown person observed plaintiff in an unclothed state during the course of the inspection. To this aspect of the suit it was determined that upon a showing that the defendant, Forest Park Police Department, "customarily" conducted such searches the plaintiff could prevail; there being a causal connection between official practice and the resulting invasion of privacy, unreasonable search, and deprivation of due process guarantees.[56]

Taking up the theoretical responsibility of the unnamed supervisory personnel, the question is why were such individuals not implicated? Why were they not held "vicariously" liable? The answer is the same. Because there was no sufficient causal relation between the official action or inaction of the supervisors and the claimed constitutional deprivations. Applying the "affirmative link" set out in *Rizzo* v. *Goode*, of course liability could flow if the supervisors had actually participated. That is, they surely would be responsible for directing or authorizing their officers to conduct strip searches on shoplifting suspects in full view of the public. Or, having actual knowledge that such a practice was occurring, could surely be held for ignoring the situation. But beyond such clear acts of malfeasance and misfeasance accountability becomes more complex. As has been established, actual personal participation in the tortious act is not the limit to potential supervisory liability. According to the factors and principles set out in *Santiago*, evidence was sufficient to allow a trier of fact to reasonably conclude that each supervisor in his own special circumstance had assumed the duty to control the specific acts of the offending officers and/or that there existed rules or customs within the agency dealing with the specific conduct that the supervisor should have been aware of such constitutional violations and failed to take appropriate action would satisfy the plaintiff's burden of proof. In such a circumstance, it could be safely concluded that the action or inaction of the defendant supervisor caused the plaintiff to be subjected to a deprivation of his rights despite the secondary causation logic. An analogy exists in the criminal law theory of accomplice liability for the facts of a principal offender. In both situations, there can be liability where a duty exists and there is either an active or negligent breach of said duty which sets into action a course of events leading eventually, in a reasonably foreseeable fashion, to harm.[57] As it happens, most supervisory liability results from official acts of omission: negligent employment, negligent retention, negligent entrustment, negligent training, negligent direction, negligent assignment, and negligent supervision.[58] Still, it must be kept in mind that there is always a legally sufficient causal connection.

1. 42 U.S.C. Section 1983, stating: "Every person who, under color of any statute, ordinance, regulation, custom, or usage, of any state or territory, subjects, or causes to be subjected, any citizen of the United States or other person within the jurisdiction thereof to the deprivation of any rights, privileges, or immunities secured by the Constitution and laws, shall be liable to the party injured in an action at law, suit in equity, or other proper proceeding for redress."
2. 365 U.S. 167 (1961).
3. Between 1961 and 1979, suits pursuant to 42 U.S.C. Section 1983 brought by plaintiffs other than state prisoners increased from 296 to 13,168. Those brought by prisoners increased from 218 in 1966 to 11,195 in 1979. Source: Administrative Office of the United States Courts, 1979 Annual Report of the Director, in Whitman, "Constitutional Torts," *Michigan Law Review* 79 (1980):6.
4. On Tuesday, December 28, 1982, an Hispanic Miami police officer shot a 20-year-old black youth during a confrontation in a video game arcade. The youth died later of a wound to the face. Though contradictory explanations abound at this

writing, the community erupted into 3 days of violence resulting in two additional deaths, 25 people reported injured, and 45 arrests. In the wake of the violence, it was reported that the officer involved had been the subject of many citizen complaints and five internal investigations in his year and one-half tenure as a Miami officer. *Time*, "Miami's New Days of Rage," (January 10, 1983), p. 20.

5. See, for example, *Parratt* v. *Taylor* 451 U.S. 527 (1981); involving a suit by a Nebraska state prison inmate against prison officials for the negligent loss of hobby materials valued at $23.50.

6. 690 F.2d 126 (7th Cir. 1982).

7. *Supra*, note 1.

8. *Iskander, supra*, note 6, at 127.

9. *Webster's Third New International Dictionary*, 1976, Springfield, Mass.: G.&C. Merriam Co.

10. Oran, Daniel. 1983. *Oran's dictionary of the law*. St. Paul, Minn.: West Pub. Co.

11. Dooley, James A. 1977. *Modern tort law: Liability and litigation*, vol. 1, Section 16.01. Chicago: Callaghan.

12. Avery, Michael, and Rudovsky, David, under the auspices of the National Lawyers Guild. 1980. *Police misconduct law and litigation*, Section 3.4. New York: Clark-Boardman.

13. *Id.*

14. *Kostka* v. *Hogg*, 560 F.2d 37 (1st Cir. 1977); *Johnson* v. *Glick*, 481 F.2d 1028, *cert. denied* 414 U.S. 1033 (2nd Cir. 1973); *Brown* v. *Sielaff*, 474 F.2d 826 (3rd Cir. 1973); *Vinson* v. *Richmond Police Department*, 567 F.2d 263 (4th Cir. 1977); *Anderson* v. *Nosser*, 438 F.2d 183 (5th Cir. 1971); *Coffy* v. *Multi County Narcotics Bureau*, 600 F.2d 570 (6th Cir. 1979); *Adams* v. *Pate*, 445 F.2d 105 (7th Cir. 1971); *Taken Alive* v. *Litzau*, 551 F.2d 196 (8th Cir. 1977); *Boettger* v. *Moore*, 483 F.2d 86 (9th Cir. 1973); *Williams* v. *Anderson*, 599 F.2d 923 (10th Cir. 1979). As applied to municipalities, see *Monell* v. *New York Department of Social Services*, 436 U.S. 658, 691 (1978).

15. *Delaney* v. *Dias*, 415 F.Supp. 1351 (D.C. Mass. 1976); *Santiago* v. *City of Philadelphia*, 435 F.Supp. 136 (E.D. Pa. 1977).

16. *Supra*, note 14.

17. *Id.*

18. 416 U.S. 232 (1973).

19. The common law is referred to here as a result of the court's earlier decision in *Monroe, supra*, where the Justices concluded, at 187, that Section 1983 "should be read against the background of tort liability. . . ."

20. *Monroe, supra*, note 2, at 246.

21. *Monell, supra*, note 14, at 690-691.

22. *Ford* v. *Byrd*, 544 F.2d 195 (5th Cir. 1976); see also *Lessman* v. *McCormick*, 591 F.2d 605 (10th Cir. 1979); *Maiorana* v. *McDonald*, 596 F.2d 1072 (1st Cir. 1979).

23. 560 F.2d 37 (1st Cir. 1977).

24. *Op.cit.*, at 40.

25. *Op. cit.*, at 41.

26. 423 U.S. 362 (1975).

27. *Op. cit.*, at 371.

28. *Santiago* v. *City of Philadelphia*, 435 F.Supp. 136 (E.D. Pa. 1977).

29. *Op. cit.*, at 151.

30. *Id.*

31. *Op. cit.*, at 152.

32. *Op. cit.*, at 153.

33. *Supra*, note 1.

34. *Monroe, supra*, note 2.

35. 466 F.2d 6 (7th Cir. 1972).

36. *Op. cit.*, at 10.

37. *Op. cit.*, at 4.

38. *McClelland* v. *Facteau*, 610 F.2d 693 (10th Cir. 1979).

39. *Supra*, note 14.

40. *McClelland, supra*, note 38, at 695.

41. *Id.*

42. *Op. cit.*, at 697.

43. *Id.*

44. 417 F.2d 358 (D.C. Cir. 1976).

45. 295 F.Supp. 1025 (D.C. 1968).

46. 368 F.Supp. 843 (N.D. Ill. 1973).

47. 684 F.2d 422 (6th Cir. 1982).

48. *See* U.S. Supreme Court docketed case #82-797. The issue before the Court is: May a defendant in an action under Section 1983 be held liable where there is no proof of personal involvement in the alleged deprivation of plaintiff's constitutional rights (51 U.S.L.W. 3487 (1/10/83)).

49. *Supra*, note 35.
50. *Bruner, supra*, note 47, at 427.
51. *Op. cit.*, at 424.
52. *Op. cit.*, at 425.
53. *Supra*, note 35.
54. *Bruner, supra*, note 47, at 426.
55. *Iskander, supra*, note 6, at 128.

56. *Op. cit.*, at 129.
57. *Johnson* v. *Duffy*, 588 F.2d 740, 743 (9th Cir. 1978).
58. See Schmidt, "Recent trends in police tort liability." *Urban Lawyer* 8, 682 (1976).

Reviewing Citizens' Complaints Against Police

James J. Fyfe

A cantankerous friend loves his work but regards as tiresome the many Washington parties and receptions it requires him to attend. He takes out his frustrations by slyly attempting to antagonize the new acquaintances he is obliged to make at these events. The technique he uses is surefire: he has carefully compiled a mental list of phrases, questions, and opinions he calls "occupational anathema," and ingenuously drops them into conversations.

At a legislative reception for union organizers, for example, he might respond to a question by stating that, yes, he lives in Washington, but will soon be moving to Virginia. There, he says, "right-to-work" laws keep the cost of constructing his new home lower than in places where construction workers are unionized. On another occasion, he asks a wealthy surgeon why we should not adopt a British-style system of nationalized medicine. The doctor opines that such a system would violate the American free-market ideal and would decrease the quality of medical care. My friend has a ready answer: "You're right, I suppose. If the government ran medicine, doctors wouldn't have to worry about malpractice suits, and they wouldn't have to answer to anybody for their mistakes. As I think about it, I guess the free-market system has its good points. At least you can take a doctor to court here if you're unhappy with him."

Civilian complaint review boards

His most lively discussion, however, occurred a few years ago, at a convention of police officials. He knew how hard it was to be a police officer, he observed, and was glad that he lived in Washington, where the city council had just voted to establish a civilian complaint review board. The board, he said, would be a good thing, because it would show all the skeptics that their charges of police brutality and official whitewashes were unfounded.

He had pricked the right nerve. There is probably no subject that so predictably raises the hackles of police as civilian investigation and review of citizens' complaints against officers.[1] Conversely, among those who most ardently challenge the efficacy of police exercise of their authority, probably the most frequently sought after curative is civilian review: if the large number of requests to the Police Foundation for information are any indicator, civilian review boards are a matter of increasing concern in American cities.

Inquiries about civilian review boards generally come from three sources. First are citizens' groups, civil liberties organizations, and government officials who perceive problems of local police accountability, and who seek to establish independent mechanisms for assuring that the last word on accusations of police misconduct does not come from in-house. Second are police officials in crisis. Typically these officials oversee agencies in which controversial incidents involving accusations of police misconduct have led to calls for establishment of civilian review boards. Most often, these officials seek ammunition for arguments that civilian review is a redundant and inhibiting form of oversight. Third are the journalists who cover these policy arguments, and who typically seek information concerning the experiences of police jurisdictions that have established and operated civilian complaint review boards.

All three of these groups are usually surprised to hear that there is little hard information available to them: as far as can be determined, there are only a few civilian complaint review boards in existence,[2] and there is no central source of data on their operations. Still, it is possible to offer some general, but necessarily anecdotal, observations about the costs and benefits of attempting to establish and operate such forums.

Police resistance to establishment of boards

As my friend knows, civilian participation in the process of reviewing complaints against police officers is a form of occupational anathema which, almost invariably, meets great resistance from police. Some of that resistance may be only a reflection of an unreasonable desire to avoid direct police accountability to the citizenry, but much of it is valid, and should be carefully heard out.

Authority of the chief   Police chiefs resist citizen review because it impinges upon their authority as chief police administrators. The reasons for this are clear where it is proposed that boards be granted power to discipline officers directly. In such instances, chiefs worry that having to share—or to lose altogether—one of the most important of their disciplinary powers will result in erosion of the rest of their authority. A composite picture of the concerns of the chiefs with whom I have spoken recently would read as follows:

"How can I run this department and get officers to do what's necessary if they know that I have nothing to say about what will happen to them if they are accused of abusing citizens? Suppose I'm at a sit-in and order officers to remove and arrest demonstrators. What happens if the demonstrators complain that they were abused? Do I testify before the board as a witness for my officers? If the people who want this board think I side with my officers now, what will happen when I do that? If I were an officer, I'd be tempted to take no action until somebody from the board was present and could see what I had done. Suppose I determine—*or see*—that an officer was wrong and should be disciplined, but the board disagrees: what happens then? Am I overruled? Will the officers learn that it doesn't matter what the chief thinks?"

Those concerns are legitimate. Even where chiefs retain direct disciplinary authority and boards serve only to advise them of their findings, such organizations are almost certain to be perceived by police as an unreasonable compromise of the authority of the chief. Further, as Herman Goldstein suggests, no civilian board can exert the kinds of immediate and day-to-day influences on officers' street performance that are traditionally the responsibilities of the chief. If the chief is not exerting those influences in a way that is acceptable to the community, Goldstein concludes, the answer is not to attempt to work around him by establishing a review board, but to fire him and replace him with someone who is more responsive to his community.[3]

"Singling out" the police   Police officers frequently resist citizen review on the grounds that they, alone among municipal employees, are being singled out for close scrutiny by lay people who have little knowledge of their work, or of the nuances of investigating allegations of professional misconduct by them.[4]

Thus, they argue that while greater civilian oversight of police conduct might be desirable, the mechanism established should take the form of an *ombudsman* rather than a police board, and it should also have jurisdiction over complaints against other municipal employees—school teachers, bus drivers, telephone operators, and clerks, for example.

One response to this suggestion is that civilian oversight of police may be more critical than for other employees, who do not have the same life-or-death powers as the police. If experience in most cities is any indicator, however, most citizens' complaints against police do not involve life-or-death questions. Instead, they allege the same kinds of discourtesy and violations of citizens' dignity of which other municipal employees are often accused.[5] Thus, absent some reason, symbolic or otherwise, for focusing solely on the police, it may be that polarization between the police and the rest of a city is best avoided by establishing an *ombudsman* or a panel that can review complaints against all city employees.

Non-professional judgments of police conduct   Police also question the appropriateness of investigation and review of professional conduct by those not a part of the profession. Here, police frequently hold the position that the skills necessary to conduct objective and thorough investigations are rare outside policing.[6] Consequently, they suggest, if the board is to have at its disposal all information relevant to the cases it is charged with reviewing, it must necessarily employ police officers as staff investigators. But if the board does so, much of its independence is lost: how can it be perceived as independent when it bases its judgments on the results of investigations conducted by employees of the department it is charged with monitoring?[7]

The question of citizen *review* of the propriety of police actions is equally complex. If we expect the police to be professional, why are they not allowed the power of judgment by peers found in other professions? If it is true that the best judges of the efficacy of a lawyer's response to a problem are his fellows, is it not also true that police actions may best be judged by other officers? Bar association panels composed of experienced attorneys rather than uninformed laymen assess the propriety of each other's actions and, where appropriate, render discipline. If a client who feels he has been wrongly treated is unhappy with their best professional judgment, he retains the option of seeking redress in the courts.

Many police officials suggest that this model of peer judgment is appropriate for policing and, indeed, that it already exists in the form of internal police disciplinary mechanisms. Several retorts to their argument are possible.

Even though the tradition of self-monitoring is strong in well-established professions such as medicine and law, there is far from universal agreement that the mechanisms involved are much more than window-dressing designed to protect a professional image. An American Bar Association committee reported of its three-year investigation of legal discipline, for example, that:

[T]he public dissatisfaction with the bar and the courts is much more intense than is generally believed within the profession. The supreme court of one state recently withdrew disciplinary jurisdiction from the bar and placed it in a statewide disciplinary board of seven members, *two of whom are laymen*. This should be a lesson to the profession that unless public dissatisfaction with existing disciplinary procedures is heeded and concrete action taken to remedy the defects, the public soon will insist on taking matters into its own hands [emphasis added].[8]

Further, James Q. Wilson suggests, because the operative controls on police behavior are internal departmental rules rather than external and universally observed codes, policing is more appropriately considered a craft than a profession. He concludes also that fundamental differences between policing and the established professions mitigate against police adoption and enforcement of external codes similar to those of the established professions:

Professionalism is a term that must be understood in a special sense when applying it to policemen. Generally speaking, a profession provides a service (such as medical aid or legal advice) the quality of which the client is not in a position to judge for himself; therefore, a professional body and a professional code must be established to protect both the client from his ignorance and the profession from the client who supposes that he is not ignorant. The policeman differs from the doctor or lawyer, however, in important respects: first, his role is not to cure or advise, but to restrain; and second, whereas health and counsel are welcomed by the recipients, restraint is not. If this is true, the professionalism among policemen will differ from professionalism in other occupations in that the primary function of the professional code will be to protect the practitioner from the client rather than the client from the practitioner.[9]

Wilson is generally correct in his assertion that efforts to develop universally acceptable police professional standards will result in documents designed to protect the practitioner from the client. Most of the widely used texts and training materials designed for use by street police officers (as opposed to police administrators) quite reasonably focus on means by which officers may defend themselves from those unwilling to submit to restraint.[10] Stated simply, the clientele who most frequently complain about police behavior are those who are dissatisfied with the results of their *adversarial* contacts with police, while those who complain about medical and legal behavior are dissatisfied with the results of their attempts to obtain aid.

Further, Wilson's argument points out the faults of the analogy between medical and legal self-monitoring and that which currently exists in the police field. It is true that surgeons and lawyers are subject to review by such internal disciplinary bodies as hospital "tissue committees," and law firms' committees that decide which associates will become partners and which will be asked to seek other employment. The *major* provisions for professional review in both these occupations, however, are *external* to immediate employers. They are, respectively, the forums convened by medical and bar associations to decide not only whether a practitioner shall continue to ply his profession with a particular employer but, on occasion, whether he will continue in his profession at all. Because there is no police analogue to either of these mechanisms, arguments that existing internal police disciplinary proceedings are comparable to those of the established professions are simply groundless.[11]

The distinction between internal organizational review and external professional review is significant because employers of police officers (or doctors, or lawyers) may have a far greater stake in demonstrating that their employees' actions were justifiable than do professional colleagues not employed by the same organization. To what extent, for example, are the deliberations of a police internal disciplinary body (or a hospital tissue committee) influenced by the knowledge that a finding that an officer used unnecessary force (or that a doctor performed unnecessary surgery) might expose its employer—or even members themselves—to civil liability? While it may be argued that existing review in the professions is less than totally objective, it certainly does not have built into it the conflicts of interest inherent in organizational review.

Unrealistic expectations

Many of those who argue for establishment of civilian complaint review boards have extremely unrealistic expectations of what they can accomplish. Except in rare, extreme cases, it is unlikely that such boards will provide a panacea for whatever police-community problems may exist.

The major reason that civilian complaint review boards are not a panacea is that, regardless of the intensity of investigation, most citizens' allegations cannot be definitely resolved one way or the other. In most cases, three bits of information are available to those who review citizens' complaints against police. The first is the citizen's allegation that he was done wrong by an officer. The second is the officer's denial of the charge against him. The third is the investigator's conclusion that there exists little or no objective evidence to support or refute the citizen's charge. Mr. Smith, for example, displays a bump on his head, and claims that Officer Jones hit him unnecessarily, and then arrested him to cover up his misdeed. Officer Jones says he used only that degree of force necessary to restrain Smith, who had taken a swing at the officer when told he was going to receive a speeding ticket. The bump on Smith's head, says Jones, occurred when he fell during their struggle. Smith's wife gives a version of the event that parallels that of her husband; Jones' partner corroborates the Jones version. How can any objective body accept either of these stories without calling the other party a liar? Consequently, unless the former review mechanism has habitually engaged in blatant whitewashes, it is unlikely that establishment of external review proceedings will significantly change the pattern of dispositions of citizen complaint investigations: most are destined to be found unsubstantiated, which is certain to come as a disappointment to people who anticipate that the board will "crack down" on brutal or discourteous police.

Thus, over the long haul, the board may be seen by some as merely another part of the official establishment that almost always finds complaints "unsubstantiated."[12] In addition, a citizen review board's long-term credibility is threatened by another problem: how does a city administration establish and operate an *independent* review board to oversee its police department? Does the city's chief executive—the same person who has selected and appointed the police chief—select and appoint board members? Are board members to be paid by the city? If so, how many of those who feel the need for civilian review will continue to view such a board as truly "independent"?

Accountability: the real issue

When one gets beyond the rhetoric on both sides of the civilian review debates, it is clear that the real issue is police accountability to the public. Those who demand civilian review do not believe the police are properly answerable to the people who pay their salaries, a charge which the police predictably deny.

Cast in that light, it is also clear that the integrity and objectivity of the process of reviewing complaints are far more important than whether the process is staffed by civilians or by sworn officers, especially when the chief reserves the final determination regarding disciplinary action. Given the polarization that accompanies the mere mention of civilian complaint review boards, and given the difficulties of establishing and maintaining such bodies, it may be desirable to seek to increase (or to demonstrate) police accountability by altering or merely opening up the process, rather than by adding another item to the city budget.

To demonstrate how that might be accomplished, it is first necessary to define the purposes of mechanisms for receipt, investigation, and review of citizens' complaints against police officers. Whether staffed by police officers or by civilians, such mechanisms should provide management with information on the quality of police service being rendered, and should serve four very specific objectives.

Documenting incidents   The first is to determine whether individual complaints against officers are founded and, where appropriate, to provide a basis for discipline or other corrective action. As suggested above, however, except in the most clear-cut and well-documented cases, it is very difficult to reconstruct definitively the events that lead to citizens' complaints. Unless the review process becomes a Star Chamber, it is unrealistic to assume that more than a very few officers will be disciplined as a result of determinations that they have acted wrongly in specific incidents.

Identifying patterns of misconduct   Thus, the second purpose—identifying patterns of wrongful conduct by officers—becomes very important. Such patterns begin to emerge when an officer becomes the subject of repeated complaints by independent citizens, none of which can be individually sustained: what should be done about the officer who has been accused on eight or ten or more different occasions of mistreating different citizens and, for want of objective evidence, has never been found in violation?

This is a ticklish problem: even though they recognize that most complaint investigations eventually boil down to irresoluble swearing contests, many police departments treat citizens' complaints as individual events occurring in a vacuum, and close each individually. But it means little to say that a complaint cannot be resolved, if it is the tenth—or the twentieth—allegation of misconduct against an officer whose colleagues are rarely if ever accused of wrongdoing. Any complaint mechanism, therefore, should have the power to review individual complaints in the context of an officer's whole career history, and to make recommendations to the chief that go beyond the findings in individual complaints. In fairness to the citizenry, those who review complaints must assume that where there is smoke, there is fire; officers with lengthy complaint histories should be looked at very closely and should be considered candidates for counseling or for reassignment to duties that do not bring them into close contact with citizens.[13]

Feedback on policies and practices   The third purpose of citizen complaint procedures is to identify poor departmental policies and practices. Some complaints against police involve officers who have offended citizens, but who have acted perfectly in accordance with departmental policy. In such cases, it might be unfair to discipline officers (who have only done what was expected of them), but it may be that a poorly conceived departmental policy should be reviewed and changed. An extreme example involves the search policies of some police departments, which specify that all arrestees be thoroughly strip-searched. In such a case, the officer who strip-searches an elderly man he has arrested on a minor traffic warrant is only doing what is expected of him: but it may be that the expectation is wrong. Thus, the complaint mechanism should also have the power to hear cases based upon allegations of counterproductive policies, and to recommend to the chief that policies (as well as police officers) be brought into line with community expectations.[14]

Credibility   The fourth purpose is to demonstrate police credibility and responsiveness and to assure citizens that their grievances (real or imagined) are welcomed and will be taken seriously. One way to help accomplish that purpose is to involve as many people as possible in the review procedure. That helps to reduce the possibility that complaint reviews will be perceived as whitewashes that occur behind the closed door of the chief's office.[15]

Another important way to demonstrate the integrity of a complaint mechanism is to encourage citizens to complain when they feel they have been wronged. How easy is it for a citizen to complain about a police officer? Must he actually go into a police facility to do so? If a citizen feels he has been abused by a police officer, it takes a lot of nerve for him to go into that officer's station (or any other police facility) to complain. What can he expect when he goes in and tells a desk officer that he wants to initiate an investigation directed at showing that one of the officer's colleagues acted wrongly?[16]

Just as hotels and airlines regularly seek feedback from their customers by encouraging them to comment positively or negatively about the quality of service, police agencies should encourage both laudatory and critical comments from the public. But they often seek out only praise, and discourage or discard criticism. In most police departments, anonymous letters of commendation become valued parts of officers' personnel jackets; in those same places, anonymous written complaints are often ignored because, in order to be considered "official complaints," they must be signed. But if police regularly accept and act upon anonymous letters of commendation and upon anonymous tips about criminal activity, why do they require that complaints about officers be signed? All feedback from the public should be considered valuable management information.

Like citizens' commendations, citizens' complaints should be taken in any form. They should be acceptable if made by telephone, by anonymous persons (it also takes a lot of courage to sign one's name to a complaint against the police in one's neighborhood), in writing, or in person. All department personnel should be required to take and forward to the proper authority any citizen's complaints.[17]

Finally, no complaint mechanism can be considered credible unless it informs complainants of the reasons that their investigations resulted in a certain finding. It is simply not adequate to tell a citizen who, rightly or wrongly, feels that he has been mistreated by the police only that the complaint has been investigated, and that "appropriate action has been taken," or that the complaint was found unsubstantiated or unfounded. When that happens, complainants are justified in feeling that their grievances have been ignored. At minimum, every complainant whose identity is known to the police deserves a written explanation of what occurred after he lodged his complaint, and of the criteria used in adjudicating it.

Thus, police complaint review mechanisms should be required to report thoroughly on the investigative steps taken to resolve citizens' complaints and to document on paper the reasons for their conclusions. It is very difficult for anybody, no matter how ill-intentioned, to support in writing the disposition of a complaint that is not warranted by the evidence he has found, or to twist facts or omit relevant evidence from a report that might be used in subsequent court proceedings.

Attaining these objectives does not require that civilians investigate or review complaints against police. Instead, it requires that citizens be strongly encouraged to make complaints; that complaints be investigated thoroughly and objectively; that departmental reporting requirements provide sufficient openness that it becomes nearly impossible to cover up misconduct, and that the system be perceived as credible and fair by citizens and officers.

The chief's responsibilities

There is no reason why those objectives cannot be attained by the person who serves as police chief. True, there are some conflicts inherent in internal organizational review of complaints against officers, but by requiring that the processes involved be open and documented, they can be minimized. They are, in fact, part and parcel of the chief's responsibilities as an agency head. If the chief does not live up to those responsibilities and is not responsive and not accountable to the citizens or their elected officials, it is difficult to see how the establishment of a board to review complaints against officers will make *the chief* more accountable and responsive. Further, if the chief is not responsive and not accountable, and does not administer the agency in a manner consonant with the reasonable expectations of the people whose taxes support it, it is difficult to see why he or she continues on the police payroll.

The person who sits in the chief's chair is best situated by experience, position, and day-to-day authority to run a police department, and to achieve the objectives of a citizen complaint review board. If the chief does not run the department satisfactorily, and is not committed to achieving those objectives, he or she should be fired and replaced by someone whose views are more congruent with those of the community.

Replacing a chief is a lot less polarizing and expensive than establishing a board that is unlikely to live up to the unrealistic expectations of its proponents.

1. Herman Goldstein (*Policing a Free Society*, Cambridge, Mass.: 1977, p. 142) distinguishes between civilian review boards (the subject of this article) and citizen participation in police policy formulation:

    "The primary objective in proposals for the creation of a civilian review board or another form of civilian review of police actions is to judge the legality and propriety of police action in an *individual* case *after* an action has been taken. In contrast, citizen participation in policy determinations has nothing to do with sitting in judgment on events that have already transpired, nor is it concerned with police action in a given case. Rather, it is a matter of citizens setting priorities and choosing from among alternatives so that the future actions of the police will be in accord with the desires of the community. Civilian review is a negative form of control over police activity. Involvement of citizens in policy determinations, by contrast, has a positive character."

2. According to Robert M. Fogelson (*Big-City Police*, Cambridge, Mass.: 1977, pp. 283–87), the approximately half-dozen cities that established civilian review boards during the 1950s and 1960s had abolished them by the late 1960s. More recently, Washington, D.C., has established a civilian review board, and review board variants exist in Kansas City, Missouri; Chicago; Detroit; Oakland, California; Miami; and Dallas. United States Civil Rights Commission, *Who Is Guarding the Guardians?* (Washington, D.C.: USGPO, 1981, pp. 124–27).

3. Goldstein, *Policing a Free Society*, p. 174.

4. See Walter Gellhorn, "Police Review Boards: Hoax or Hope?," 9 *Columbia Forum* 10 (summer 1966).

5. The United States Civil Rights Commission (*Who Is Guarding the Guardians?*, p. 168) reports that 18.903 percent of the internal and external complaints against Houston police officers during a two-year period alleged "use of excessive force" or "use of unnecessary force."

6. A related complaint was frequently voiced by the police officers interviewed during an evaluation of the Los Angeles County District Attorney's "Rollout Program." (Craig D. Uchida, Lawrence W. Sherman, and James J. Fyfe, *Police Shootings and the Prosecutor in Los Angeles County: An Evaluation of Operation Rollout*, Washington, D.C.: Police Foundation, 1981). Following public controversy over several police shootings and related investigations conducted by the departments involved, the district attorney established this program under which teams of one deputy district attorney and one district attorney investigator (DAI) from his Special In-

vestigations Division (SID) would be available twenty-four hours a day to "roll out" and commence immediate investigations of police shootings. In this way, it was reasoned, prosecutors would not subsequently be forced to rely so heavily on police internal investigations in determining whether to initiate criminal charges against officers. As one might expect, police officers were generally unenthusiastic about this form of oversight. A recurrent complaint, especially among those responsible for conducting internal police investigations of shootings, was that DAIs were unqualified, inexperienced, and incompetent, despite considerable evidence to the contrary. Given the negative and near universal police view of even these apparently highly qualified investigators, it is not hard to imagine the response of police to less credentialed civilian complaint investigators.

7. Ironically, the experiences of the Rollout investigators speak to this issue as well. While they were generally perceived by police as incompetent "headhunters," community activists held a very different view. First, these activists believe that reliance on the police for investigative information prevents an objective fact-finding investigation. Second, they argue that since the DA investigators have law enforcement backgrounds, they cannot be objective in their investigation of officer-involved shootings.

8. American Bar Association Special Committee on Evaluation of Disciplinary Enforcement (Tom C. Clark, chairman), *Problems and Recommendations in Disciplinary Enforcement* (final draft, 1970), p. 2.

9. James Q. Wilson, "Police and Their Problems: A Theory," in *Public Policy*, Yearbook of the Harvard University School of Public Administration, (Cambridge, Massachusetts), pp. 200–201.

10. See, for example, Thomas F. Adams, *Police Patrol: Tactics and Techniques*, (Englewood, N.J.: Prentice-

Hall, 1971); Ronald J. Adams, *Street Survival: Tactics for Armed Encounters* (Northbrook, Ill.: Calibre Press, 1980); Robert J. Downey and Jordan T. Roth, *Weapon Retention Techniques for Officer Survival* (Springfield, Ill.: Charles C. Thomas, 1981).

11. There are, however, notable (if isolated) exceptions to the general rule that all police discipline is internal. The State of Florida presently licenses local police officers and conducts investigations and hearings into misconduct that may result in license suspension or revocation.

12. A careful distinction should be drawn between findings that complaints are "unsubstantiated" or "not sustained" and findings that complaints are "unfounded." As the United States Civil Rights Commission points out (*Who Is Guarding the Guardians?*, p. 169), complaints are "unsubstantiated" or "not sustained" when "the evidence is insufficient to either prove or disprove the allegation"; complaints are "unfounded" when "the allegation is false or not factual."

13. See Hans Toch, J. Douglas Grant, and Raymond T. Galvin, *Agents of Change* (New York: John Wiley and Sons, 1975) for an account of how social scientists worked with police to attempt to identify and modify the behavior of violence-prone police officers.

14. Goldstein, (*Policing a Free Society*, p. 171) points out that, "[f]or the progressive administrator, citizen complaints are often the best indicators of long-standing practices in need of correction. They bring to light police procedures that are often more traditional than necessary."

15. The New York City Police Department provides a good model for investigation and review of police firearms discharges. Before a case is closed, written reports with findings, recommendations, and the

reasons therefor are sequentially prepared by the patrol captain on duty at the time the firearms discharge occurred; the commander of the precinct in which it occurred; the alternating members of "area-level" firearms discharge review boards, and the members of the headquarters firearms discharge review board. In all, approximately 12 officials ranging from the rank of the officer who discharged the firearm through the department's highest uniformed official are required to document and to be held accountable for their determinations during this process. This broad participation minimizes room for speculation that these reviews are secretive whitewashes of unjustifiable police actions. New York City Police Department, *Interim Order 118* (1973).

16. In one case with which I am familiar, a citizen called a police station to complain about an officer's allegedly abusive conduct at a traffic stop. The official who took his call requested that he proceed to the police station to file a formal complaint. When he arrived, he was arrested for disorderly conduct by the officer in question, who had apparently been summoned by the station official.

17. Compliance with this requirement may be tested by investigators who periodically pose on the telephone as wronged citizens and attempt to lodge complaints with department personnel. Determining whether complaints are processed appropriately then becomes a simple matter of checking the records. In New York City, such "integrity tests" have virtually ended the inappropriate "quashing" of complaints by officers: after a few widely publicized disciplinary actions against officers who failed to act correctly, more recent tests of the system have reported virtually total compliance.

Police Agency Handling of Citizen Complaints: A Model Policy Statement

Police Executive Research Forum

The following model policy on police agency handling of citizen complaints was adopted by the members of the Police Executive Research Forum in September 1981. It is intended to provide police officials with precise guidelines for the development of effective agency mechanisms to handle citizen complaints. Further, it aims to establish standards for these mechanisms which will ensure effectiveness as well as fairness to officers and citizens alike. Some of the provisions in this policy will conflict with state law, municipal ordinances and collective bargaining agreements in some jurisdictions and, as such, cannot be implemented. Other provisions may be inappropriate for the unique traditions of certain communities and police agencies and, as such, should not be adopted. Thus, this policy statement can serve as a blueprint for the development of effective discipline procedures as well as a framework for the review and revision of existing practices.

Model policy statement

Statement of purpose   The purpose of this policy is to improve the quality of police services. This is accomplished in three ways. First, through the provision of meaningful and effective complaint procedures, citizen confidence in the integrity of police actions increases and this engenders community support and confidence in the police department. Improving the relationship between the police and the citizens they serve facilitates police-citizen cooperation, an element vital to the department's ability to achieve its goals. Second, disciplinary procedures permit police officials to monitor officers' compliance with departmental procedures. Adherence to departmental procedures assists officers in meeting departmental objectives and a monitoring system permits managers to identify problem areas in which increased training or direction is necessary. Finally, the third purpose is to clarify rights and ensure due process protection to citizens and officers alike. Heightening officer awareness of the rights afforded them when charged with misconduct will increase the appreciation of the comparable rights afforded citizens accused of a crime.

In light of these purposes, the objective of this policy is to provide citizens with a fair and effective avenue for redress of their legitimate grievances against law enforcement officers, and, by the same token, to protect officers from false charges of misconduct or wrongdoing and provide accused officers with due process safeguards. The agency seeks to maintain its integrity and that of its employees. In so doing, the agency shall not hesitate to impose disciplinary actions on guilty officers, to remove from employment those officers who prove to be unfit for law enforcement work, and to dismiss unjustified allegations against innocent officers.

It is the policy of this agency to accept and investigate all complaints of officer misconduct or wrongdoing from any citizen or agency employee. Following a thorough and impartial examination of the available factual information, the officer shall be found innocent or guilty of the allegation. Guilty officers shall be disciplined according to the degree of misconduct.

The imposition of corrective actions and necessary penalties are among the methods available to management to achieve agency goals and compliance with agency policies and procedures. Use of this authority is intended to eliminate the particular behavior and to censure the individuals that account for the misconduct. Furthermore, the discipline process shall be used to identify and correct unclear or inappropriate agency procedures, as well as organizational conditions that may contribute to the misconduct, such as poor recruitment and selection procedures or inadequate training and supervision of officers.

This agency is committed to providing law enforcement services that are fair, effective, and impartially applied. In so doing, officers are held to the highest standards of official conduct and are expected to respect the rights of all citizens. Officers' voluntary adherence to these standards, motivated by a moral obligation to perform their job to the best of their ability, is eminently desirable and an ultimate objective of this agency.

If an officer does not adhere to the standards of official conduct, either through deliberate action or negligence, disciplinary action shall be applied in a prompt and certain manner.

Prevention of misconduct It is the policy of this agency to emphasize the prevention of misconduct as the primary means of reducing and controlling it. While disciplinary actions are properly imposed on officers who have engaged in wrongdoing, they are of limited utility if they shield organizational conditions which permit the abuses to occur. Too often inadequate training and lack of supervision are factors that contribute to the officers' improper behavior. This agency shall make every effort to eliminate the organizational conditions which may foster, permit, or encourage improper behavior by its employees.

Recruitment and selection   Finding and appointing the highest quality of individuals to serve as law enforcement officers is a priority for this agency.

During the selection process, written psychological tests and individual interviews shall be completed by each candidate in an attempt to identify those who would be unsuited for police work. These procedures may also be used for promotional testing, as well as prior to assignments that are especially sensitive or that pose the greatest opportunities for abuse and wrongdoing.

Training   Recruit training and in-service training for veteran officers shall emphasize the sworn obligation of police officers to uphold the laws and provide for the public safety of the citizenry. Police ethics shall be a major component in the training curricula, as well as an in-depth examination of the rules, procedures and outcomes of the disciplinary process. Periodic training bulletins shall be issued to each officer to explain any new statutory requirements or significant procedural changes.

Written directives manual   Each officer shall be given an official, agency-written directives manual which contains specific directions for conducting all aspects of police work. Categories of misconduct shall be clearly described and defined. The directives shall emphasize the officer's responsibility and accountability to the citizens of the community, and their obligation to protect the civil rights of all citizens.

The disciplinary process shall be thoroughly explained in the manual, including precise descriptions of the proper authority of the internal affairs office, the interrogation process, the officer's rights, the hearing board, and all appeal procedures.

Supervisory responsibility   Proper training of agency supervisors is critical to the discipline and performance of patrol officers. Emphasis shall be placed on anticipating problems among officers before they become manifest in improper behavior or debilitating conditions, identifying potentially troublesome officers, identifying training needs of officers, and providing professional support in a consistent and fair manner.

Community outreach   Commanding officers shall strive to remain informed about and sensitive to the needs and problems in the community. Formal and regularly scheduled meetings with advisory councils composed of citizens, meetings with citizens and informal meetings with community leaders shall be used to hear the concerns of citizens, to identify potential crisis situations, and to keep open channels of communication between the agency and the community. The disciplinary process is publicized and clearly explained in these forums, and the availability of a secure post office box for hesitant citizens to file grievances is publicized.

Data collection and analysis   Monthly reports shall be prepared by the internal affairs office for submission to the agency's chief executive that summarize the nature and disposition of all misconduct complaints received by the agency. Further, notation will be made of age, sex and racial characteristics of the complainants and the officers, as well as the complainants' residential neighborhoods. Terminated complaints shall be recorded and reasons for the termination explained.

Copies of the report shall be distributed to all command and supervisory personnel, as well as to training commanders. Notations shall be made for corrective actions of any developing patterns of abuse of a similar nature in a particular neighborhood.

An annual report, summarizing the types of complaints received and the dispositions of the complaints, shall be prepared and made available to members of the public and the press. The names of complainants and accused officers shall not be published in this report.

Purpose   The system that has been established to investigate officer misconduct and to impose disciplinary actions is intended to be fair, thorough and objective. In order to maintain the integrity of this system, precise rules governing the process for receiving, investigating and adjudicating misconduct complaints are published and in effect. These rules are written in clear and easy to understand language, and adequately publicized in both the community and the agency. The rules are internally consistent, realistic and provide due process protections for the person who files the complaint and for the accused officer.

The disciplinary system is open to all persons who wish to file a complaint. It is located in an accessible, clearly marked office and operates week days, from early morning to early evening. During weekends and nights, supervisory personnel are directed to accept complaints. Procedures are explained to the person making the complaint, who is then kept informed of the status of the complaint at each stage of the process. The complaint disposition process is limited to 120 days, unless granted 30-day extensions by the agency's chief executive. While some citizens will be satisfied only if their complaints result in a guilty finding, others will accept a non-guilty finding if they perceive the process has been open, objective, rigorous and thorough.

In order to maintain high morale among agency personnel, the disciplinary system is designed to function in a consistent and prudent manner. It does not challenge or interfere with the prerogative of law enforcement administrators to supervise officers and it gives full support to officers who perform their law enforcement duties in a thorough and effective manner.

Code of conduct Specific categories of misconduct that are subject to disciplinary action are precisely defined. These include:

Crime: Complaint regarding the involvement in illegal behavior, such as bribery, theft, perjury or narcotics violations.

Excessive force: Complaint regarding the use or threatened use of force against a person.

Arrest: Complaint that the restraint of a person's liberty was improper or unjustified.

Entry: Complaint that entry into a building or onto property was improper and/or that excessive force was used against property to gain entry.

Search: Complaint that the search of a person or his property was improper, in violation of established police procedure or unjustified.

Harassment: Complaint that the taking, failing to take, or method of police action was predicated upon factors irrelevant, such as race, attire, sex, age, etc.

Demeanor: Complaint regarding a department member's bearing, gestures, language or other actions which are offensive or of doubtful social propriety or give the appearance of conflict of interest, misuse of influence or lack of jurisdiction or authority.

Serious rule infractions: Complaint such as disrespect toward supervisor, drunkenness on duty, sleeping on duty, neglect of duty, false statements or malingering.

Minor rule infractions: Complaint such as untidiness, tardiness, faulty driving, or failure to follow procedures.

Penalties   A scale of progressive penalties permitted by law and/ or bargaining agreements is used by the agency to punish guilty officers. These are: (1) counseling; (2) verbal reprimand; (3) letter of reprimand; (4) loss of vacation time; (5) imposition of extra duty; (6) monetary fine; (7) transfer; (8) suspension without pay; (9) loss of promotion opportunity; (10) demotion; (11) discharge from employment; (12) criminal prosecution.

The disciplinary process

Receipt and processing of complaints   Complaints shall be accepted from any source, whether made in person, by mail or over the telephone. Individuals are encouraged to submit their complaints in person in order to obtain as complete a report as soon as possible after the incident. In cases in which the complainant cannot file the report in person, agency personnel may visit the individual at his or her home, place of business or hospital in order to complete the report.

Complaints shall be accepted from anonymous sources, juveniles and persons under arrest in police custody so long as the complaint contains sufficient factual information to warrant an investigation. Each complaint shall be investigated to its logical conclusion and the investigation results properly placed into the appropriate category of completed cases.

Any individual who files a complaint shall receive a written brochure or form that explains the disciplinary process in clear and concise language. Individuals who file written complaints or those made over the telephone shall receive a written confirmation of the receipt of their complaint, signed by the internal affairs office director, including a unique case reference number and the name of the staff member who will handle their case. The name of an internal affairs staff member with whom to discuss the investigation termination decision and the office telephone number shall be included on the form. Also, a complaint description form, to be reviewed and signed by the complainant and returned to the agency, shall be sent to the complainant. Persons who file complaints charging excessive use of force shall be asked to sign a form authorizing release of their relevant medical records to the police agency.

While encouraging the filing of legitimate complaints against officers as means by which they can be held accountable to the public, the department simultaneously seeks to hold members of the public responsible for the filing of false and malicious allegations against police officers. In cases of this nature, the complainants will be informed that appropriate legal proceedings will be instituted to remedy such action.

In cases where the identity of the officer is unknown, the internal affairs office investigator shall use all available means to determine proper identity. Complaints should be referred to the internal affairs office where they shall be recorded in a central log and assigned a unique case number. If, however, an officer receives a complaint and the department is able to resolve the situation, through an explanation of rules or procedures, to the complainant's satisfaction, a termination of complaint form shall be completed, signed by the complainant and the officer, and sent to the internal affairs office. If such a complaint is not filed in person, the termination of complaint form shall be mailed for signature and returned to the internal affairs office.

Investigation and adjudication of complaints   Complaints of harassment, demeanor and all rule infractions shall be forwarded from the internal affairs office to the accused officer's commanding officer who, in turn, shall require the officer's supervisor to investigate the allegation of misconduct. The supervisor shall interview the complainant, all witnesses and the accused officer, as well as review relevant reports, activity sheets, or dispatcher forms. The supervisor shall then submit a report to the commander summarizing the matter and determining if the complaint is sustained. If it is, the commander shall determine disciplinary action and forward notification of the action through the chain of command to the agency's chief executive for approval. If, however, the commander determines that the required disciplinary action exceeds a verbal reprimand, he shall forward the investigation report and his recommendations to the director of the internal affairs office for review.

The commander's recommendation shall be submitted to a Review Council of the internal affairs office for concurrence. The Review Council shall be composed of three senior officers appointed for two-year terms by the agency's chief executive. Following Council concurrence, the recommendation shall be sent to the agency's chief executive for approval.

If, however, the supervisor determines that the complaint is not sustained, his or her report is sent to the commander for review and, if approved, forwarded to the internal affairs office for review and to the chief executive for approval. The complainant shall be sent a letter from the agency's chief executive explaining the outcome of the complaint, the reasons for the decision not to fault or discipline the officer, and available appeal procedures.

Complaints of repeated harassment, demeanor and serious rule infractions, and complaints of a serious nature shall be handled by the internal affairs office. An office investigator shall conduct confidential investigation of the complaint and assemble the necessary materials, such as:

1.   Physical evidence
2.   Statements or interviews from all witnesses
3.   Statements or interviews from all parties of specialized interest, such as: doctors, employers, lawyers, teachers, legal advisors, parents, etc.
4.   Investigative aids, such as the various reports, activity sheets, complaint cards, and dispatcher's forms.

In cases where preliminary investigative data indicate the possibility of a criminal act on the part of the officer, the case shall be referred to the district attorney. This should be accomplished prior to the lodging of a formal accusation against an officer. In all other cases, after the gathering of preliminary investigation data, the accused officer shall then be notified of the complaint and an appointment scheduled for questioning. The officer shall be entitled to be accompanied by one other person of his or her choosing to attend the questioning session in order to provide counsel and to ensure protection of the officer's civil rights. The questioning shall take place at a time when the officer is on duty or during his or her normal working hours. In extremely serious cases that involve the public interest or which may bring the agency into disrepute, the accused officer may be questioned during non-working or non-waking hours.

Before the questioning begins, the accused officer shall be informed of the nature of the complaint, the name of the person in charge of the investigation, and the names of all persons who will be present during the questioning. The questions shall be specifically, directly and narrowly related to the performance of the officer's official duties. Also, the officer shall be advised that failure to answer questions will result in disciplinary action, but that his or her answers and the fruits of these answers cannot be used against him or her in a criminal proceeding. If, at any time during the questioning session, the officer becomes a suspect in a criminal act, the administrative questioning shall end, and the officer shall be so informed and read the *Miranda* warnings. The case shall then be referred to the district attorney. Otherwise, the officer shall be expected to answer questions or submit materials and statements to the investigator when so directed. The officer shall be given an opportunity to respond to the complaint orally or in writing. No more than two investigators shall question the officer at one time and they shall not subject the officer to offensive language, threaten punitive action, or make promises of reward as an inducement to answer questions. The questioning session shall be conducted for a reasonable duration, taking into consideration the complexity and gravity of the matter being investigated. The officer shall be allowed time for meal breaks and to attend to physical necessities.

The agency shall protect the accused officer from contact with the news media unless he or she gives written consent. Neither the home address nor a photograph of the accused officer shall be released without the officer's written consent.

All questioning sessions may be tape recorded. The accused officer may review the tapes or purchase copies of a transcription, if any are made, before any subsequent statements are made in furtherance of the investigation of the same case.

Where not precluded by state or local law or by the bargaining agreement, the police chief executive shall have the right to require the use of a polygraph examination as a condition of continuing employment.

No officer shall have his or her locker or other department-assigned storage space searched, except in his or her presence, or with his or her written consent, unless a valid search warrant has been obtained or the officer has been notified that a search will be conducted in the presence of an internal affairs officer and a property control officer.

All documents concerning complaints of officer misconduct shall be considered confidential. They may not be removed from the internal affairs office by any person without express consent of the office director, or on the written order of a court of competent jurisdiction or the agency chief executive.

Conclusions of fact   The investigator shall consider all relevant documents, testimony and evidence in order to determine what actually happened. He or she shall prepare a summary report that provides a complete account of the situation. Gaps or conflicts in evidence and testimony shall be noted and the investigator shall not draw conclusions of fact from them.

At the end of the report, the investigator shall state a conclusion of fact for each allegation of misconduct from among the following dispositions:

Proper conduct: The allegation is true, but the action of the agency or the officer was consistent with departmental policy, and the complainant suffered no harm.

Improper conduct: The allegation is true and the action of the agency or the officer was inconsistent with department policy, and the complainant suffered harm.

Policy failure: The allegation is true, and although the action of the agency or the officer was not inconsistent with department policy, the complainant suffered harm.

Insufficient evidence: There is insufficient evidence to prove or refute the allegation.

Unfounded complaint: Either the allegation is demonstrably false or there is no credible evidence to support it.

If the investigator concludes that the conduct of any officer was improper, he or she shall cite in the disposition report the agency rule, regulation, or order which was violated. He or she shall also note any mitigating circumstances surrounding the situation, such as unclear or poorly drafted agency policy, inadequate training, or lack of proper supervision.

The investigation report shall be sent to the director of the internal affairs office who, in turn, shall request the officer's commanding officer to recommend an appropriate disciplinary action. The investigation report and the commander's recommendation shall then be sent to the internal affairs office's Review Council for concurrence and to the agency's chief executive for approval. In cases involving sustained complaints of misconduct that involve disciplinary actions more severe than a verbal reprimand or counseling, the officer's commanding officer shall send a written notification of the intended disciplinary action to the accused officer.

In addition to existing appeal procedures, an officer may, within 30 days, file a written response to any adverse comment entered in his or her personnel file. Such written response shall be attached to the document containing the adverse comment.

Imposition of a disciplinary action   Following the determination of a sustained complaint of officer misconduct, and allowing for any appeals, agency executives shall act swiftly and deliberately to impose a proper and just disciplinary action on the officer. The final determination of disciplinary actions exceeding summary punishments shall be the prerogative of the agency's chief executive.

The disciplinary action to be taken shall be determined by the seriousness of the misconduct and by the extent of wrongdoing or injury to the victim. It shall also be commensurate with the circumstances surrounding the total incident and with the officer's service record or prior sustained complaints. If the complaints were for incidents of misconduct similar or identical to the current incident, the disciplinary action shall be more severe than for a first offense.

External factors, such as the officer's service record and any sustained complaints for the past three years, shall be considered for a possible referral to appropriate counseling programs. To make such a referral, the officer's physical, emotional and psychological health shall be determined by competent professionals.

Participation in a counseling program may be required of an officer in lieu of a more serious disciplinary action if, in the determination of the agency's chief executive, the officer would benefit. Such a disposition may be revoked in favor of the more severe penalty, however, if the officer fails to participate or to participate successfully in the program.

Once the officer has waived his or her right to an appeal or has exhausted the appeal process, his or her supervisor shall impose the disciplinary action and then forward a summary report to the officer's commander for approval. Once approved, the report shall be sent to the director of the internal affairs office for case closure. The agency's chief executive shall notify the complainant explaining the outcome of the investigation.

Conclusions of fact and of the imposed penalty will be noted in the officer's personnel file after he or she has the opportunity to read and sign it.

High-Speed Chases: In Pursuit of a Balanced Policy

Erik Beckman

During the spring of 1981, a car driven by a 13-year-old boy went out of control and struck a concrete pillar while being chased by a police car, killing six teenagers. Police explained that the youths had tried to outrun a pursuing police car and that they were traveling at an extremely high rate of speed.[1] In Massachusetts, a stolen vehicle driven by a teenager was pursued by an officer who "buried the needle at 140 mph" in a 30-minute chase covering 26 miles, involving 20 units, and resulting in an accident.[2] In Wisconsin, a sheriff's unit pursued a teenager in a stolen car at 105 mph over 19 miles, resulting in an accident in which one youth was killed and five injured.[3] Court records in a large Michigan city tell of a city police car pursuing a "suspicious" vehicle off the freeway onto city streets at 110 mph in medium evening traffic, resulting in an accident in which an infant in a different vehicle was killed.[4]

Existing research

High-speed police chases are a serious matter that have become a concern for citizens, police administrators, city managers, and legal advisers. It is an issue which deserves the same degree of attention as deadly force—for it can be deadly force. However, if one were to turn to research to ascertain the causes, frequency, and consequences of pursuits, one would be disappointed. Little research exists on this subject, and the existing research is of questionable quality.

A 1970 U.S. Department of Transportation study presents the following findings:[5]

Reproduced from *The Police Chief* magazine, January, 1983, issue, with permission of the International Association of Chiefs of Police, P.O. Box 6010, 13 Firstfield Road, Gaithersburg, Maryland 20878.

1. Each year between 50,000 and 500,000 "hot" pursuits occur in the United States.
2. 6,000 to 8,000 of these pursuits result in crashes.
3. 300 to 400 people are killed in such crashes.
4. 2,500 to 5,000 people are injured in these crashes.

The report further states:

1. In 90 percent of the cases, the offense leading to the pursuit was a traffic offense.
2. The suspect is most likely to be a male under the age of 24 with a poor driving record.
3. Alcohol plays a substantial role in more than 50 percent of the cases.
4. The majority of the pursuits occur at night and on weekends.

This transportation department study is based on (1) review of prior research, (2) a one-month field study in four police agencies, and (3) available police data. When one looks behind this data collection, one finds that the so-called "prior research" consisted of a highway patrol study of one week duration, a state police study mentioned in literature but the original of which could not be found, and a study by Physicians for Automotive Safety. The one-month field study in the four agencies was based on only 46 pursuit cases. And the "available police data" were so limited (less than 5 percent of police agencies maintain a records system on pursuits) that the study itself terms them "unworkable."[6]

Another research project on pursuits occasionally referred to in the press and in the police literature was done by an organization calling itself Physicians for Automotive Safety.[7] Its findings regarding the reasons for pursuit were as follows:

Traffic offense or mere suspicion	50 percent
Non-violent crime	6 percent
Stolen vehicle	20 percent
Leaving accident scene	20 percent
Response to complaint	2 percent
Suspicion of violent crime	1 percent
Not stated	18 percent

The study reports that 512 pursuits resulted in 118 fatalities, 272 major injury cases, and 237 minor injury cases. Seventy percent of pursuits were found to result in accidents with injuries to a person involved or a bystander. The physicians recommend training police in accordance with national standards, restricting pursuits to no more than 20 mph over the speed limit, placing speed control governors in private vehicles, maintaining police records on pursuits, and increasing penalties for fleeing from police.

Although the recommendations may have merit and although the findings may be based on an accurate analysis of the data, the method of data collection subjects the study to question. The data were collected by (1) retaining a newspaper clipping service for a three-month period of April through June 1967 to clip all articles on police pursuits and (2) sending questionnaires to "national and state law enforcement officers and the attorney generals ... and major police departments." The study does not reveal why national law enforcement was included in the sample together with attorneys general or how or which "major police departments" were selected; nor is there any indication of the sample size or response rate. There is also no recognition of the fact that newspaper clippings do not constitute a scientific sampling method. The methodological weaknesses are obvious; yet the study is often cited and was made a part of the transportation department's data in its own study previously discussed.

Problem recognition

The absence of good research, however, should not be confused with the absence of an issue or a problem. In this matter, as in all other police operations, there is an obligation to reexamine constantly our philosophy, goals, policies, practices, training, and control. This is particularly important in operations which affect the life and limb of citizens and officers.

The police community knows from its own experience that pursuits are synonymous with hazard.

"Dangers are inherent in pursuit driving. At its best it can be a risky business. At its worst it can be a menace to the people on the highways. This must be avoided at all cost."[8]

"A 4,000-pound automobile traveling at 120 miles per hour has almost two million pounds of energy."[9]

"Every second that a high-speed chase continues will increase the chances for death, injury, or property damage."[10]

"Sometimes the pursued driver escapes and sometimes he even stops. But most often, either he or the police (frequently both) end up in an accident that usually involves some innocent third party who just happened to be in the way."[11]

Given the obvious hazards of conducting the high-speed pursuit, some basic philosophical questions must be asked. What value do we place on the life of the officer, the suspect, a bystander? Assuming they have value, to what degree are we prepared to endanger them and under what circumstances? On the one end of a continuum, it can be asserted that no human life is so valuable that it should prevent us from capturing any violator of the law, no matter how minor his offense. On the other end of the continuum, one can argue that any human life has so much worth that no circumstance would justify placing it in any danger. Most would probably agree that the answer lies somewhere in between; i.e., that society's interest in the immediate capture of an offender may be so great that it is moral to take a certain amount of risk with the welfare of others.

A reasonable position appears to be one which places a high value on any human life. Not even the attempt to effect the immediate capture of a serious offender is worth the death of an innocent bystander, and one must seriously question the prolonged, high-speed pursuit of a traffic violator, misdemeanant, or non-violent felon. There is always the speculation that the minor violator who flees may have something else to hide. He may. He most often does not.[12] In either case, society is not served by the killing or maiming of a third party to effect his capture.

The answers to these basic questions should be codified at the state level. Just as the right to use deadly force is a matter for the state legislature, so should there be state law on pursuit.[13] We do not allow police in one city to shoot misdemeanants while disarming police in another city. Similarly, each state legislature has the duty to address the life and death issue of pursuits. In the absence of state legislation, it is mandatory that every police chief establish a detailed and carefully formulated policy. If state law is enacted, the chief has the option of establishing a more restrictive policy for his department.

Assuming that law and policy will permit some type of pursuit in certain cases, training of all officers is, of course, a necessity. Just as no police agency should allow an officer to carry a firearm if not regularly trained and certified, so should no police agency allow an officer to operate a police vehicle if he is not regularly trained and certified in its operation under all possible conditions. Such training must include classroom theory as well as initial practical training and regular refresher training. Experience must be acquired through long hours of correct driving practices under close supervision.[14] The chief of Washington State Patrol envisions a 40-hour behind the wheel beginner's course.[15] There are side-benefits in such training. Washington, D.C., police[16] as well as the Georgia State Patrol[17] experienced a general reduction in accidents with patrol cars after their officers went through pursuit driving training.

Once the philosophy has been translated into policy supported by training, control through supervision and discipline must follow. All pursuits must be monitored by a supervisor who has the authority to order the pursuit terminated. Granted, the supervisor may not be at the scene of the pursuit, but a pursuing officer easily gets so emotionally involved that his judgment may be impaired. The supervisor, informed of the details by radio, is in a better position to take into account all the factors and make a judgment. Violations of the department policy by an officer must be reported, investigated, and punished. Should the officer's actions constitute a prima facie violation of the vehicle code or other state law, the case should be presented to the prosecutor for his evaluation and possible criminal action.

Every pursuit should be critiqued by management to ascertain what can be learned from it. The findings may well lend themselves to a modification of the training program or the policy.[18]

Department pursuit policies

There are a number of excellent pursuit policies in various police agencies in the nation which could serve as models for other departments. Among the better and more carefully written are policies for Los Angeles Sheriff's Department; Anaheim, California, Police Department; and Southfield, Michigan, Police Department. The model pursuit policy adopted by the International Association of Chiefs of Police in 1973 should be reviewed by police administrators. When it was issued, the IACP passed a resolution urging the adoption by local agencies of a written pursuit policy.

The better policies share some qualities. They appear to be carefully written; they cover many associated issues; they urge consideration of the seriousness of the offense balanced against the danger of the pursuit; and they provide for discontinuance of the pursuit.

The issues normally include: (1) when to initiate pursuit; (2) number of units permitted; (3) responsibilities of primary and secondary units; (4) driving tactics; (5) helicopter assistance; (6) communications; (7) capture; (8) discontinuance of pursuit; (9) supervisory responsibilities; (10) firearms use; (11) offense categories—traffic misdemeanors, felonies (types and differing seriousness); (12) blocking, ramming, boxing, roadblocks; (13) absolute speed limits; (14) interjurisdictional considerations; (15) conditions of vehicle, driver, roadway, weather, traffic; (16) hazards to users of highway; and (17) reporting and post-pursuit analysis.

If a police administrator carefully covers these points, his policy should be quite complete.

On initiation of pursuit for traffic offenses and misdemeanors, one policy cautions the officer against a high-speed chase and states:[19]

The officer shall slow down, and in some cases, cease the pursuit because the apprehension of the violator is not as important as the safety of the citizen and the police officer himself. Some may say that when a suspect attempts to elude the police there may be deeper factors, such as possession of narcotics, a stolen vehicle, or a car containing stolen items. This is just an assumption and would not justify a high-speed chase which resulted in an accident. It is better to let the suspect get away than to jeopardize the lives of so many others. . . . All pursuits originating as a result of traffic infractions will be terminated within a reasonably short distance.

With respect to felonies, the same policy states:[20]

In the case of a major felony such as murder or armed robbery, or if there is reason to believe the suspect might kill or injure someone if allowed to escape, then a pursuit might be justified depending on the circumstances involved.

A supervisor from the same department comments:[21]

If you think the suspect has killed somebody, or taken a hostage, or committed rape, it is better to do everything you can to get the guy. But if it is a stolen car, or even somebody who has robbed a bank and has $100,000 in his car, maybe you are better off letting him go.

Another policy emphasizes:[22]

The immediate apprehension of the violator is never more important than the safety of innocent motorists or the deputy himself. When it becomes apparent that the immediacy of apprehension is out-weighed by a clear and unreasonable danger to the deputy and others, the pursuit must be abandoned.

The same policy states under "abandonment of pursuit":[23]

The decision to pursue is not irreversible, and it is the intelligent deputy who knows when to call off the chase. Deputies must continually question whether the seriousness of the crime justifies continuing the pursuit. A pursuit shall be discontinued:

When there is a clear and unreasonable danger to the deputy and other users of the highway. A clear danger exists when speeds dangerously exceed the normal flow of traffic or when vehicular or pedestrian traffic necessitates dangerous maneuvering exceeding the performance capabilities of the radio car or the driver.

After a reasonably short distance when the only known reason for the pursuit is traffic violations or other misdemeanors, or known or suspected grand theft auto suspects.

When the violator can be identified to the point where an apprehension can be more safely made at a later time.

The policy also suggests a maximum speed of 60 mph on urban surface streets and 80-90 mph on rural roads or freeways. It emphasizes that "any doubt concerning the propriety of a pursuit should be resolved in favor of the safety of departmental members and other users of the highway."

As for the other common policy rules for pursuit driving, they can be summarized as follows. Pursuing units are limited to two and "caravanning" is not permitted. Helicopter assistance is encouraged. Communications must be frequent, giving the type of offense, description of suspect and vehicle, direction of travel, speed, traffic, and other pertinent conditions. The information is evaluated by a supervisor who has authority to order discontinuance of the pursuit. However, he does not order continuance if the pursuing officer decides to abandon the pursuit. After capture of the suspect other units remain away from the scene unless assistance is requested. Use of firearms is generally prohibited unless officers are fired upon. Ramming is generally prohibited, and boxing in is discouraged but allowed by some departments, not by others. Roadblocks are permitted by some departments as a last resort.

There is some trend, then, toward providing officers with a detailed policy for pursuit driving, reflecting the recognition of the need to balance the known offense and the need for immediate capture against the risks for officers and other citizens.

Further considerations

Some police officers will resent any restriction on their ability to pursue any and all fleeing offenders. This is understandable, for it goes against our sense of police tradition, part of which is that "we get our man." Some will say that if an accident occurs, it is the fault of the fleeing suspect, not the officer. Certainly the suspect is at fault. But if the officer abandons the pursuit, the need for the suspect to continue his reckless driving is removed, and a serious accident involving an innocent citizen may be prevented. It really goes back to the earlier philosophical question: What kind of offense makes the need to attempt an immediate capture so great that other lives should be endangered?

Others will say that a restrictive policy will be an open invitation to people to run from the police. They assume that large numbers of previously law-abiding citizens will suddenly start to try to outrun the police, an assumption difficult to believe. In any event, regardless of how many misdemeanants try to outrun the police on foot, our social policy and law do not allow us to use deadly force against them or to endanger other citizens to effect their capture. We ought to adhere to a similar policy when the flight is attempted in a motor vehicle; or, if anything, stricter standards should apply because of the inherent danger of a vehicle.

It would, of course, be very helpful if police administrators in all jurisdictions would maintain statistical records on all their pursuits, including such information as the known offense, other offenses later discovered, speed, length, injuries, fatalities, and other consequences in cases where pursuits were completed to apprehension and in cases where they were abandoned. Such information would be of great assistance in further policy formulation and modification.

1. *The Flint Journal,* "Chase Ends in 6 Deaths, 13-year-old at Wheel," May 31, 1981, p. A-3.
2. Kim Chapin, "If a Guy Goes Flying By, The Decision is to Get Him," *Police Magazine,* Vol. 1, No. 5 (Nov. 1978), pp. 36-7.
3. *Drescher* vs. *Employers Mutual, et al.*
4. *Roberson* vs. *City of Detroit, et al.*
5. The Center for the Environment and Man, Inc., *A Study of the Problem of Hot Pursuits by the Police* (Washington, D.C.: U.S. Department of Transportation, July 1970), p. 2.
6. Center, p. 6.
7. Physicians for Automotive Safety, *Rapid Pursuit by the Police: Causes, Hazards, Consequences* (Springfield, N.J., Mimeographed, undated document).
8. Edward E. Doughtery, "Training the Police Pursuit Driver," *Police* (Nov.-Dec. 1966), p. 76.
9. Doughtery, p. 78.
10. Edward Byrne, "Safety Considerations in Traffic Police Work," *Law and Order* (June 1974), p. 45.
11. D.P. VanBlaricom, "A Sensible Alternative to Those High Speed Police Chases," *The Seattle Times* (Nov. 25, 1980), p. A-11.
12. Louis H. Barth, "Police Pursuit: A Panoply of Problems," *The Police Chief* (Feb. 1981), p. 55.
13. We recognize that the states have vehicle code sections dealing with exemptions for emergency vehicles. These codes do not begin to address the issue.
14. Doughtery, p. 76.
15. Will E. Bachofner, "Safe Driving," *FBI Law Enforcement Bulletin* (June 1966), p. 2.
16. Carolyn S. Tweed, "Washington, D.C. Police Use Old Air Force Runway for Pursuit Driving Course," *The Police Chief* (April 1978), p. 85.
17. Chapin, p. 41.
18. The same practice should be followed in other types of operations such as shootings, barricaded gunman situations, hostage situations, major crime scene investigations, etc. Citizen complaints should also constitute a similar learning process.
19. Anaheim Police Department, "Procedure-Operation of Police Vehicles," June 1978, section 11a and b.
20. Anaheim, section 12a.
21. Chapin, p. 40.
22. Los Angeles County Sheriff's Temporary Departmental Order, "Emergency Driving Policies," October 23, 1979, section 5-09/081.00.
23. Los Angeles County, section 5-09/081.05.

PART 3

Operational
Considerations

The Newark Foot Patrol Experiment: Executive Summary

Police Foundation

This is a description of an experiment in foot patrol in Newark, New Jersey. This evaluation came about as a result of an invitation from Governor Brendan Byrne to Patrick Murphy, president of the Police Foundation, to observe a unique program: the Safe and Clean Neighborhoods Program, which provides funds for foot patrol officers and for upgrading and stabilizing neighborhoods in 28 cities in New Jersey. This evaluation concerns only the foot patrol aspect of the program.

The planning of the evaluation began in mid-1976, and all participants agreed on an evaluation design late in 1977.

The state of New Jersey paid for all the program costs and the Police Foundation bore all the evaluation costs. No funds were paid by the state of New Jersey to the Police Foundation, nor by the Foundation to the state.

The major portion of this evaluation was an experiment conducted in Newark. The evaluation rests heavily on this experiment. During its final stages, fiscal conditions in Newark necessitated that 200 Newark police officers be laid off. Although the experimental interventions were not affected, the announcement of this drastic personnel issue created an extremely serious conflict between the police (as represented by their unions) and the mayor and police director. Beyond calls for the resignation of the police director, the unions vociferously proclaimed the extreme dangers these layoffs would create for citizens in Newark. The uproar was prominently presented in the press. There is no alternative but to assume that

Reprinted with permission from: Police Foundation, *The Newark Foot Patrol Experiment* (Washington, D.C.: Police Foundation, 1981).

these circumstances did affect the experimental outcomes. The report addresses the probable effects.

Evaluation design

Three designs were used to evaluate the effects of foot patrol.

Design I   This design was to compare the attitudes of officers assigned to foot patrol with those of officers assigned to motor patrol in all 28 cities receiving state funding for foot patrol.

Design II   In Elizabeth, two basic patterns of foot patrol coverage were found to exist. Some areas had steady foot patrol coverage both before and after the Safe and Clean Neighborhoods Program began; other areas had no foot patrol coverage before the program began. The levels of reported crime in these areas before and after foot patrol coverage was implemented were compared in those two types of areas. Initially, the plans were to use reported crime statistics from three additional cities. Although the cooperation of these other cities was high, the difficulty and cost of acquiring these additional data became prohibitive.

Design III   In Newark, assignment logs of all existing foot posts were examined to determine which had been patrolled on foot consistently since the beginning of the Safe and Clean Neighborhoods Program. There were eight such beats. These beats were matched into four sets of two beats each, based on the number of residential and nonresidential units found on each beat. Out of each pair of beats, one beat was randomly assigned to continue foot patrol, and foot patrol was discontinued in the other. In addition, foot patrol was instituted in four areas (similar to those previously patrolled on foot) which had not had it before. Outcome measures included reported crime, arrests and victimization, fear, and satisfaction of residents and representatives of commercial establishments.

Summary of findings

1. The first major finding, significant regardless of analytic approach used, was that *residents were aware of levels of foot patrol.* Although people seem to be only modestly aware of the levels of motor patrol, and are not particularly sensitive to team policing, they seem to be acutely aware of the presence of foot patrol. Given the different sizes of beats and speed of movement, perhaps this is not surprising. It does suggest that, if a goal of a program is to make citizens more aware of police presence, foot patrol is especially useful.

Commercial respondents reported drops in their awareness of foot patrol in all three conditions. This is not surprising: the experimentally manipulated foot patrol posts were covered during times when most commercial establishments were closed. In addition, extensive press coverage of the reduction in the total number of police officers contributed to the fear campaign.

2. *Generally, crime levels, as measured by the victimization survey and reported crime* (to the extent that reported crime measures it) *are not affected for residents or commercial respondents at a significant level.* There seem to be no strong trends in the data.

3. In measures dealing with citizens' perception of crime, a different pattern emerges. *Consistently, residents in beats where foot patrol was added see the severity of crime problems diminishing in their neighborhoods at levels greater than the other two areas.* Street disorders, serious crime, drug usage, vandalism, victimization of the elderly, and auto theft all are perceived to be less of a problem. The greatest decreases occur in perceptions about street disorders, victimization of the elderly, and auto theft, all of which are street crimes potentially controllable by foot officers.

Commercial respondents report a different pattern. *When statistical significance is found (street disorder, drugs, teenage loitering, prostitutes, auto theft, rape, and shoplifting), the trend is that the perceived severity of the problem is greatest in the "added" beats (with the exception of auto theft) and least in the "dropped" beats.* Again, this finding is consistent with the fact that most commercial respondents were not exposed to the foot patrol experiment, but *were* exposed to the "fear city" campaign.

4. *In looking at the perceived safety of the neighborhood for residents, a pattern similar to that for perceived severity of crime problems emerges. Of the six times statistical significance is found, five favor the "added" beats.* The perceptions regarding likelihood of crime, of serious nighttime crime, of day street robberies, of daytime assaults, and of general feelings of personal safety either go down or increase less in the "added" areas. The second pattern was that the level of safety in the beats with new foot patrol increased in eight of the nine measures.

The pattern for commercial respondents again differs. Although no items were found to be of statistical significance, the perceived safety of *all* conditions decreased.

5. *A similar pattern emerges in responses to questions about what protective measures residents and merchants take to avoid crime. In three cases—crime avoidance efforts during the day, a composite of crime avoidance efforts, and non-weapon protection against theft—residents of the beats that added foot patrol indicated a greater reduction in the use of protective measures than persons in the other two conditions. No items of significance appeared in the analysis of the commercial respondents' responses.* However, 28 of the 42 measures were positive, indicating that there was a general trend in businesses to take protective measures.

6. *The final attitudinal dimension is the evaluation of police services by residents and commercial respondents. For residents, statistical significance is obtained in all 12 measures; more positive or less negative responses occur in the areas that added foot beats in 10 of the 12 measures.* Of these ten, two of the questions deal with police services generally and the rest deal with residents' evaluation of motor patrol services. The overwhelming impression is that positive attitudes gained from foot patrol generalize to other patrol services, an important finding in inner city urban areas, where both citizens and police protest police-citizen alienation.

The pattern is again different in the commercial sample, where only five items achieve statistical significance. This failure to achieve strong effects is consistent with the fact that the foot patrol experiment did not take place during normal business hours.

Thus, the general impression is gained that while foot patrol may not have a significant effect on crime, it does affect citizens' fear of crime, the protective measures they take to avoid crime, and the perceived safety of their neighborhoods in consistent and systematic ways. In general, when foot patrol is added, citizens' fear of typical street crimes seems to go down and generalized feelings of personal safety go up.

False Alarms: Do We Cope or Control?

Robert E. Lovell

"Car 8 handle a signal 2 at 100 Turner Street. Respond code 4 time 2230 hrs."

"Cars 1 and 3 handle a signal 2 at 207 Main Street. Respond code 1 time 2235 hrs."

To someone listening in to the police frequency, these two calls may seem to be alike, but to the responding radio cars they are vastly different. A signal 2 indicates that a business alarm has been activated, code 4 instructs the responding units to handle the call as routine, while a code 1 puts the call into an emergency handling condition. The two calls, and the responses to them, are indicative of a problem which is common to almost every police department—the false burglar alarm signal.

At 100 Turner Street, a national paint company maintains its corporate headquarters, while 207 Main Street has on its ground floor a large jewelry store. A study showed that 100 Turner Street was one of the most abused alarms in the city of Danbury. The jewelry store alarm rarely, if ever, went off unless a burglary was in progress. The dispatcher, realizing this, sends the cars accordingly —one man for Turner Street, two for Main Street—since he perceived the latter to be potentially a more dangerous situation.

Every police department is faced with the problem of false burglar alarms. Departments can generally do one of two things, cope with them as being a necessary evil or make an attempt to control those which, by poor design and/or installation or through improper use by employees, seem to go off almost every day. After realizing

Reproduced from *The Police Chief* magazine, February, 1982, issue, with permission of the International Association of Chiefs of Police, P.O. Box 6010, 13 Firstfield Road, Gaithersburg, Maryland 20878.

the drain on police manpower caused by false alarm problems, Danbury Police Chief Nelson F. Macedo commissioned the writer to do a study of the problem and to suggest a way to control it.

The first step was to measure the impact of alarms, false and real, on total services. Using the calendar year of 1979 as a base, we began to draw a profile of alarm responses as they affected total police service. Danbury is a city of just under 60,000 people covering 43 square miles with a police department of just over 100 men, of which 70 are assigned to the patrol division. Danbury is the largest city in the area and is the hub of northern Fairfield County, Connecticut.

During 1979, the department responded to 34,031 police service calls of which 3,965, or 12 percent, were burglar or holdup alarms. This figured out to 3.62 alarm responses of all types per eight-hour working shift. Working on the assumption that an average of two patrol cars are sent on each call with the officers spending an average of thirty minutes on each call, we estimated that the cost in officer salaries alone was $29,856 per year. We did not attempt to take into account the cost of the telephone operator and dispatcher, air time, or motor vehicle costs. Nor did we consider the possible costs arising from officer injuries at the scene or being involved in a motor vehicle accident on the way.

The problems

In building a case for some type of control, we took a random sample of 1,796 alarms, 45 percent of the total alarm responses. The sample was then broken down into four categories: actual burglaries or holdups, equipment malfunctions, human error, and undetermined reasons. We found the figures broke down as follows:

Reason	Number	Percent
Burglaries/holdups	21	0.01%
Malfunctions	354	19.70%
Errors	786	46.80%
Undetermined	635	35.40%

For our purposes, we considered a malfunction as a breakdown within the system which caused the alarm to activate, as well as outside problems such as power failures or other problems in the electric or telephone lines away from the source. A mistake or error was differentiated as action by the owner or employee of the building which caused the alarm to activate.

Some of the common human errors we found were failure to shut down the system before entering the building, re-entering after the alarm was set, or entering secured areas and testing the equipment without first notifying the department and getting approval. We also found intentional abuse such as tripping a holdup alarm located in a business when the only problem was an unruly customer.

In a few instances, we found persons intentionally tripping the alarm to check on the response time of police units. It was noted that one company had as many as 35 false alarms in the sample which could be traced solely to human error. In order to be fair to the alarm holders, we listed as human errors only those responses which could be proven by the officer at the scene as definite action by a person at the location. If any doubt existed as to the true cause of the alarm, it was listed as being undetermined.

In addition to the costs in manpower, it was also necessary to look at the inherent risk factor to the responding officers. Ideally all alarm responses should be handled as a live call by the assigned officers. In practice, once an alarm at a certain location has proven to be false on a regular basis, the responding officers will tend to take a less than fully cautious attitude. They will approach the building with less than the normal regard for routine safety, thereby opening themselves to the possibility of injury should a holdup or burglary truly be in progress. In addition dispatchers, on a busy night, may tend to stack the call on an abused alarm, opening the department to criticism should the call be valid.

The solution

Having compiled all the data, we felt that there was more than enough evidence to support a request for a new city ordinance. Rather than merely request an ordinance and have the city's corporation counsel draft something that we would find difficult to work with, we decided to draw up our own law, working with samples taken from other locations and incorporating those items we felt best suited our situation.

We began by giving a detailed description of all the terms used in the proposed ordinance so that there could be no misinterpretation. We explained exactly what a burglar and holdup alarm was, including the description as shown in the Connecticut General Statutes. From there, we defined exactly what would constitute an error or mistake, a malfunction, and intentional misuse. By describing in lay terms precisely what each term meant, no one could claim s/he did not understand the ordinance.

We also added a clause giving the chief of police, or a designate, the right to inspect the design and installation of any proposed system and to reject those which appeared to be poorly conceived or constructed.

A provision required that the police department have at all times the names of at least two persons who would have the knowledge and ability to reset the alarm and secure the building in case of a burglary or false alarm. A provision was then written in to hold the police department harmless should a keyholder refuse to respond to the location when notified of an alarm. In that case, the units on the scene would be returned to service and we would not respond to that location again until the building was properly secured and the alarm reset.

Having laid the groundwork, we then established a system of fines for violating the various provisions. At first a three-tier fine schedule was considered, but was later discarded as being too confusing and unwieldy. Working with the city common council, the legislative arm of city government, we settled on a single fine of $25.00 for each error or malfunction over three occasions in any calendar month. After the second incident, the records bureau sends a registered letter to the alarm holder warning that s/he has only one false alarm left. After the third alarm, and for each subsequent unfounded alarm, the fine of $25.00 is automatic.

Since the intentional activation of an alarm was felt to be a more serious offense, we established a separate section which made it unlawful to intentionally activate any burglar or holdup alarm when no crime is occurring or to test any alarm without first notifying the department and getting approval for the test. To insure security, a rigid code number system was assigned each alarm company which they would have to give to the dispatcher before the start of any test. Due to the more serious nature of this situation, a fine of $100.00 was established and provisions were made for additional prosecution under the Connecticut General Statutes for Falsely Reporting an Incident.

In order to insure payment of fines, a provision was included requiring payment within 30 days and giving the chief of police the right to order the alarm removed from the Varitech notification panel at police headquarters for nonpayment. (That is the source of the bulk of our alarms.)

An attempt was made to establish a training and equipment fund within the police department budget into which the fines would be paid. This fund, under the control of the chief of police, could be used only for training programs and equipment purchase once the annual budget was set. This idea was dropped when the city director of finance pointed out that, under city ordinance, all money must go into the general fund except for sewer and water usage fees. At best, we were able to get a gentlemen's agreement that a fund transfer request would be given a favorable reply if requested for equipment or training.

Passage

After the original draft was written, I spoke to several local alarm companies and found, to my surprise, that they were not only in favor of the ordinance but were willing to help modify it and iron out any flaws. Once we had a workable form, the report and sample ordinance were submitted by the chief of police to the full common council for consideration. After several public hearings and a few more modifications, which the department did not necessarily agree with but had to accept, the council passed the ordinance on February 3, 1981. Thirty days after it was published in the local newspaper on March 9, 1981, almost one full year after I first began the study, the ordinance became law.

False alarms: a Canadian problem too

According to Cst. Gene Janzen, writing in the *British Columbia Police Journal* (Winter 1981), "A major problem to police departments in Canada (and the U.S.) is the increasingly large number of false burglar alarms. The concern to a police department, primarily, is the waste of man hours. In addition, the individual police member must also cope with the frustration . . . "

Janzen recommends, "It is of vital importance that we, the police, initiate and work toward attaining a more agreeable relationship with alarm companies. A good basis for this could be provided through a better understanding of each other, our roles, and procedures."

In seeking a better relationship, Janzen argues that "it is always beneficial to air the complaints." He lists police complaints in Canada as focusing on the following issues: (1) Alarm companies are not concerned if police waste time and effort; (2) alarm companies are using police as runners; (3) if the reference (runner) doesn't attend when called, why then should police be concerned; and (4) incorrect information about an alarm is sometimes given; for example, audible alarm, however, on arrival, all is found quiet.

On the other hand, Janzen points out alarm companies complain about the incomplete investigation of an alarm call. "After a perimeter check, a police member may report a building secure. It is later discovered by someone else that the building has been entered or an attempted entry has been made."

"Another complaint," according to Janzen, "occurs when a police officer offers an opinion about an alarm system when the member's knowledge of alarm systems and causal factors is limited."

Janzen recommends these basic rules:

"The subscriber should always treat his alarm system with the responsibility it demands and keeping in mind the consequences of a moment's carelessness.

"The alarm company should always reach for the highest standards possible. . . .

"The police member should always turn in a false alarm report so the call can be properly documented and acted upon by follow-up members."

The Minneapolis
Domestic Violence
Experiment

———————— Lawrence W. Sherman and Richard A. Berk

Under a grant from the National Institute of Justice, the Minneapolis Police Department and the Police Foundation conducted an experiment from early 1981 to mid-1982 testing police responses to domestic violence.[1] A technical report of the experiment can be found in the April 1984 issue of the *American Sociological Review*. This report summarizes the results and implications of the experiment. It also shows how the experiment was designed and conducted so the reader may understand and judge the findings.

Findings in brief

The Minneapolis domestic violence experiment was the first scientifically controlled test of the effects of arrest for any crime. It found that arrest was the most effective of three standard methods police use to reduce domestic violence. The other police methods—attempting to counsel both parties or sending assailants away from home for several hours—were found to be considerably less effective in deterring future violence in the cases examined. These were not life-threatening cases, but rather the minor assaults which make up the bulk of police calls to domestic violence.

The findings, standing alone as the result of the experiment, do not necessarily imply that all suspected assailants in domestic violence incidents should be arrested. Other experiments in other settings are needed to learn more. But the preponderance of evidence in the Minneapolis study strongly suggests that the police should use arrest in most domestic violence cases.

Why the experiment was conducted

The purpose of the experiment was to address an intense debate about how police should respond to misdemeanors, cases of domestic violence. At least three viewpoints can be identified in this debate:

1. The traditional police approach of doing as little as possible, on the premise that offenders will not be punished by the courts even if they are arrested, and that the problems are basically not solvable.
2. The clinical psychologists' recommendations that police actively mediate or arbitrate disputes underlying the violence, restoring peace but not making any arrests.
3. The approach recommended by many women's groups and the Police Executive Research Forum[2] of treating the violence as a criminal offense subject to arrest.

If the purpose of police responses to domestic violence calls is to reduce the likelihood of that violence recurring, the question is which of these approaches is more effective than the others?

Policing domestic assaults

Police have been typically reluctant to make arrests for domestic violence,[3] as well as for a wide range of other kinds of offenses, unless a victim demands an arrest, a suspect insults an officer, or other factors are present.[4] Parnas' observations of the Chicago police[5] found four categories of police action in these situations: negotiating or otherwise "talking out" the dispute; threatening the disputants and then leaving; asking one of the parties to leave the premises, or, very rarely, making an arrest.

Similar patterns are found in many other cities. Surveys of battered women who tried to have their domestic assailants arrested report that arrest occurred in only 10 percent or 3 percent of the cases.[6] Surveys of police agencies in Illinois and New York[7] found explicit policies against arrest in the majority of the agencies surveyed. Despite the fact that violence is reported to be present in one-third to two-thirds of all domestic disturbances police respond to,[8] police department data show arrests in only five percent of those disturbances in Oakland, six percent of those disturbances in a Colorado city, and six percent in Los Angeles County.[9]

The best available evidence on the frequency of arrest is the observations from the Black and Reiss study of Boston, Washington, and Chicago police in 1966.[10] Police responding to disputes in those cities made arrests in 27 percent of violent felonies and 17 percent of the violent misdemeanors. Among married couples, they made arrests in 26 percent of the cases, but tried to remove one of the parties in 38 percent of the cases.[11]

The apparent preference of many police for separating the parties rather than arresting the offender has been attacked from two directions over the past 15 years. The original critique came from clinical psychologists who agreed that police should rarely make arrests in domestic assault cases[12] and argued that police should mediate the disputes responsible for the violence. A highly publicized demonstration project teaching police special counseling skills for family crisis intervention[13] failed to show a reduction in violence, but was interpreted as a success nonetheless. By 1977, a national survey of police agencies with 100 or more officers found that over 70 percent reported a family crisis intervention training program in operation. Although it is not clear whether these programs reduced separation and increased mediation, a decline in arrests was noted for some.[14] Indeed, many sought explicitly to *reduce* the number of arrests.[15]

By the mid-1970s, police practices were criticized from the opposite direction by feminist groups. Just as psychologists succeeded in having many police agencies respond to domestic violence as "half social work and half police work," feminists began to argue that police put "too much emphasis on the social work aspect and not enough on the criminal."[16] Widely publicized lawsuits in New York and Oakland sought to compel police to make arrests in every case of domestic assault, and state legislatures were lobbied successfully to reduce the evidentiary requirements needed for police to make arrests for misdemeanor domestic assaults. Some legislatures are now considering statutes requiring police to make arrests in these cases.

The feminist critique was bolstered by a study showing that for 85 percent of a sample of spouse killings, police had intervened at least once in the preceding two years.[17] For 54 percent of those homicides, police had intervened five or more times. But it was impossible to determine from the data whether making more or fewer arrests would have reduced the homicide rate.

How the experiment was designed

In order to find which police approach was most effective in deterring future domestic violence, the Police Foundation and the Minneapolis Police Department agreed to conduct a classic experiment. A classic experiment is a research design that allows scientists to discover the effects of one thing on another by holding constant all other possible causes of those effects. The design of the experiment called for a lottery selection, which ensured that there would be no difference among the three groups of suspects receiving the different police responses.[18] The lottery determined which of the three responses police officers would use on each suspect in a domestic assault case. According to the lottery, a suspect would be arrested, or sent from the scene of the assault for eight hours, or given some form of advice, which could include mediation at an officer's discretion. In the language of the experiment, these responses were called the arrest, send, and advise treatments. The design called for a six-month follow-up period to measure the frequency and seriousness of any future domestic violence in all cases in which the police intervened.

The design applied only to simple (misdemeanor) domestic assaults, where both the suspect and the victim were present when the police arrived. Thus, the experiment included only those cases in which police were empowered, but not required, to make arrests under a recently liberalized Minnesota state law. The police officer must have probable cause to believe that a cohabitant or spouse had assaulted the victim within the past four hours. Police need not have witnessed the assault. Cases of life-threatening or severe injury, usually labeled as a felony (aggravated assault), were excluded from the design.

The design called for each officer to carry a pad of report forms, color coded for the three different police responses. Each time the officers encountered a situation that fit the experiment's criteria, they were to take whatever action was indicated by the report form on the top of the pad. The forms were numbered and arranged for each officer in an order determined by the lottery. The consistency of the lottery assignment was to be monitored by research staff observers riding on patrol for a sample of evenings.

After a police action was taken at the scene of a domestic violence incident, the officer was to fill out a brief report and give it to the research staff for follow-up. As a further check on the lottery process, the staff logged in the reports in the order in which they were received and made sure that the sequence corresponded to the original assignment of responses.

Anticipating something of the background of victims in the experiment, a predominantly minority, female research staff was employed to contact the victims for a detailed, face-to-face interview, to be followed by telephone follow-up interviews every two weeks for 24 weeks. The interviews were designed primarily to measure the frequency and seriousness of victimizations caused by the suspect after police intervention. The research staff also collected criminal justice reports that mentioned suspects' names during the six-month follow-up period.

Conduct of the experiment

As is common in field experiments, the actual research process in Minneapolis suffered some slippage from the original plan. This section recounts the difficulties encountered in conducting the experiment. None of these difficulties, however, proved finally detrimental to the experiment's validity.

In order to gather data as quickly as possible, the experiment was originally located in two of Minneapolis's four precincts, those with the highest density of domestic violence crime reports and arrests. The 34 officers assigned to those areas were invited to a three-day planning meeting and asked to participate in the study for one year. All but one agreed. The conference also produced a draft order for Chief Anthony Bouza's signature specifying the rules of the experiment. These rules created several new situations to be excluded from the experiment, including whether a suspect attempted to assault police officers, a victim persistently demanded an arrest, or both parties were injured. These additional exceptions allowed for the possibility that the lottery process would be violated more for the separation and mediation treatments than for the arrest treatment. However, a statistical analysis showed that these changes posed no threat to the validity of the experiment's findings.

The experiment began on March 17, 1981. The expectation was that it would take about one year to produce about 300 cases. In fact, the experiment ran until August 1, 1982, and produced 314 case reports. The officers agreed to meet monthly with Lawrence W. Sherman, the project director, and Nancy Wester, the project manager. By the third or fourth month, two facts became clear: Only about 15 to 20 officers either were coming to meetings or turning in cases, and the rate at which the cases were turned in would make it difficult to complete the project in one year. By November, it was decided to recruit more officers in order to obtain cases more rapidly. Eighteen additional officers joined the project. But like the original group, most of these officers turned in only one or two cases. Indeed, three of the original officers produced almost 28 percent of the cases, in part because they worked a particularly violent beat and in part because they had a greater commitment to the study. A statistical analysis showed that the effects of police actions did not vary according to which officer was involved. Since the lottery was by officer, this condition created no validity problem for the cases in the study.

There is little doubt that many of the officers occasionally failed to follow fully the experimental design. Some of the failures were due to forgetfulness, such as leaving report pads at home or at the police station. Other failures derived from misunderstanding about whether the experiment applied in certain situations; application of experimental rules under complex circumstances was sometimes confusing. Finally, there were occasional situations that were simply not covered by experimental rules.

Whether any officer intentionally subverted the design is unclear. The plan to monitor the lottery process with ride-along observers broke down because of the unexpectedly low frequency of cases meeting the experimental criteria. Observers had to ride for many weeks before they saw an officer apply one of the treatments. An attempt was made to solve this problem with "chase alongs," in which observers rode in their own car with a portable police radio and drove to the scene of any domestic call dispatched to any officer in the precinct. Even this method failed.

Thus, the possibility existed that police officers, anticipating from the dispatch call a particular kind of incident and finding the upcoming experimental treatment inappropriate, may have occasionally decided to ignore the experiment. In effect, they may have chosen to exclude certain cases in violation of the experimental design. Such action would have biased the selection of the experiment's sample of cases, but there is little reason to believe it actually happened. On the other hand, had they, for example, not felt like filling out extra forms on a given day, this would not affect the validity of the experiment's results.

Table 1 shows the degree to which the three treatments were delivered as designed. Ninety-nine percent of the suspects targeted for arrest actually were arrested; 78 percent of those scheduled to receive advice did; and 73 percent of those to be sent out of the residence for eight hours actually were sent. One explanation for this pattern, consistent with experimental guidelines, is that mediating and sending were more difficult ways for police to control a situation. There was a greater likelihood that officers might have to resort to arrest as a fallback position. When the assigned treatment is arrest, there is no need for a fallback position. For example, some offenders may have refused to comply with an order to leave the premises.

This pattern could have biased estimates of the relative effectiveness of arrest by removing uncooperative and difficult offenders

Designed treatment	Delivered treatment			
	Arrest	Advise	Separate	
Arrest	98.9% N=91	0.0% N=0	1.1% N=1	29.3% N=92
Advise	17.6% N=19	77.8% N=84	4.6% N=5	34.4% N=108
Separate	22.8% N=26	4.4% N=5	72.8% N=83	36.3% N=114
Total	43.3% N=136	28.3% N=89	28.3% N=89	100% N=314

Table 1. Designed and delivered police treatments in domestic assault cases.

from mediation and separation treatments. Any deterrent effect of arrest could be underestimated and, in the extreme, arrest could be shown to increase the chance of repeat violence. In effect, the arrest group would have too many "bad guys" *relative* to the other treatments.

Fortunately, a statistical analysis of this process shows that the delivered treatments conformed very closely to the experimental design, with no problems of bias.

Things went less well with interviews of victims; only 205 (of 330, counting the few repeat victims twice) could be located and initial interviews obtained, a 62 percent completion rate. Many of the victims simply could not be found, either for the initial interview or for follow-ups. They had left town, moved somewhere else, or refused to answer the phone or doorbell. The research staff made up to 20 attempts to contact these victims and often employed investigative techniques (asking friends and neighbors) to find them. Sometimes these methods worked, only to have the victim give an outright refusal, or break one or more appointments to meet the interviewer at a "safe" location for the interview.

The response rate to the biweekly follow-up interviews was even lower than for the initial interview, as response rates have been in much research on women crime victims. After the first interview, for which the victims were paid $20, there was a gradual falloff in completed interviews with each successive wave; only 161 victims provided all 12 follow-up interviews over the six months, a completion rate of 49 percent. Whether paying for the follow-up interviews would have improved the response rate is unclear; it would have added over $40,000 to the cost of the research. When the telephone interviews yielded few reports of violence, every fourth interview was conducted in person.

Fortunately, there is absolutely no evidence that the experimental treatment assigned to the offender affected the victim's decision to grant initial interviews. Statistical tests showed there was *no* difference in victims' willingness to give interviews according to what police did, race of victim, or race of offender.

In sum, despite the practical difficulties of controlling an experiment and interviewing crime victims in an emotionally charged and violent social context, the experiment succeeded in producing a promising sample of 314 cases with complete official outcome measures and an apparently unbiased sample of responses from the victims in those cases.

Results

The 205 completed initial interviews provide some sense of who the subjects involved in domestic violence are, although the data may not properly represent the characteristics of the full sample of 314.

They show the now familiar pattern that domestic violence cases coming to police attention disproportionately involve unmarried couples with lower than average educational levels, who are disproportionately minority and mixed race (black male, white female) and who are very likely to have had prior violent incidents with police intervention. The 60 percent unemployment rate for the experiment's suspects is strikingly high in a community with only about 5 percent of the workforce unemployed. The 59 percent prior arrest rate is also strikingly high, suggesting (with the 80 percent prior domestic assault rate) that the suspects generally are experienced law-breakers who are accustomed to police interventions. But with the exception of the heavy representation of Native-Americans due to Minneapolis' proximity to many Indian reservations, the characteristics in Table 2 are probably close to those of domestic violence cases coming to police attention in other large U.S. cities.

Two kinds of measures of repeat violence were used in the experiment. One was a police record of an offender repeating domestic violence during the six-month follow-up period, either through an offense or an arrest report written by any officer in the department or through a subsequent report to the project research staff of an intervention by officers participating in the experiment. A second kind of measure came from the interviews in which victims were

Relationship of suspect to victim		Unemployment		
Divorced or separated husband	3%	Victims		61%
Unmarried male lover	45%	Suspects		60%
Current husband	35%			
Wife or girlfriend	2%	**Mean Age**		
Son, brother, roommate, other	15%	Victims		30 years
		Suspects		32 years
Prior assaults and police involvement				
Victims assaulted by suspect, last six months	80%	**Education**		
Police intervention in domestic dispute, last six months	60%		Victim	Suspect
		<high school	43%	42%
Couple in counseling program	27%	high school only	33%	36%
		>high school	24%	22%
Prior arrests of male suspects		**Race**		
Ever arrested for any offense	59%		Victim	Suspect
Ever arrested for crime against person	31%	White	57%	45%
		Black	23%	36%
Ever arrested on domestic violence statute	5%	Native-American	18%	16%
Ever arrested on alcohol offense	29%	Other	2%	3%

N=205 (Those cases for which initial interviews were obtained)

Table 2. Victim and suspect characteristics: initial interview data and police sheets.

asked if there had been a repeat incident with the same suspect, broadly defined to include an actual assault, threatened assault, or property damage.

The technical details of the analysis are reported in the April 1984 *American Sociological Review*. The bar graphs in Figures 1, 2 and 3 approximate equations presented in that article, which made statistical adjustments for such problems as the falloff in victim cooperation with the interviews. Figure 1 shows the results taken from the police records on subsequent violence. The arrest treatment is clearly an improvement over sending the suspect away, which produced two and a half times as many repeat incidents as arrest. The advise treatment was statistically not distinguishable from the other two police actions.

Figure 2 shows a somewhat different picture. According to the victims' reports of repeat violence, arrest is still the most effective police action. But the advise category, not sending the suspect away, produced the worst results, with almost twice as much violence as arrest. Sending the suspect away produced results that were not statistically distinguishable from the results of the other two ac-

N = 314

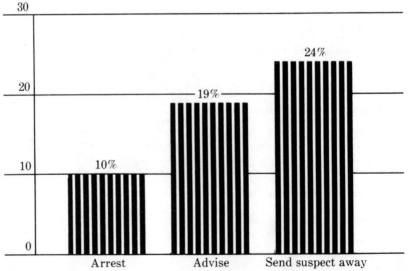

Figure 1. Percentage of repeat violence over six months for each police action: official records.

N = 161

Percent of suspects repeating violence

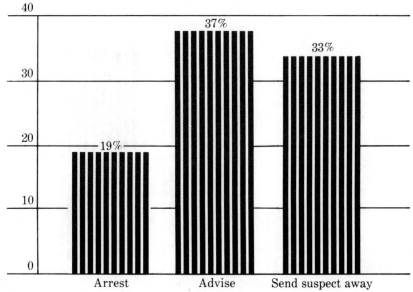

Figure 2. Percentage of repeat violence over six months for each police action: victim interviews.

tions. It is not clear why the order of the three levels of repeat violence is different for those two ways of measuring the violence. But it is clear that arrest works best by either measure.

Additional statistical analysis showed that these findings were basically the same for all categories of suspects. Regardless of the race, employment status, educational level, criminal history of the suspect, or how long the suspect was in jail when arrested, arrest still had the strongest violence reduction effect. There was one factor, however, that seemed to govern the effectiveness of arrest: whether the police showed interest in the victim's side of the story.

Figure 3 shows what happens to the effect of arrest on repeat violence incidents when the police do or do not take the time to listen to the victim, at least as the victim perceives it. If police do listen, that reduces the occurrence of repeat violence even more. But if the victims think the police did not take the time to listen, then the level of victim-reported violence is much higher. One interpretation of this finding is that by listening to the victim, the police "empower" her with their strength, letting the suspect know that she

N = 194

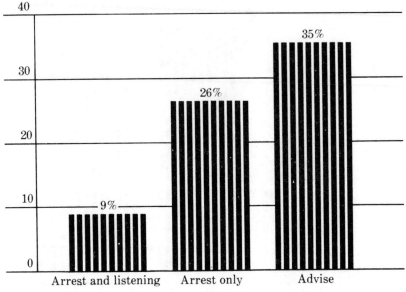

Percent of suspects repeating violence

Police action

All bars are approximate, and drawn from a multivariate model that includes the effects of the prior number of arrests for crimes against persons.

Figure 3. Percentage of repeat violence over six months for each police action and listening to victim: victim interviews

can influence their behavior. If police ignore the victim, the suspect may think he was arrested for arbitrary reasons unrelated to the victim and be less deterred from future violence.

Conclusions and policy implications

It may be premature to conclude that arrest is always the best way for police to handle domestic violence, or that all suspects in such situations should be arrested. A number of factors suggest a cautious interpretation of the findings:

Sample size   Because of the relatively small numbers of suspects in each subcategory (age, race, employment status, criminal history, etc.), it is possible that this experiment failed to discover that for some kinds of people, arrest may only make matters worse. Until subsequent research addresses that issue more thoroughly, it would be premature for state legislatures to pass laws requiring arrests in *all* misdemeanor domestic assaults.

Jail time   Minneapolis may be unusual in keeping most suspects arrested for domestic assault in jail overnight. It is possible that arrest would not have as great a deterrent effect in other cities where suspects may be able to return home within an hour or so of arrest. On the other hand, Minneapolis seems to have the typical court response to domestic violence: only three out of 136 of the arrested suspects ever received a formal sanction from a judge.

Location   Minneapolis is unusual in other respects: a large Native-American population, a very low rate of violence, severe winters, and low unemployment rate. The cultural context of other cities may produce different effects of police actions in domestic violence cases.

Interviewer effect   Strictly speaking, this experiment showed the effects of three police responses *plus* an intensive effort by middle class women to talk to victims over a six-month follow-up. It is possible that the interviewers created a "surveillance" effect that deterred suspects. Whether the same effects would be found without the interviews is still an open question.

A replication of the experiment in a different city is necessary to address these questions. But police officers cannot wait for further research to decide how to handle the domestic violence they face each day. They must use the best information available. This experiment provides the only scientifically controlled comparison of different methods of reducing repeat violence. And on the basis of this study alone, police should probably employ arrest in most cases of minor domestic violence.

Legislative implications   The findings clearly support the 1978 statutory reform in Minnesota that made the experiment possible. In many states the police are not able to make an arrest in domestic violence cases without the signed complaint of a victim. In at least one state (Maryland), police cannot make an arrest without a warrant issued by a magistrate. This experiment shows the vital importance of state legislatures empowering police to make probable cause arrests in cases of domestic simple assault.

Impact of the experiment   As a result of the experiment's findings, the Minneapolis Police Department changed its policy on domestic assault in early March of 1984. The policy did not make arrest 100 percent mandatory. But it did require officers to file a written report explaining why they failed to make an arrest when it was legally possible to do so. The policy was explained to all patrol officers in a roll call videotape. The initial impact of the policy was to double the number of domestic assault arrests, from 13 the weekend before the policy took effect to 28 the first weekend after. On one day in mid-March there were 42 people in the Minneapolis jail on spouse assault charges, a record as far as local officials could remember.

The experiment apparently has done more than contribute to knowledge. It also has helped to change police behavior in Minneapolis, and possibly in other cities as well. If the findings are truly generalizable, the experiment will help ultimately to reduce one of the most common forms of violent crime.

1. The experiment was conducted under grant number 80-IJ-CX-0042 from the Office of Research and Evaluation Methods, Crime Control Theory in Policing Program, National Institute of Justice, U.S. Department of Justice. Points of view or opinions stated in this article do not necessarily represent the official position of the U.S. Department of Justice, the Minneapolis Police Department, or the Police Foundation.

2. Nancy Loving, *Responding to Spouse Abuse and Wife Beating: A Guide for Police* (Washington, D.C.: Police Executive Research Forum, 1980).

3. Sarah Fenstermaker Berk and Donileen R. Loseke, "Handling Family Violence: Situational Determinants of Police Arrest in Domestic Disturbances," *Law and Society Review* 15(1981):315–46.

4. Lawrence W. Sherman, "Causes of Police Behavior: The Current State of Quantitative Research," *Journal of Research in Crime and Delinquency* 17(1980):69–100.

5. Raymond I. Parnas, "The Police Response to the Domestic Disturbance," pp. 206–36 in *The Criminal in the Arms of the Law*, ed. L. Radzinowics and M. E. Wolfgang (New York: Basic Books, 1972).

6. M. Roy, ed., *Battered Women* (New York: Van Nostrand Reinhold, 1977) p. 35; and Richard Langley and Roger C. Levy, *Wife Beating: The Silent Crisis* (New York: E. P. Dutton, 1977), p. 219.

7. Illinois Law Enforcement Commission, "Report on Technical Assistance Project—Domestic Violence Survey [abstract]" (Washington, D.C.; National Criminal Justice Reference Service, 1978); and State of New York, Office of the Minority Leader, "Battered Women: Part I [abstract]" (Washington, D.C.: National Criminal Justice Reference Service, 1978).

8. Morton Bard and Joseph Zacker, "Assaultiveness and Alcohol Use in Family Disputes—Police Perceptions," *Criminology* 12(1974):281–92; and Donald Black, *The Manners and Customs of the Police* (New York: Academic Press, 1980).

9. Jeanie Keeny Meyer and T. D. Lorimer, *Police Intervention Data and Domestic Violence: Exploratory Development and Validation of Prediction Models*, report prepared under grant number RO1MH27918 from the National Institute of Mental Health (Kansas City, Mo.: Kansas City Policy Department, 1977), two citations: Hart, p. 21, and Patrick, Ellis, and Hoffmeister, p. 21; and Charles D. Emerson, "Family Violence: A Study by the Los Angeles County Sheriff's Department," *Police Chief*, June 1979, pp. 48–50.

10. Black, *Manners and Customs*, p. 182.

11. *Ibid.*, p. 158.

12. Jane Potter, "The Police and the Battered Wife: The Search for Understanding," *Police Magazine* 1(1978):46; and James A. Fagin, "The Effects of Police Interpersonal

Communications Skills on Conflict Resolution," Ph.D. diss., Southern Illinois University (Ann Arbor: University Microfilms, 1978), pp. 123-24.

13. Morton Bard, *Training Police as Specialists in Family Crisis Intervention* (Washington, D.C.: U.S. Department of Justice, 1970).

14. P. B. Wylie et al., "Approach to Evaluating a Police Program of Family Crisis Interventions in Six Demonstration Cities—Final Report [abstract]" (Washington, D.C.: National Criminal Justice Reference Service, 1976).

15. University of Rochester, "FACIT—Family Conflict Intervention Team Experiment—Experimental Action Program [abstract]" (Washington, D.C.: National Criminal Justice Reference Service, 1974); and Thomas Ketterman and Marjorie Kravits, *Police Crisis Intervention: A Selected Bibliography* (Washington, D.C.: National Criminal Justice Reference Service, 1978).

16. Langley and Levy, *Wife Beating*, p. 218.

17. Police Foundation, *Domestic Violence and the Police: Studies in Detroit and Kansas City* (Washington, D.C.: The Police Foundation, 1976).

18. Thomas D. Cook and Donald T. Campbell, *Quasi-Experimentation: Design and Analysis Issues for Field Settings* (Chicago: Rand McNally, 1979).

Police and Community Participation in Anti-Crime Programs

———————— Richard R. Bennett and Sandra Baxter

Since the mid-1960s and the occurrence of the urban riots, crime and crime prevention have become major political and social issues. Reported national crime rates increased each year during the 1960s and 1970s. In numerous opinion polls conducted during the two decades, the public consistently ranked crime as one of the most pressing problems facing America.

The government's response to the growing problem was to increase spending on the criminal justice system, particularly the police, through the Law Enforcement Assistance Administration (LEAA). The strategy reflected the prevailing public belief that the job of crime prevention and control rested solely with the justice system, and especially with the police.

Continued increases in the level of street crime, however, began to shake the public's confidence that police, given even extraordinary resources, could reduce crime. This shift in attitude coincided with the emergence of research findings suggesting that the police in fact had little effect on the prevention or control of crime.

Research findings from Kansas City, Newark, and other studies on team policing, the investigatory process, and response time indicated that the police were, by and large, powerless to prevent crime. These findings were not surprising to those in the field for three reasons. First, the police traditionally respond reactively, based on such external demands as citizen calls for service and justice system priorities, rather than proactively to stop crime from occurring.[1] Second, constitutional limitations on search and seizure and surveillance bar the police from using many methods that could pre-

The authors gratefully acknowledge Robert Johnson's comments on an earlier draft.

vent individuals from committing crimes. Third, and most important, the police have not had control over the factors that actually
cause crime. They are powerless to ameliorate poverty and discrimination, not to mention the psychological forces at work in families
and neighborhoods which translate social pressures into criminal
behavior. Thus, while in the public's eye the police were not fulfill-
ing their function, to the more trained eye the police were faced with
an impossible mandate.

The apparent inability of police to stem rising crime rates, coupled with a worsening national economy, moved citizens, researchers, and policymakers in the 1970s to devise less costly means of
controlling and preventing crime. The Reagan administration's
themes of decreased federal services and increased local volunteerism introduced in 1980 coincided with (some say justified) substantial budget cuts to states and municipalities. Crime prevention and
control became the joint responsibility of financially weakened local
police agencies and the residents they served.

The shift from federal support to community-based initiatives,
however, was neither realized overnight nor attributable solely to
economic problems or federal policy shifts. Neighborhood crime
prevention had been a topic for community organizers and justice
researchers since the President's Crime Commission of 1968. Oscar
Newman's work on defensible space,[2] which viewed the physical
environment as contributing to crime and its control, was one of the
first to shift responsibility away from the police. Residential and
commercial security surveys and property marking programs (e.g.,
Operation Identification) were being implemented in many neighborhoods. The apparent success of these programs continued the
movement away from sole reliance on the police and toward greater
emphasis on community-based programs.

These programs came under close scrutiny. Researchers soon
realized that the major preventive elements of the programs were
not simply physical changes such as target hardening and environmental redesign, but rather the attitudinal and behavioral changes
they generated. Newman, for example, acknowledged the importance of citizen involvement when he stated that "through manipu-
lation of building and spatial configuration, one can create areas for
which people adopt concern."[3] By the mid-1970s there was widespread belief that organized, neighborhood-based (or block-based or
building-based) crime prevention programs worked. Yin documented the existence and focus of more than 100 of these programs
in a Justice Department–funded study.[4] The programs involved such
activities as clubs, watches, patrols, escort services, and public education campaigns. During the late 1970s and early 1980s, the number of anti-crime programs that included some type of neighborhood control effort continued to increase across the country. In one

county bordering on the nation's capital, over one thousand neighborhood watch programs existed in 1984.

The impetus for the creation of community-based programs has stemmed in part from citizens' fear of crime, their lack of confidence in police effectiveness, and their belief that volunteerism is one of the few untapped resources available. The impetus has also sprung from an apparent effect of the programs: a downward trend in crime rates. The Uniform Crime Reports for 1981–83 indicated that the crime rate for index offenses decreased at approximately 4 percent per year. Many federal, state, and local law enforcement officials attributed part of the reduction to the efforts and proliferation of community crime programs. FBI Director William Webster stated, "With citizens taking an active part, . . . those efforts are finally having an impact on the crime problem."[5] The police chief of Alexandria, Virginia, contended that "after the implementation of the crime Neighborhood Watch program done by the community with the assistance of the police, the crime stats reflected a 98.2 percent decrease in crime, with no added police surveillance or deployment."[6]

These claims are questioned in a great deal of literature reporting evaluations of neighborhood anti-crime programs and showing little or no lasting effect. The early evaluations funded by the National Institute of Law Enforcement and Criminal Justice did document a decline in burglaries, but the results have either been refuted by the same researchers several years later[7] or criticized on methodological grounds by other evaluators.[8] Experts in criminal justice have attributed the drop in crime rate to a decline in the number of men age 16–24 in the population, a group that disproportionately accounts for crime.[9]

There are at least three reasons for the public's failure to understand that citizen-based programs have little impact on crime. First, the number of credible program evaluations (i.e., those not suffering fatal design or measurement flaws) is very small and these tend to be published in quantitative and hard-to-obtain reports. Second, many programs have claimed responsibility in the media for drops in crime rates without eliminating alternative explanations. It could be, for instance, that similar drops were recorded in comparable neighborhoods without anti-crime programs, that police deployment changed, or that criminal activity was displaced to nearby neighborhoods. Third, participants in community programs argue convincingly that something positive happened in their neighborhoods because residents feel and act differently now. Researchers have documented that organized programs do lower the perceived fear of crime, that residents are more visible on the streets, and that neighbors come to each other's aid more often. These are positive benefits and perhaps reason enough for community programs to be launched and maintained.

The purpose of this article is three-fold. First, it distinguishes between crime control and crime prevention in order to be clearer about realistic goals for these programs. It then presents a classification scheme for categorizing the types of community anti-crime activities. The activities have been initiated by residents in some communities, by police in others, and as a police–resident partnership in still others. Next, it discusses those characteristics of the community, the police role, and the program strategy that appear to lead to programs that participants define as successful.

Distinguishing crime control from prevention

In order to understand why neighborhood programs might be failing to reduce crime, one must first grasp the difference between crime prevention and crime control. Although these terms are frequently used interchangeably, they refer to different anti-crime approaches. Crime prevention efforts are directed toward the factors believed to cause crime in the community. Accepting the sociological explanation of crime, prevention programs seek to reduce such problems as poverty and discrimination. The rationale is that these social conditions foster criminal behavior and that improved conditions will reduce the frequency of crime.

Crime control, on the other hand, refers to reducing the opportunity to commit crime. Under this definition, crime is diminished by (1) decreasing the chances that it will be committed against a particular target and (2) minimizing the cost (monetary, psychological, and physical) once a crime has occurred.[10] This approach does not attempt to weaken or eliminate the individual's desire to commit crime but rather to reduce the opportunity for its expression.

By mounting a control program, a neighborhood should be able, in principle, to reduce crime without confronting the social bases of it. Once the program ends or loses support among residents, the crime rate should return to the level experienced by comparable communities. In contrast, community efforts directed at crime prevention would entail massive corrective programs that would generate more stable and lasting reductions in crime without the need for constant vigilance by residents.

It is clear that logically, the more effective crime reduction strategy employs the crime prevention approach. However, what is more effective is not always what is most socially or politically acceptable. The crime prevention approach requires long-term programs of social reassessment and change with few short-term positive effects. Further, evidence from the War on Poverty era suggests that even when social and political support exists, policymakers may not know how to design effective programs. Nevertheless, some community groups conduct crime prevention programs in addition to their crime control efforts. One of the better known groups to offer both types of programs is the Midwood Kings Highway Development Corporation (MKDC) in Brooklyn, New York. Organized by residents to seek ways to revitalize the housing and business district in their area, the MKDC sponsors job training and recreation programs as part of its multi-issue agenda. The athletic programs, cadet corps, and runaway hotlines sponsored by many police departments are also crime prevention efforts.

Most fearful neighborhoods and understaffed police agencies are not interested, however, in programs that require large amounts of their time or money or that will require a generation to be successfully implemented. For these reasons, crime control programs have become the more popular form of neighborhood anti-crime activity even though they are, in principle, less effective. A perusal of the relevant literature indicates that with the exception of the Chicago Area Projects,[11] almost all "community crime prevention programs" in fact have adopted the crime control approach.

These neighborhood programs involve a vast constellation of activities. To simplify the discussion, these activities can be grouped according to *level of interaction* (that is, whether the activity involves the individual or the neighborhood) and by *goal* (whether it seeks to effect social or physical changes). Using these two groupings, a table can be constructed to categorize the various activities (see Figure 1). It should be noted that the cells in the table do not reflect mutually exclusive anti-crime activities. Rather, it is typical for programs to include activities drawn from several cells.[12]

Activities falling in cell A are enacted on the individual level and are directed at the physical environment. These include attempts to harden the target of crime and in most cases focus on burglary. Typical measures to increase home and business security involve installing new and stronger locks, window bars, and other physical barriers to illegal entry. Citizens often take these actions after a security check. Police departments can conduct such checks themselves, train residents to do them for their neighbors, or distribute a form that individuals can use to conduct their own.[13]

| | | Level of interaction | |
		Individual	Neighborhood
Goal of activity	**Physical change**	A Target hardening	B Environmental redesign
	Social change	C Coping behaviors	D Cooperative activities

Figure 1. Classification of community crime control activities.

Activities found in cell B also focus on physical changes, but these changes are directed toward the neighborhood rather than a single household. Newman's approach to defensible space falls within this category, as do improved street lighting,[14] neighborhood clean-ups, and changes in traffic patterns and street widths.[15] The underlying notion is to harden an *area* by changing the physical environment.

Activities in cell C shift to the social plane. Here, individuals develop "coping behaviors"[16] intended to reduce the chances and costs of victimization, such as walking in the neighborhood only during the day, avoiding certain areas entirely, and engraving major possessions with a number filed with the police (Operation Identification). Many of these actions can reduce vulnerability, but they do so at the cost of weakening informal social ties by isolating individuals from traditional neighborhood life. In this regard, they differ from the actions suggested in the other three cells.

Finally, cell D activities focus on crime control at the neighborhood level. Unlike the activities in cell C, these tend to increase social interaction by encouraging neighbors to look out for one another's personal safety and property. The cooperative activities grouped here include escort services, citizen patrols, compilation and distribution of neighborhood directories, block watch programs, and safe houses. The underlying assumption is that a potential crime can be foiled or a perpetrator caught by residents who know their neighbors and are willing to help them. New crime control programs, whether initiated by citizens, by the police, or by the two jointly, have a lengthy list of activities from which to choose the ones most appropriate for the area. The following section suggests a number of factors program designers should consider.

Implementing a community crime control program

Implementing a successful community anti-crime program requires consideration of three interrelated elements: the community, the police, and the program. Since anti-crime programs are voluntary and their success depends on community support and participation, it is mandatory that the values, norms, attitudes, and behavior of the residents be understood. A program not tailored to the needs of the community, not sensitive to its dynamics (relations among existing organizations, land usage, residents' demographics, and the prevailing sense of community), and not consistent with the neighborhood's resources or the citizens' motivation is doomed to failure.

Similarly, a program that does not consider police officers and their department cannot function long or effectively. It is the police who wield the ultimate power over the program's future. It is their ability to use legitimate coercive force to arrest suspects, disperse crowds, and maintain public order that gives a community program its muscle. Program designers must give consideration to police factors such as resource allocation, technical expertise, motivation and reward, and organizational structure. Without the cooperation and participation of police, a community anti-crime program becomes a vigilante activity that finds itself confronted not only by crime but by the legitimate agents of social control.

In short, each anti-crime program must be designed with the unique needs and abilities of both citizens and the police in mind. For the program to really succeed, both sets of players must work toward a partnership; without a sharing of their critical but limited resources, the program will not succeed.

But what is success? In almost all descriptions of community anti-crime programs it is defined as the reduction of the incidence of a target crime or crime(s) that the program was designed to reduce. Overall assessment of these programs indicates, however, that success so defined is largely elusive.[17] According to the formal evaluations that were most rigorously undertaken, crime levels in the communities studied show little if any immediate decline and *no* long-term reduction.[18] In short, anti-crime programs appear to have no effect on crime! Does this mean that the programs were a failure and that the concept of community anti-crime is without merit? Or could it mean that the wrong criteria of success were used to evaluate their impact?

To answer these questions, one must look at the relationships among actual crime, the perception of crime, fear, and sense of personal efficacy (or the feeling of power over one's environment). The findings of a five-year study on the fear of crime coupled with various evaluations of anti-crime efforts supply an unexpected answer. Data from the Reactions to Crime Project show that people's concern about crime is disproportionate to the actual chances of becoming a victim. The people least likely to be victimized (the elderly, women, and the middle class) are the most concerned about crime, while those most likely to become victims (the young, urban dwellers, and the poor) manifest the least fear.[19]

This overestimation of vulnerability to crime directly affects citizens' quality of life and sense of personal efficacy. It produces a feeling of isolation, suspicion, and anxiety that makes people reluctant to venture from the security of their homes. They forgo interacting with their neighbors and using their neighborhood for shopping and recreation. In short, their immediate environment becomes a source of threat and fear rather than a source of pride and enjoyment. Research indicates that reaction to this fear produces a variety of behavior changes, some of which are destructive to the maintenance of a sense of community.[20] If Wilson and Kelling[21] are correct, fear and isolating coping behaviors tend to reduce even further the community's control over the security of the neighborhood. As law-abiding residents fearfully retreat to their homes, the streets are left to the whims of the hoodlums and thugs, and crime and incivilities increase further.

Although community programs appear to have no effect on the incidence of crime, they do influence people's perceptions of the amount of crime in their neighborhood. Fowler and Mangione document a change in the perceptions of Hartford residents concerning the seriousness and incidence of local crime as the direct result of an anti-crime program. The residents were bringing their assessment of the level of crime more in line with its actual incidence, and their fear declined as well. Since behavior is based on perceptions, the residents began to walk on the neighborhood streets, visit the park, and socialize in public places. Furthermore, they reported that the neighborhood was safer and that they enjoyed an enhanced quality of life.

Again, if Wilson and Kelling are right, the increased use of a neighborhood, the heightened sense of personal efficacy, and freedom from fear will in the long run reduce the disorder and crime there. Improved quality of life, then, might not only be a significant benefit of anti-crime programs, but may be the only functional outcome that can be expected from a crime control as compared to a crime prevention program.

For purposes of this discussion, therefore, we define success of a community anti-crime program as an enriched quality of life for residents. Further, we define a successful program as one that addresses those neighborhood conditions which reduce perceived quality: fear, little use of the neighborhood, minimal social interaction among residents, and a weak sense of personal efficacy.

This definition of success forces a program designer to seriously consider what characteristics of the community, the police, and the program can be combined to produce an enhanced quality of life for the residents. Each of these three interrelated components is addressed in greater detail below.

The community   Since anti-crime programs are voluntary and require widespread popular support and participation, their success depends on three community factors: the social characteristics, the physical design, and the perceived crime problem.

The social characteristics of a neighborhood are divided into those of individual residents and those of the social networks. Feins suggests careful consideration of the residents' characteristics (age mixture, race and ethnicity, household composition, income and education, mix of owners and renters, and turnover). An area populated largely by homeowners, the elderly, and those of high socioeconomic status offers a stable base for program development. In contrast, an area in which most of the residents are renters, young, and from a variety of ethnic backgrounds will probably lack the community ties that would support an anti-crime program. Skogan and Maxfield echo this contention. They found that neighborhoods with high residential turnover and minimal ownership lacked a concern with neighborhood maintenance and recorded higher levels of fear of criminal victimization. Flight of some of the remaining homeowners to the safety of the suburbs only exacerbated an already deteriorating condition.

In addition to individual characteristics of the residents, the social networks of the neighborhood determine the ease or difficulty of mounting an anti-crime program. According to Schoenberg and Rosenbaum,[22] two factors account for success in implementation. First, a neighborhood that has a formal, internal organizational structure that facilitates communication among residents, identification of neighborhood leaders, and a definition of neighborhood norms and values is in an optimal position to create and maintain a successful program. Formal structures include churches, business organizations, social clubs, and community self-help associations. Second, the members of these structures must be willing to establish a common definition of acceptable public behavior. Such behavior entails use of public areas as well as the behavior of local residents concerning the maintenance of their private property.[23] In addition to the establishment of common definitions, mechanisms must exist to enforce them. Such mechanisms usually include peer pressure and the selected use of local ordinances.

Second, the physical characteristics of the neighborhood must be considered. Again, Schoenberg and Rosenbaum maintain that a viable community must have recognizable boundaries, whether they are physical barriers or just clearly defined geographic perimeters. A formal name for the neighborhood strengthens the sense of identification and feelings of territoriality. In addition, the physical characteristics of the area must be analyzed to understand where crime occurs (in private dwellings or apartment buildings) and how criminals enter and exit the area. Is most of the housing single family or apartment? If the latter, how many stories high? Is the population densely housed or not? Are there natural boundaries such as rivers or ravines that surround the area and keep nonresidents out? Are there major thoroughfares that allow many nonresidents to stop in the area? Is there a commercial strip? If so, is it healthy, dying, or abandoned? A successful anti-crime program will create physical barriers where none exist. For example, if significant amounts of crime occur in apartment building hallways because there is no security in the lobbies, the program can install lights and mirrors, organize the tenants into teams to screen lobby visitors, and provide telephones for lobby watchers to report suspicious persons to the police. If alleyways are known to serve as escape routes for burglars, neighborhood watch groups can be organized across alleys instead of across streets.

Finally, the third community factor to consider during the program design phase is the type of crime problem residents perceive. Residential burglary is the major concern of most programs, followed by minor larceny and auto theft. But as Lewis points out,[24] conditions of social disorder (such as groups of youths loitering on a streetcorner or graffiti-marred buildings) may also influence how safe residents feel. Collective crime control activities must deal with issues of public order as well as legal behavior.

The effort to understand the exact nature of a neighborhood's crime problem must draw on information from a variety of sources. In addition to the residents' perceptions, program designers must talk with the police and if possible should gain access to detailed crime reports. Residents' assumptions about crime patterns are often faulty, but most victimization surveys indicate that police records show only about half of the crime events.

In summary, a successful anti-crime program should take the community into consideration because the program must be tailored to the area's needs. Although some community factors are easy to manipulate, such as restricting entrance to an apartment house lobby, there are ways to change more difficult factors such as sense of community boundaries. A report in *Newsweek*[25] cited the activities of a patrol officer in Brooklyn who worked with the residents to clean up vacant lots and stimulate repair of dilapidated properties. The residents took new pride in their community. Successful programs require innovative techniques to mobilize citizens to take an active part in shaping their community destiny.

The police   Among the many factors controlled by the police that can serve as enhancers or retardants of program success are resource allocation decisions, technical expertise, motivation and rewards, and organizational structure. Resource decisions include the personnel, time, and budget directly allocated to work with citizen anti-crime activities, as well as decisions with only indirect implications for them. For instance, limited resources in numerous localities have forced police agencies to reduce overall patrol strength or to reallocate existing patrols to problem areas irrespective of the needs of citizen anti-crime activities.[26]

Since the backbone of any successful program is the police, their lack of complete commitment signals inevitable doom for the program. This does not mean that a department has to allocate all or a majority of its forces to programs attempting to improve the quality of life for residents. It does mean that the agency must view quality of life issues as an important aspect of its mission. Rather than accept the traditional, narrow view of their mandate as enforcers of major sections of the criminal law, the police must expand their mission to include combating incivilities in the neighborhood, such as rowdiness, vandalism, and general disorder. The police must act as a catalyst to win back the neighborhood streets for the residents.

Expansion of the traditional police mission has been tried in several cities. The results of these efforts are very promising. In one Brooklyn precinct, a more neighborhood-oriented definition of mission was so well-received in the summer of 1984 that the New York Police Department enlarged its COP (Community Oriented Policing) project to seven more precincts.[27] This pilot program reduced community fear and improved neighborhood life by cleaning up the trash and reducing the noise in a neighborhood park, rousting boisterous groups of drunks, and displacing street drug activity. One of the techniques employed by COP is the use of foot patrol allowing officers to learn first-hand about the neighborhood's problems. The COP strategy is a legacy of the Newark Foot Patrol Study, which demonstrated that foot patrol positively affected residents' fearfulness, although it did not reduce the incidence of crime, which was the experiment's primary goal.[28]

Police also must have, or be willing to gain, technical expertise in several areas. First, they must know enough about target hardening strategies to make useful recommendations during security surveys of residences (and perhaps businesses), one of the most popular components of many anti-crime programs. This technical expertise issue quickly becomes a resource question if a department lacks the personnel to respond to all requests for surveys. This was a problem for the precincts in the MKDC area. As the program gained acceptance, the police were flooded with requests for surveys. A substantial backlog was created which may have negatively influenced citizens' perceptions of cooperation from the police force. Second, departments must have expertise in organizing and communicating with citizens' groups. These are skills not taught in traditional police academy curricula but are critical to achieving a partnership with residents. One of the more useful services a department can provide is crime report information compiled for the neighborhood area. This requires both statistical and communication skills.

The police must also build motivation within their ranks for making community crime control a priority. Individual officers must come to see that local programs require more than standard police-community relations work; they require a fundamental shift from reactive to proactive policing. Further, they require an expansion of the definition of police work to include public disorder and vandalism as problems worth fighting even though such activities do not boost arrest statistics.

In addition, officers will develop the motivation to work with citizens if they see such cooperation as benefiting their careers. Work with citizens must parallel the traditional performance criteria of good felony arrests and competent paperwork in decisions regarding promotions and favored assignments. Involvement in this form of police work must be viewed as a rewardable career path and not as a "place to retire" or a "dumping ground" for misfits. For example, the Minneapolis police chief made assignment to the special platoon that conducted crime control and surveillance activities a reward for good performance elsewhere in the department.[29]

The police organization must also develop the motivation to partner community crime control programs. The motivation may stem from an awareness that both parties have limited but complementary resources. However, historical hostilities between citizens and a department can blind both sides to their needs for the other.

The MKDC project was initiated amid such hostility.[30] Each side perceived the other as a cause of the spiraling crime rate and neighborhood deterioration. Recognizing the importance of good relations with the police department, the program's developers hired a former police detective as its first director. He in turn scheduled meetings at the three precincts in the area immediately after the program began. It soon became clear that one barrier to a working partnership was the officers' fears of losing their jobs as citizens began to perform crime control functions. To counteract this, MKDC told the New York Police Department that its volunteers would not tolerate being used to justify cutbacks in police personnel or services, and the organization monitored local deployment patterns to ensure that changes did not occur.

The way a police organization chooses to structure its community anti-crime effort can increase or decrease the overall program's chances of success. Feins describes the Detroit and San Diego police departments as presenting two models of successful structuring. A new chief of the Detroit department created a 150-officer Crime Prevention Section that reported directly to him. He permanently assigned a large number of staff to offices in targeted areas of the city so their ties to the community would solidify. Even though he incorporated crime prevention and control training into the police academy curriculum, the department gives further training to some officers to make them specialists. In contrast, the San Diego Police Department has decentralized many crime control responsibilities to eight storefront offices with a few permanently assigned community relations staff. Both programs are successful because (1) the chiefs share the philosophy and goals of neighborhood crime control with the residents; (2) crime prevention and control training is given to all new recruits; (3) crime control work is weighed in officer performance and promotion decisions and in Detroit constitutes a distinct career path; (4) the officers assigned to the programs have considerable discretion regarding ways to help a community organize and maintain anti-crime programs; and (5) the departments work cooperatively with, not independently of, the citizen groups.

In summary, the police are an integral part of neighborhood anti-crime programs. Police commitment is manifest in a variety of ways, many requiring some restructuring of attitudes, behaviors, personnel policies, or organizational diagrams. The research indicates that innovative partnerships with the community are cost effective and may dramatically affect citizens' evaluations of the threats and benefits of neighborhood living. It is time for the police and program designers to realize that this goal should replace the traditional and unachievable one of crime reduction.

The program   As the previous sections have emphasized, crime control programs must be designed from scratch to fit the communities where they will be implemented. The variety of activities conducted, drawn from any or all four cells in Figure 1, must reflect the needs and capacities of the residents, police, and the neighborhood itself. There are some organizational issues relevant to any program, however, which deserve attention at the design stage.

One of the program's first projects should be a full-scale needs assessment. Respondents should include business owners, professionals such as social workers familiar with the area, and police officials as well as local residents. The results of the assessment can provide the information on perceptions regarding crime and characteristics of the residents that will serve as the basis for many of the program design decisions.

Similarly, the program should incorporate periodic surveys of residents to ascertain whether their attitudes and behavior show a reduced fear of crime. Additional information can be collected through observation of sidewalk and street traffic, business receipts, and use of park facilities. These data should complement official police statistics that detail crime events and pinpoint their occurrence. Reports to the community based on a compilation of this information should be made regularly, to keep the program visible and to show (hopefully) its positive impacts.

Whether a program is initiated by a community organization or by the police, it will be effective only as long as citizen participation is maintained. People grow bored of constantly being watchful or patrolling the neighborhood streets. The program should also include activities intended primarily to keep the interest and morale of participants high. These may range from certificates of appreciation to publicly awarded citations, annual dinners, and holiday parties. Some programs built around youth patrols of buildings and grounds have created strong group identity by purchasing jackets with the organization's name on them. Even fund-raising activities can increase neighborhood awareness of the program beyond the level established by explicit public education campaigns.

Several publications intended for designers of community crime patrol (and prevention) programs have very useful lists of the steps required for implementation, and the considerations important at each step.[31] They also describe fully the specific activities of programs conducted across the nation. The publications emphasize the importance of partnerships between residents and police in mounting effective, successful programs.

1. Donald J. Black and Albert J. Reiss, Jr., "Patterns of Behavior in Police and Citizen Transactions" in *Studies in Crime and Law Enforcement in Major Metropolitan Areas*, vol. II, section I. Report submitted to the President's Commission on Law Enforcement and Administration of Justice (Washington, D.C.: U.S. Government Printing Office, 1967).

2. Oscar Newman, *Defensible Space: Crime Prevention through Urban Design* (New York: Macmillan, 1972).

3. Ibid., p. 206.

4. Robert K. Yin et al., *Patrolling the Neighborhood Beat: Residents and Residential Security: Case Studies and Profiles* (Santa Monica, Calif.: Rand, 1976).

5. *The Washington Post*, April 20, 1983.

6. *The Washington Post*, February 2, 1984.

7. Floyd J. Fowler, Jr., and Thomas W. Mangione, *Neighborhood Crime, Fear and Social Control: A Second Look at the Hartford Program* (Washington, D.C.: U.S. Department of Justice, 1982). This is a reassessment of: Floyd J. Fowler, Jr., Mary Ellen McCalla, and Thomas W. Mangione, *Reducing Resident Crime and Fear: The Hartford Neighborhood Crime Prevention Program* (Washington, D.C.: U.S. Department of Justice, 1979).

8. Richard R. Bennett and Sandra Baxter, "Preventing Crime or Building a Sense of Efficacy: The Effects of Neighborhood Crime Control Activities," paper presented at the Academy of Criminal Justice Sciences Meeting, Chicago, Illinois,

1984. This paper dealt with: Paul Cirel et al., *An Exemplary Project: Community Crime Prevention Program, Seattle, Washington* (Washington, D.C.: U.S. Department of Justice, 1977).

9. See: James Q. Wilson, *Thinking about Crime* (New York: Random House, 1975).

10. Paul J. Lavrakas and Dan A. Lewis, "The Conceptualization and Measurement of Citizens' Crime Prevention Behaviors," *Journal of Research in Crime and Delinquency* 17 (1980): 160–89.

11. Anthony Sorrentino, *Organizing against Crime* (New York: Human Sciences Press, 1977).

12. Robert K. Yin, "What Is Citizen Crime Prevention?" in *How Well Does It Work? Review of Criminal Justice Evaluation, 1978* (Washington, D.C.: U.S. Department of Justice, 1979).

13. International Training, Research and Evaluation Council, *Crime Prevention Security Surveys* (Washington, D.C.: U.S. Department of Justice, 1977).

14. James M. Tien et al., *National Evaluation Program, Phase I Report: Street Lighting Projects* (Washington, D.C.: U.S. Department of Justice, 1979).

15. Judith D. Feins, *Partnerships for Neighborhood Crime Prevention* (Washington, D.C.: U.S. Department of Justice, 1983).

16. Wesley G. Skogan and Michael G. Maxfield, *Coping with Crime: Individual and Neighborhood Reactions* (Beverly Hills: Sage Publications, 1981).

17. For a survey of evaluation findings, see: Bennett and Baxter, "Preventing Crime."

18. See: Fowler and Mangione, "Neighborhood Crime."

19. Skogan and Maxfield, *Coping with Crime.*

20. Ibid.

21. James Q. Wilson and George L. Kelling, "Broken Windows," *Atlantic Monthly,* March 1982, pp. 29–38.

22. Sandra Perlman Schoenberg and Patricia L. Rosenbaum, *Neighborhoods that Work: Sources for Viability in the Inner City* (New Brunswick, N.J.: Rutgers University Press, 1980).

23. Feins, *Partnerships.*

24. Dan Lewis, ed., *Reactions to Crime* (Beverly Hills, Calif.: Sage Publications, 1981).

25. "The 'Blues' Beat Street," *Newsweek,* January 28, 1985, p. 49.

26. Fowler and Mangione, "Neighborhood Crime."

27. "The 'Blues' Beat Street."

28. Police Foundation, *The Newark Foot Patrol Experiment* (Washington, D.C.: Police Foundation, 1981).

29. Feins, *Partnerships.*

30. William DeJong and Gail A. Goolkasian, *The Neighborhood Fight Against Crime: The Midwood Kings Highway Development Corporation* (Washington, D.C.: U.S. Department of Justice, 1982).

31. See: Feins, *Partnerships,* and Georgette Bennett, *A Safe Place to Live: A Management Manual to Help Communities Plan Crime Prevention Programs* (New York: Insurance Information Institute, 1982).

PART 4

Personnel Management

Affirmative Action in Police Organizations

Candace McCoy

In *Bakke* v. *Regents of the University of California*,[1] the Supreme Court apparently held that public organizations' affirmative action plans do not violate the equal protection clause of the Fourteenth Amendment as long as the preferential programs do not utilize quotas. "Apparently" is an appropriate adverb here, because in that famous case the Court split 5-4, filing no majority opinion; a patchwork plurality on key issues—such as the quota question—tipped the scales against the California program.

The problem defined

It is scarcely surprising that public administrators are often frustrated when considering the legality of affirmative action plans. If the courts can't define what type of plan constitutes repugnant reverse discrimination and what type exemplifies praiseworthy affirmative action, how can a beleaguered public executive do so? Police administrators, especially, have had reason to lament the lack of definite legal standards on affirmative action in police hiring and promotion, because the Supreme Court recently declined to decide *Detroit Police Officer's Association*.[2] In that case, which many observers had believed would dispel some ambiguities of post-*Bakke* law, the Court unanimously let stand a Sixth Circuit opinion approving an affirmative action plan in the Detroit Police Department that reserved for blacks half of all promotions to the rank of lieutenant.

"Affirmative Action in Police Organizations: Checklists for Supporting a Compelling State Interest," reprinted with permission of *Criminal Law Bulletin*, copyright 1984, Warren, Gorham & Lamont, 210 South Street, Boston, Massachusetts 02111.

The Court has sidestepped cases raising similar issues before. In 1981, the justices granted certiorari in a case challenging a preferential hiring plan for California prison guards,[3] but, as in *Detroit Police*, they later declined to hear the case. The guards' affirmative action plan survived, but local criminal justice administrators still lacked a clear interpretation of federal affirmative action principles.

Yet the Court has consistently approved affirmative action ideals. (By default, the justices supported the Detroit plan when they refused to review it, despite vehement opposition by the Justice Department.) With respect to the law of equal employment opportunity, then, police administrators' most pressing task is not to ascertain whether affirmative action is legal—it is. The task is to design and adopt affirmative action plans matching those that have withstood legal attacks. Preferential hiring, training, and promotion have been litigated carefully in nonpolice contexts, and the topic will soon come to the Court once more in a case involving firefighters.[4] It is not too early to compile a general checklist of the components of a constitutionally acceptable affirmative action program; the firefighter case, when it is decided, will add to the list.

The factors involved

This article will outline five factors to consider when designing or improving an affirmative action plan for a police department, and will explain why they are important from legal and practical standpoints. The five are:

1. Voluntary adoption of a quota or goal for a specified level of minority participation in the police department's work force. The choice of either a quota system or a goal system will depend on the history of the department and the character of the decision-making body that mandates adoption of the affirmative action program.
2. Analysis of differing standards for affirmative action in hiring and for promotion, if any.
3. Careful adherence to Equal Employment Opportunity Commission guidelines for implementing an affirmative action plan. For public employers, these involve analysis of the available work force, close examination of the public agency's hiring and/or promotion policies, and initiation of a program tailored to the facts found by this self-analysis.[5]
4. Promulgation of the affirmative action plan by a "competent" or "politically responsible" public agency—i.e., a political body having factfinding and rulemaking powers—preferably the city council or equivalent legislative body.
5. Explicit statement of the compelling state interest to be served by the preferential program.

To explore fully why these "checklist items" are important, police executives can begin by reviewing two factors likely to influence policy: the law concerning affirmative action and practical reasons that the policing profession would embrace the concept. To begin, consider some basic definitions. "Affirmative action" is a broad term that describes any system of hiring, training, or promotion in which members of selected minority groups are given special preferential consideration and treatment; its goal is to achieve the minority work force participation that most closely approximates what would have obtained but for unfair discrimination against these groups in the past.

Methods of implementation

Under this broad definition fall three general methods of implementing affirmative action ideals. They employ quotas or goals. (It is important to grasp at the outset that there is a difference between quotas and goals—both are means of achieving affirmative action, but they are distinct devices with different legal consequences.)

Court-ordered quota   One method of achieving affirmative action is by a court-ordered quota. This device is a compensatory remedy ordered to rectify proven intentional illegal discrimination practiced by a specific defendant organization.[6]

Voluntary quota system   Another method is voluntary use of a quota system—for example, the procedure that was attacked in the *Detroit Police* case. There, the Board of Police Commissioners promulgated a rule requiring that, from all candidates eligible for lieutenant positions, 50 percent of those promoted would be black. Thus, for every white who received a promotion, a black would also be promoted. The Board said that this measure was taken to counter proven past discrimination in minority hiring by the police department. (At the time the Board announced the rule, 50 percent of Detroit's population was black but only 5 percent of the police force was black.) Thus, though no court found that there had been past discrimination, the quota system was voluntarily instituted after an organizational self-assessment by police executives; such voluntary assumption of a quota system is, then, the second method of affirmative action implementation.

Voluntary preferential hiring   The third method involves voluntary preferential hiring or promotion pursuant to a *goal* of minority work force representation. If the Detroit Police Commissioners had announced that they would prefer blacks for promotions until approximately 50 percent of the lieutenants were black (i.e., until the police force racial makeup roughly matched the city's black population), this would have been an example of an affirmative action goal. The goal system is usually considered more flexible than the quota system; its supporters claim that whereas quotas may result in preferential treatment for individuals who may not be as qualified as competing majority group members, goals simply require that, of all *similarly qualified* applicants, a member of a minority group will always be chosen until the goal is reached.[7]

Legal considerations

The law of affirmative action begins where any constitutional law concerning equal protection does—with the Fourteenth Amendment. Furthermore, in regard to employment, Title VII of the 1964 Civil Rights Act is involved. Title VII requires employers to follow a policy of nondiscrimination in employment-related matters—hiring, testing, evaluation, promotion, and the like.[8] The federal Equal Employment Opportunity Commission was constituted to act as an implementation and enforcement agency for Title VII.

The Supreme Court has never squarely tested whether public employers using affirmative action plans developed in accordance with Title VII of the Civil Rights Act of 1964 have engaged in unconstitutional "reverse discrimination," but in *Bakke*, discussed earlier, it decided a Title VI case. Opponents of affirmative action claim that the equal protection clause of the Fourteenth Amendment supersedes the Act and EEOC guidelines based on it, and that under the controlling equal protection standards, no particular group of citizens may be given unfair advantages over other groups. These critics consider affirmative action to be one such unfair, illegal preference.

The *Bakke* case

But the Court has refused to say that affirmative action, in principle, is unfair reverse discrimination.[9] The issue in *Bakke* was whether a public university that used a quota system for admitting minority students to medical school had violated either the Civil Rights Act of 1964 or the equal protection clause of the Fourteenth Amendment. The equal protection question was whether an affirmative action plan that designated a set percentage of seats in a medical school class for minority students was unconstitutional racial discrimination against applicants from the white majority. Title VI of the Civil Rights Act also applied; it prohibits discrimination by agencies receiving federal funds in the same way that Title VII of the Act prohibits discrimination by any employer. The only difference here between the medical school admissions question and affirmative action in police hiring is that a different provision of the

1964 Act was involved. The *Bakke* Court held that the quota system was unconstitutional because it absolutely barred whites from certain medical class seats, but that the concept of affirmative action was constitutional. A plurality of the justices said that Title VI neither altered nor conflicted with the Fourteenth Amendment. "Title VI ... proscribe[s] only those racial classifications that would [also] violate the Equal Protection Clause," Justice Powell opined.[10] Accordingly, constitutional case law on equal protection controls. Unless the Supreme Court in a case like *Detroit Police* holds otherwise, equal protection reasoning will apply to the constitutionality of affirmative action plans formulated under Title VII as well as *Bakke*'s Title VI.

That reasoning involves by-now-familiar strict scrutiny and rational basis tests. That is, an employment criterion sensitive to an applicant's ethnicity, gender, or religion is illegally discriminatory *unless* the employer can prove some good reason for discriminating. If discrimination is based on a status other than race (e.g., having been convicted of a felony), an employer must prove that the policy is "rationally related to a state interest."[11] Because of the long history of racial discrimination in this country, and because the Thirteenth, Fourteenth, and Fifteenth Amendments were written to address it, constitutional law requires any discrimination based on race to survive an even more exacting "strict scrutiny." Employers who racially discriminate must prove the practice to be "necessary to further a compelling state interest."

Cases are very few, indeed, where a compelling state interest has been proven so that racial considerations survive. One of these few cases was *Bakke*. There, race-sensitive university acceptance procedures were approved in principle, because the educational advantage of congregating an ethnically diverse student body was a sufficient compelling state interest to justify discrimination. However, this statement of compelling state interest was dictum. On the precise facts of the case, the *quota* system for admissions could stand only if (1) it were taken in response to proven past illegal discrimination by the defendant institution, and (2) that discrimination had been assessed, admitted, and addressed by a government body with authority to do so. The Board of Regents had approved the medical school quota plan for the general purpose of "rectifying historic inequities"—an aim perhaps not specific enough to constitute a compelling state interest—but there had been no factfinding or debate regarding past discrimination at this particular university. Furthermore, it was doubtful that the Board of Regents would have been competent objectively to gather and assess such evidence.

The trick for public employers to master in formulating affirmative action plans, then, is to avoid quotas—or, if quotas are used, to have the plans promulgated by some public body more "politically responsible" than the Board of Regents was in *Bakke*.[12] The *Detroit Police* case resembled *Bakke* in its use of a quota for promotions to lieutenant, but Detroit's affirmative action plan had been developed by the Board of Police Commissioners, in response to factfinding, a review of the history of discrimination in the police department, a statistical assessment of the black work force available in the city, and a statement that the compelling state interest in the case that rendered the affirmative action plan constitutional was that police departments serving predominantly black communities need many black officers in order to function effectively. The *Detroit Police* affirmative action plan was different from *Bakke*'s because the Board of Police Commissioners acted in accordance with EEOC guidelines in designing the plan, the Board was a "politically competent body" to assess the evidence of past discrimination, and a compelling state interest more specific than "general historical inequities" was alleged.

This "compelling state interest" involves an "operational needs" test.[13] Under this analysis, police departments might hire blacks by using quotas—even though in other public agencies quotas would be unconstitutional—because police departments have particular characteristics that justify racial preferences. These "operational needs" involve the necessity of employing black officers to police black neighborhoods effectively. Although other city agencies—highway repair departments, for example—have no particular reason to employ workers of any particular race, police departments, it is argued, need officers of the same race as the predominant ethnicity of the neighborhoods to be policed. Relying on the recent history of black urban discontent with mostly white police departments, proponents of this "operational needs" analysis say that black citizens will not trust white officers, and that inferior policing in black neighborhoods will therefore be the norm unless large numbers of blacks are hired.

In sum, the law of affirmative action for public organizations is that a preferential program is legal if it utilizes goals. If it uses quotas, it will be legal if a compelling state interest (for racial quotas) or a rational basis (for nonracial quotas) exists that justifies the "reverse discrimination." That interest or basis may involve police department "operational needs," or it may involve a general finding of past discrimination in the department. If an agency other than a court makes this finding, it must be a governmental body closely tied to the electorate, having wide factfinding powers.

Inside this broad legal framework, police executives may carve affirmative action plans that most clearly meet the requirements of particular police departments and that most carefully address the practical obstacles they are likely to face in promulgating the plans they formulate.

Practical considerations

Within the equal protection legal framework, consider the five factors for designing or improving an affirmative action plan that were outlined above. Given the history of *Bakke* and *Detroit Police*, choosing between a goal system and a quota system is an important first item for this "checklist." A quota system must be justified by a more carefully enunciated history of past discrimination by the police department than a goal system requires, and quotas should probably be approved by the city council if they are to withstand an equal protection attack. A goal system will not raise these touchy political issues, but it might not be as effective in maintaining steady progress toward integration of the police work force.

In practice, a goal system is arguably fairer and less rigid than a quota, but it is also more easily ignored. As an illustration, consider the *Minnick* prison guards case.[14] The California prison authorities decided to increase the numbers of blacks and Hispanics serving as correctional officers. An affirmative action plan was instituted; its goal was to achieve a certain percentage of minority guards in the work force. A timetable of minority "hires" that would lead to this goal was established. Hiring began with identical assessment of each applicant's qualifications and experience, and each individual was rated on a point system. Minority candidates received extra points for ethnicity. (In this, the plan resembled the civil service point ranking system, where an applicant who is a veteran of the armed services receives extra points—a special preference that has withstood equal protection challenges by women.) In other words, of those candidates judged equally qualified for the job of correctional officer, members of minority groups would be given preference in hiring until the goal percentage of minority work force representation was reached.

Shortcomings of goal system   Critics of the goal system aver that minorities are unfairly examined at the hiring stage. At the outset, they say, minorities do not receive the points necessary to place them on a par with the majority applicants because the tests and job criteria are biased. This is an important objection, and to a great extent it has been addressed nationwide by more careful attention to testing procedures and instruments and more conscientious definition of job-related qualifications in police departments.[15] Nevertheless, no amount of attention to testing will save a goal system that does not enjoy the support of police executives. Goals can be evaded by shifting selection criteria or by simply falling behind on the timetables. Quotas, at least, offer the police department no alternative; it must hire a precise, certain number of minorities.

Certainly, a goal system is less likely to produce as rapid an increase in minority representation as a quota system like *Bakke*'s would. (There, 15 percent of the medical school seats were reserved exclusively for minorities, regardless of how the minority applicants compared with majority applicants on admissions tests.) But it is also less likely to stir animosities about "reverse discrimination" among police personnel and the public. If all the applicants are equally qualified, and a choice must somehow be made among them, race is as valid a criterion as any—given the compelling state interest in increasing minority police representation.

The case of police promotions   These distinctions between goal systems and quota systems are less clear, though, when we consider the second checklist item: police promotions. Was the *Detroit Police* 50/50 plan a quota or a goal? Because it mandated that a set percentage of blacks be promoted (50 percent—one black for every white), it seems to be a quota. But since the pool from which the promotions were made presumably included identically qualified personnel, and the 50/50 promotions were to be made until the police force minority representation approximated that of the Detroit population, it resembles a goal.

Goals and quotas can shade into each other, and police promotions represent a particularly muddy example of affirmative action. If promotional criteria include a written test and general fitness review, as is true in hiring, the affirmative action prescription would be the same as in hiring. But promotions are not as easily granted, based on numerical rankings, as new hires are. Promotions require individual assessments of long service records. Promotional criteria include test scores and also subjectively assessed material from fat personnel files. One commentator[16] has gone so far as to say that affirmative action should apply only at the promotional level, not at the hiring level, since at least the victims of the reverse discrimination at the promotional level still have jobs! Probably few police department administrators would agree; they would argue the opposite—that affirmative action is more appropriate at hiring. As a group-sensitive remedy, affirmative action would apply to a group of untried job applicants among whom few job-related distinctions can be made, but on the promotional level, the history of individual officers would be paramount. After reviewing the history and current needs of their own departments, police executives must unravel this difficult issue. They must decide whether affirmative action standards will apply with equal force on the hiring and promotional levels and must recommend a standard to the governmental body promulgating the affirmative action plan.[17]

Promulgation process   The promulgation process embraces the third and fourth points on the checklist—following EEOC guidelines for designing an affirmative action plan, and consideration by a political body having factfinding and rulemaking powers. Most of the following discussion applies to affirmative action plans that use quotas because these are the most likely to be challenged in court and therefore it is quite important to be able to prove that the department followed proper procedures in promulgating the plan. However, immunizing a goal system from legal attack by following the same procedures couldn't hurt.

Statistical groundwork   For public employers, a statistical assessment of the available work force is the starting point in deciding whether an affirmative action plan is needed. This may include a simple comparison of the city's ethnic composition to that of the police force,[18] and it also should include a review of past hiring, noting the ethnicity and gender of new hires to the percentage of particular minority groups that actually applied for the police jobs. (A recruitment drive for minority candidates may also be a good idea.) Furthermore, the history of the department in minority hiring and promotion should be assessed. If minority representation has always been minuscule compared with the available minority work force, a court might someday be willing to impose a quota system to remedy historic discrimination, if the department has not already done so itself. Most police executives would prefer to avoid court entanglement and the publicity arising from it.

Again, the EEOC guidelines[19] provide guidance. Note that once the affirmative action plan is completed, it should be put in writing, dated, and included as an official police department policy in manuals of procedure. Departments that have adopted plans and can show good faith efforts to follow them are presumed to be blameless in claims brought against them under Title VII.[20]

The political body promulgating the plan need not be the police department itself. In fact, considering the *Bakke* statement that quotas are acceptable only if approved by an "authoritative governmental body,"[21] any quota system should probably be designed and approved by a city council—and then only after full hearings on whether the police department (or all city agencies, if a citywide plan is being adopted) has discriminated in the past.

Deference to legislatures   Proponents of affirmative action may claim that if all preferential plans needed the stamp of approval from popularly elected bodies, no affirmative action will ever occur. This reasoning is faulty on two counts. First, a goal system probably can be instituted by the police department on its own initiative. Second, a quota system must counter equal protection challenges with a clearly defined compelling state interest that justifies the discrimination. This should be announced by a public body with constitutional power to define a state interest, not by nonelected officials. If a popularly elected council decides that remedying historic discrimination is a compelling state interest, there should be no second-guessing from other governmental branches. Of course, we are treading on the unquiet waters of judicial review here, and naturally the courts could strike down any legislature's affirmative action plan if it violated the equal protection clause. But affirmative action case law indicates that the courts will defer to legislatures on these issues. Drawing, perhaps, on the work of John Hart Ely,[22] the Supreme Court is developing a "politically responsible body" doctrine.[23] Where a legislature elected by a majority takes affirmative action in favor of the minority, the preferential plan may stand. (Note that a city council that is predominantly black, under this analysis, could not design an affirmative action program for blacks, because blacks there would not be a minority.)

Practically speaking, it may be a very difficult undertaking to pass an affirmative action plan through a white-male-dominated city council. But that's the point. If the plan survives, it is solid evidence that the public believes affirmative action to be a "compelling state interest."

"Operational needs" factor   Of course, a police department could avoid the trip to council chambers and set up an affirmative action plan using quotas, claiming that the compelling state interest justifying this discrimination is the "operational needs" of the department. This is a policy judgment for police executives. Surely the easiest way to set up an affirmative action plan is to use goals; to state that the compelling state interest justifying them is the "operational need" to have black officers police black neighborhoods; and to take this action only within the police department itself. But the operational needs justification has never been squarely approved by the Supreme Court, and perhaps it should not be. To say that only blacks can police blacks, or whites police whites, or women police women is to step dangerously close to the reverse discrimination that opponents of affirmative action incorrectly claim is the foundation of the concept. A well-trained police officer can work anywhere; departments should hire minorities because they are qualified for the jobs and have much to contribute to public service. That is a compelling state interest, and police agencies should say so.

Afterword

Since this article was written, *Memphis Fire Department* v. *Stotts*, 104 S.Ct. 2576 (1984) was decided.[24] In that 6–3 decision, the Supreme Court struck down a local federal district court's injunction that forbade the city from laying off black firefighters before whites, even though many whites had more seniority. The city fire department had been operating under a consent decree imposed by the district court, under which affirmative action in hiring and promoting black firefighters was mandated. The injunction later handed down in accordance with that decree was in response to a municipal fiscal crisis that had caused layoffs in the fire department.

The case certainly is not sympathetic to the concept of affirmative action, but it does approve the use of preferential hiring achieved by consent decrees. The snag in *Stotts* was twofold: first, though the consent decree itself was legal, the injunction fashioned to handle the particular seniority crisis was not; second, when seniority conflicts with an affirmative action plan, the seniority system must prevail because individual employees with particular provable employment rights may not be denied those rights by the group-oriented affirmative action plan.

This most recent case underscores points developed in this article. First, affirmative action is certainly legal and appropriate in police hiring, where administrators choose between equally qualified candidates by taking race or sex into account. The issue is stickier in promotions, however, where individual service records—like seniority records—are major factors governing conditions of employment. Second, affirmative action plans are most likely to withstand challenge if they are promulgated by local legislative bodies. Although the court consent decree survived, a policy arguably designed to be completely in accordance with it and intended to further its purposes was struck down. Had the Memphis city council and not a court adopted the "preferential" layoff provision, the Supreme Court would perhaps have had a much harder time in overturning it. Unfortunately for Mr. Stotts, the Court said that "there is no merit to the argument that the District Court ordered no more than that which the city could have done by way of adopting an affirmative action program, since the city took no such action."

1. 438 U.S. 265 (1978).
2. *Detroit Police Officers' Ass'n* v. *Young*, 608 F.2d 671 (6th Cir. 1979), *cert. denied*, 452 U.S. 938 (1981).
3. *Minnick* v. *Department of Corrections*, 95 Cal. App. 3d 506 (1979), *cert. granted*, 448 U.S. 910, *declined without comment*, 452 U.S. 108 (1981), *cert. dismissed with opinion*, 449 U.S. 947 (1981).
4. *Stotts* v. *Memphis Fire Dep't*, 679 F.2d 541 (6th Cir. 1982), *cert. granted*, 103 S. Ct. 2451 (1983). The case involves a quota for hiring black firefighters, to which the city agreed in a consent decree settling a lawsuit brought by blacks. White firemen sued when they lost their jobs during city layoffs while blacks retained their jobs under the protection of the decree.
5. These EEOC guidelines are found at 29 C.F.R. §§ 1607.17-1607.18 (1980). 29 C.F.R. § 1608 is also helpful reading, although it applies more closely to private employers.
6. Actually, in the 1970s, when affirmative action was a lively focus of scholarly and popular media attention, few commentators even labeled the court-imposed compensatory quota as affirmative action; it was considered to be simply a form of legal damages. Lately, though, it has received attention because it is the only form of preferential treat-

ment that the Justice Department currently admits would be constitutional, according to briefs filed on behalf of the Justice Department in *Detroit Police.*

7. Some commentators hold that the goals and quotas become identical in practice; once governmental entanglement into employment decisions is permissible, affirmative action zealots will push goals until they become quotas. If this is the case, the remedy is to hold carefully to the original plan, not to discard it entirely because it might be misused. A quick discussion of this is found in Fried, "Questioning Quotas," *New Republic,* Dec. 26, 1983, and responses to Fried in later issues.

8. The Civil Rights Act of 1964 is found at 42 U.S.C. §§ 2000 *et seq.* Originally, Title VII applied only to private employers, but in 1972 the statute was amended to cover public employers, including county and city agencies. As for the EEOC, its operational guidelines are found in 29 C.F.R.; the guidelines applicable to nondiscriminatory testing and hiring and to affirmative action are included in 29 C.F.R. § 1607.

9. Quotas were upheld in *United Steelworkers of America* v. *Weber,* 443 U.S. 193 (1979) (quota plan was part of collective bargaining contract), and *Fullilove* v. *Klutznick,* 448 U.S. 448 (1980) (quotas for minority hiring in federal government contract jobs will stand because specifically approved by Congress).

10. *Bakke,* 438 U.S. at 287 (Powell, J., concurring).

11. Whether gender-based discrimination should be tested under strict scrutiny or under rational basis analysis has been a difficult topic for the Court. The justices have refused to include women as a "suspect class" for whom special scrutiny is necessary, in the absence of a constitutional provision specifically pointed to their needs. In other words, race is a "suspect class" because its constitutional authority is found in the Thirteenth, Four-

teenth, and Fifteenth Amendments, but women as yet have no Equal Rights Amendment. However, the justices often accord gender-based discrimination more careful scrutiny than the rational basis test demands. A middle-ground "rather careful scrutiny" approach seems to have developed. In cases challenging affirmative action for women, the Court has taken the middle approach and upheld gender-based preferences. See *Kahn* v. *Shevin,* 416 U.S. 351 (1974); *Schlesinger* v. *Ballard,* 419 U.S. 498 (1975).

12. Plevin, "The Constitutionality of Affirmative Action in Public Employment: Judicial Deference to Certain Politically Responsible Bodies," 67 Va. L. Rev. 1235 (1981).

13. "Race as an Employment Qualification to Meet Police Department Operational Needs," 54 N.Y.U. L. Rev. 413 (1979).

14. See note 3 *supra.*

15. EEOC guidelines on selection procedures may help here. See 29 C.F.R. § 1607.5.

16. Comment, "Voluntary Affirmative Action Under Title VII: Standards of Permissibility," 28 U.C.L.A. L. Rev. 291, 312 (1980).

17. One general approach that has emerged throughout the country is that a promotional authority will review all candidates and pick a set number (fifteen, by way of illustration) that are deemed equally qualified for appointment to the higher post. The chief executive will choose from these the six (again, a hypothetical number) that will fill six available positions. The chief has discretion to apply a variety of job-related selection criteria in choosing one candidate over the other, and using race or sex as a selection criterion, in accordance with a departmental affirmative action goal system, is acceptable.

18. The Sixth Circuit opinion in *Detroit Police* is a detailed analysis of the statistical comparison technique. The trial court opinion in that case is found at 446 F. Supp. 979 (E.D. Mich. 1978). See also the companion

case, *Baker* v. *City of Detroit*, 483 F. Supp. 919 (E.D. Mich. 1979).

19. 29 C.F.R. §§ 1607.17–1607.18.
20. Civil Rights Act of 1964, Title VII, § 713(b)(1).
21. *Bakke*, 438 U.S. at 309 (Powell, J., concurring).
22. J. H. Ely, *Democracy and Distrust* (1981). Ely builds a theory of judicial review holding that activism is appropriate only when courts intervene to protect the rights of discrete minorities. In the case of affirmative action plans set up by legislatures, the minorities are protected at the outset by the legislation; courts would have no reason to interfere.
23. Plevin, note 12 *supra.*
24. This afterword was prepared by the author after publication of the article.

Management: Labor's Most Effective Organizer

Walt H. Sirene

Employee organizations are made, not born. Rarely does the seed of organized labor sprout in a well-managed organization which has as one of its major objectives the welfare of its employees. Whether intentional or not, the best organizers of labor are managers who, through poor management, lack of concern for legitimate grievances, or plain ignorance, antagonize the workers to the point where their only alternative is to form collectively so as to bargain. It's fair to say that throughout the history of the police labor movement, few police officers promoted unionism as the ultimate solution. Most likely, they were forced to reluctantly change their fraternal organization into a collective bargaining unit.

Police today have even taken a further step. As they become more and more frustrated at the bargaining table, they are turning toward affiliation with the Teamsters and the AFL–CIO to gain power through intimidation, experience in bargaining, and broader financial resources by which to gain their demands. The Teamsters and the AFL–CIO are both making a concerted effort to organize a national police union. This is evidenced by the fact that the AFL–CIO has recently granted a charter to its first police union affiliate—the International Union of Police Associations (IUPA)— to compete with the Teamsters' bid to organize law enforcement. The IUPA already claims a membership of more than 40,000 police officers throughout the country. As for the Teamsters, at least 10,000 police officers are presently members of their locals. Teamsters' officials estimate that they bargain on behalf of 15,000 police officers in approximately 225 municipalities.[1]

In the 1980's, the question is posed, "How can this occur?" Can

Reprinted with permission of the *FBI Law Enforcement Bulletin*, January 1981.

we learn from the history of law enforcement labor relations or must we repeat the mistakes which have been made from city to city, from jurisdiction to jurisdiction, since the Boston police walk-out in 1919? How many times must city officials and police managers be reminded that bad faith bargaining with local, independent police associations will lead to the introduction of organized labor unions in the labor/management equation? On the other hand, how many times must inexperienced members of employee organizations representing their membership in collective bargaining allow emotion to overrule judgment, promoting irresponsible job actions? The prime responsibility for good management of an organization lies with managers, not employees. Therefore, when local employee organizations are formed and subsequently affiliate with organized labor, one usually finds the prime cause to be the outgrowth of a management problem. This article identifies for managers the warning signals which lead police employees to unionize and seek organized labor's influence to force city officials to improve police pay and benefits. The following case study is typical of many cities and depicts why more and more police are joining the nation's largest labor unions.

Case study

Dellwood, a community with a population of 55,000, has 50 police officers. It is located in the heartland of the United States and has had collective bargaining legislation in force since early 1973. Its law provides a system whereby a state agency certifies a democratically selected "union" or "association" as the employee's sole representative in collective bargaining. In 1973, very few of Dellwood's police officers foresaw the day when they would begin bargaining collectively for wages, hours, and working conditions, let alone be represented by organized labor. After all, they were one of the highest paid departments in the area. Their chief of 12 years was considered to be somewhat autocratic and tough, but he was fair and consistent. Furthermore, he was a pillar of integrity and had established respect and support throughout the community for both the department and himself. This apparently was the lull before the storm.

The chief died unexpectedly, and his successor was a lieutenant with 20 years' experience on the Dellwood police force. The new chief was respected by the department's employees and was dedicated to law enforcement. The employees hoped that an already good situation would improve. This was not realized, however, as communications and morale began to deteriorate shortly after he took office. It became popular in the early tenure of the new chief to refer to the barriers to communication as the "brass walls." Officers began complaining openly that the brass was unwilling to listen to their concerns or grievances.

Another source of dissatisfaction voiced by the officers pertained to the lack of planning and training. They cited the example of the purchase of a new radio system through Law Enforcement Assistance Administration (LEAA) funds. By the time the system was installed and activated, no one had received any instruction on its use, adding to the frustration level.

As unrest increased in the department, neighboring police agencies were unionizing and engaging in collective bargaining. Dellwood's officers repeated, with envy, the rumors about the contract provisions that provided formalized grievance procedures and new financial benefits being obtained by other agencies through negotiations. Needless to say, the stage was set, and Dellwood's officers began talking about forming a union to bargain with the city.

PBA vs. Teamsters   As the concept of unionizing gained momentum, factions developed within the department over who would represent them. Should the Teamsters or the Police Benevolent Association (PBA), which had existed as a social organization in the department for 20 years, be elected as the exclusive bargaining agent? A group of young officers sought Teamster representation, while PBA support came from "the old guard."

A heated campaign preceded the election, resulting in further polarization of the department. Each side developed their arguments:

In favor of the PBA

1.   Better results with local people dealing with local problems
2.   Lower dues
3.   More control over expenditures
4.   More personal relationship between union and management
5.   No conflict of interest when enforcing laws involving organized labor
6.   More positive image for professionalism.

In favor of the Teamsters

1.   More experience in bargaining
2.   More influence
3.   Management respect for union power
4.   More money, experts, and legal support
5.   Political impact through lobbying and candidate support
6.   More benefits, such as union insurance programs.

Issues concerning the effect of the Teamsters image on public opinion and the officers' own self-images continued to be mentioned in locker room debates. Officers frequently questioned the Teamster's negative image and asked, "What about *our* image?" The responses heard included, "More police officers are indicted every year than Teamster officials," and "If you want results, choose a union with power. The only union more powerful than the Teamsters is the Soviet Union."

Management's mistake   The election was held in January 1974, and the PBA won with a 2–1 margin. Out of 40 persons eligible to vote, only 3 voted "no union." In city hall, the chief of police, the city manager, and the mayor were quietly rejoicing because the Teamsters lost. They anticipated a local PBA, unskilled in the bargaining process, would be easier to negotiate with and would lack the financial resources to employ a labor consultant, whom they refer to as a "hired gun." The city administration viewed collective bargaining as undesirable, but they were confident they could "win" by outwitting the PBA.

By summer 1974, the first labor contract was negotiated. Personalities aside, the bargaining was primarily a battle rather than a negotiation. Both parties came to the bargaining table ready to reject the other's demands and proposals as being unreasonable. By expecting these things and preparing for them, each set a tone which brought about the expected conduct. Neither party wanted to lose, and as a result, a bitter fight or a stalemate usually occurred. Numerous grievances were filed in the next three years concerning overtime, court-time pay, and past practice issues which were the product of poorly written contracts. The officers during this period were frequently talking about the city's bad faith in both bargaining and contract administration. The city, according to Dellwood's officers, continually had indicated "there was no more money in the budget," when in fact there was. As a result, Dellwood's police officers were now one of the lowest paid in the area.

By 1977, after three contracts, "teamsters" were saying, "I told you so," and officers who had previously promoted the PBA were now silent.

The weight of self-image   When the contract was about to expire, officers supporting the Teamsters obtained over 30 percent of their fellow officers' signatures on a petition to compel an election to determine who would be the bargaining agent for the next contract. Both the PBA and the Teamsters once again qualified for the ballot.

On this occasion, the Teamsters won the election hands down. During this period, there was little discussion regarding the Teamsters' impact on the police public image. As one officer put it, "We just balanced the sensitivity of our image and appearance of professionalism against the desire to make management sit up and listen." In four short years, Dellwood's police department has unionized and become affiliated with the nation's largest labor union. City administrators were at a loss to understand why its police officers had unionized or sought affiliation in organized labor. One thing was certain, they all agreed it wasn't going to be easy to outwit the Teamsters.

Analysis

An analysis of the case study reveals the most common reasons why police unionize and why they eventually become affiliated with organized labor. If management is to be successful in deterring unionization or keeping labor/management conflict at a minimum, they will have to address these issues.

Low salary   Salary is not generally recognized as a major cause for forming employee organizations. However, salary becomes an employee dissatisfier if wages and benefits received are not comparable to those of other organizations in the surrounding areas and significantly less than neighboring police agencies. From this dissatisfaction, other employee grievances form, much as electrons around a nucleus. Managers must realize that the true cost of dealing with the union is not higher wages but having to share management practices with the union. Once an employee association is formed, management loses its right to act unilaterally; valuable time must now be spent in negotiations. The real cost then lies in negotiations concerning disciplinary actions, personality clashes, or patrol assignments. When added up, one could argue it would be less expensive to pay the prevailing wage than to bear the expense of shared management. The other benefits of competitive wages are the attraction of better qualified personnel to the organization, a more content work force, the removal of wages as a rallying point, and the belief that management is concerned with the welfare of the workers' families. Adequate compensation for employees should not, however, be construed by management to be merely a cynical process used to buy off employees. It must be accompanied by a genuine concern for the employees' welfare. The concern can be illustrated by periodic wage reviews in order to keep wages in line with the cost of living. Management should also insure that each employee understands what they may be able to anticipate in terms of wage increases so that sound economic planning by the employee can occur. In general, salary can be identified as one triggering cause of employee dissatisfaction; rarely, though, does money promote job satisfaction. Adequate compensation is a reflection of management concern for employee welfare. The more management understands the role of money as a motivator, the less salary will be a causative factor in the formation of employee associations. Consider this statement by Gus Tyler in *Public Administration Review:*

Among the first to unionize are the better paid, better situated employees, while the very last to organize are the most deprived and aggrieved. The cycles of unionism seem to come not when a new outrage is perpetrated against employees, but when the class or subclass is ready and times are propitious.[2]

Personnel problems   Personnel problems are often cited as the "trigger mechanism" in police job actions. Pent-up employee frustrations concerning policies which they consider unfair, poorly administrated by a rotating cadre of managers or administered solely to still dissent, often combine around a single instance. The emotions generated inevitably lead to more serious dissatisfaction, or in the extreme case, a strike. "Each organization should have one person who has direct, personal responsibility for employee relations."[3] If the organization is widespread geographically or relatively large in size, it should have one representative for each precinct or department, as Joseph Latham in *Employee Law Relations Journal* correctly points out:

The appointment of one person will facilitate development of a rapport with all the employees. He or she should take the time to get to know the employees and listen to their questions and problems, providing relief for complaints when possible and, when relief is not possible, explaining why. In addition, the person responsible for employee relations should:

Train and evaluate supervisory personnel to handle employee relations;

Keep informed about local wage and benefit surveys; and

Ascertain that the employer is getting a good compensation package for its money."[4]

A labor relations individual can assist not only the aggrieved employee in reaching a just solution to his problem but also the organization in learning firsthand the type and scope of employee problems. It would seem far better to trade this management prerogative to the employee rather than surrender it later to the labor organizer.

Lack of a grievance procedure   Separate from the appointment of one or more individuals to handle employee relations, each organization should have a separate path for employees to air grievances. This more formal path allows employees to present their grievance in the manner of their choice. History is replete with examples of organizations which deemed grievance procedures a sign of weakness. Adoption of such procedures was considered an insult to enlightened management and a right to be denied a mere employee.

Such arrogance has led to the formation of employee associations or unions in a number of organizations in both private and public sectors. Rather than indulge in the belief that grievance procedures are a sign of inherent weakness, management should recognize the necessity of establishing a procedure by which complaints can be heard by managers sympathetic to employee concerns. If organizations do not have such procedures in place, it is logical to anticipate some degree of employee dissatisfaction.

Poor working conditions   Poor working conditions are not a concern of a satisfied employee. However, once employees become dissatisfied with other circumstances, poor working conditions intensify discontent. Working hours, poor equipment, fringe benefits, discipline procedures, and the condition of the work environment all influence morale. While it is probably true that poor working conditions will not cause employees to organize, they do become a sustaining factor for employee complaints until a more substantive issue comes along. Of all the expenses incurred by a police organization, the maintenance of good working conditions is minimal. There is little doubt that a poor working environment is a direct reflection of poor management.

Lack of identity and recognition

The desire for self-expression is a fundamental human drive for most people. They wish to communicate their aims, feelings, complaints, and ideas to others. Most employees wish to be more than cogs in a large machine. They want management to listen to them. The union provides a mechanism through which these feelings and thoughts can be transmitted to management.[5]

The police believe they are playing an important role in society, and in return, they are not receiving the compensation or recognition they believe they deserve and the responsibility they want. This belief of nonappreciation can have a far-reaching impact on police work itself. As the police begin to feel less and less important they begin to accept the idea that theirs is just another profession, and at that point, the romance, glory, and commitment go out of the job.

Lack of administrative leadership   At the 1967 Conference of Mayors, Jerry Wurf, President of American Federation of State, County and Municipal Employees (AFSCME) stated:

You [the mayors] represent our best organizers, our most persuasive reason for existence, our defense against membership apathy and indifference, our perpetual prod of militancy, and our assurance of continued growth. . . . Unions would be unable to sign up a single employee if he were satisfied, if his dignity were not offended, if he were treated with justice. . . . [6]

Mr. Wurf could also have leveled his charge against some police managers. If organizations lack individuals who exhibit the quality of leadership, again the potential for employee dissatisfaction is increased. Of all organizational problems, this is probably the most vexing. Simply put, the foundation of all leadership is knowledge. Some leadership qualities can be imparted through the process of training, while other more subtle qualities are seemingly genetic in origin and can only be obtained by a careful selection procedure for individuals as managers.

Lack of internal communications   No better statement on this problem exists than one made by Commissioner Don Pomerleau of Baltimore:

Employee organizations develop many times because we have not established all inclusive and progressive communications. We and our subordinates have not listened, nor have we provided our personnel with a means to seek redress for their real or imagined problems. The old autocratic and dictatorial approach to problem solving has come under severe criticism, and rightly so.

Opening lines of communication is an effective means of creating a stable labor environment. Communication between the police administrator and his officers gives each an understanding of the other's problems. Two-way communication is best facilitated by periodic, informal discussions. An informal discussion offers three decided advantages: officers are able to express their needs and dissatisfactions; more time-consuming and costly methods of achieving changes in employment conditions, such as lobbying and collective bargaining, are avoided; police officers develop a better understanding of management problems.[7]

Suffice it to say, if managers are dedicated to improving channels of communication, the labor relations battle is more than half over.

Organized labor   Public officials, having ignored the causes of unionization, now maintain that if the police must join a union, they would prefer it to be a local, independent association. The majority of city and police administrators are, therefore, opposed to organized labor's efforts to step up their drive to unionize the police. Yet, by adopting a win/lose bargaining philosophy that eventually evolves into a losing situation of frustration and job dissatisfaction, management once again falls prey to helping the union in its organizing efforts.

When management fails to negotiate in good faith with a local, independent police association, they invite and are, in fact, the catalyst for its subsequent affiliation with organized labor. The scenario presented in the previous case study is typical of many cities in the country today. Many city officials have been approaching collective bargaining in a negative manner, and a self-fulfilling prophecy results. Good faith bargaining doesn't mean giving in to the union's demands—it does mean attempting to develop an atmosphere of trust and cooperation, opening lines of communication, and working toward common goals where the needs of both parties can be realized. Cities that fail to recognize this basic principle of good faith bargaining push the local independent police association to its tolerance point. Frustrated with their inability to have the city fathers listen to what they perceive to be legitimate demands, the police look for other alternatives to gain the city's attention. One alternative in such an emotionally tense situation is for the police to participate in some type of job action—a slowdown, speedup, or blue flu. Another alternative, less radical than a job action, is to affiliate with organized labor. The police realize that the power of organized labor is its ability to intimidate the city administration. It is no wonder, therefore, that more and more police are joining the Teamsters and the AFL–CIO in order to "force" cities to listen to their demands and bargain openly. If cities prefer not to deal with organized labor, then they must recognize that the answer to this dilemma is to learn to deal with the local, independent police association in an atmosphere of trust and cooperation, promoting the true tenets of good faith bargaining. It is unfortunate that it often takes an act of intimidation to cause a shift from a competitive or combative approach to collective bargaining to one of collaboration. Needless to say, if management were truly wise, it would direct its efforts toward identifying the cause of unionization and eliminating the need for a union in the first place.

1. Alan Dodds Frank, "When All Else Fails, Call the Teamsters," *Police Magazine*, September 1978, vol. 1, no. 4, pp. 21-34.
2. Gus Tyler, "Why They Organize," *Public Administration Review*, March/April 1972, p. 98.
3. Joseph Al Latham, Jr., "Susceptibility to a Successful Union Organizing Campaign—The Seven Warning Signals," *Employee Relations Law Journal*, Autumn 1980, vol. 6, no. 2, p. 231.
4. *Ibid.*
5. Dale S. Beach, *Personnel—The Management of People at Work*, 2d ed. (New York: The MacMillan Co., 1970), p. 83.
6. John H. Burpo, *The Police Labor Movement* (Springfield, Ill.: Charles C. Thomas, 1971), p. 11.
7. *Ibid.*

Forced Arbitration: Why Cities Worry

The local governments [in California] that regularly negotiate with police and firefighter unions—cities, counties, and special districts—have consistently opposed forced arbitration.

Why are local governments concerned? With public safety personnel costs comprising close to half or more of the typical city's total budget, it is an expense item that requires careful handling. All other aspects of city services and functions are directly affected by how effectively the costs in public safety can be controlled. And if the groups representing police officers and firefighters believe they can get more from an arbitrator than from the bargaining table, legislation giving them the power to force arbitration would, in effect, hand over control of a major portion of the city's budget to a single individual who is not elected, not accountable for the decision made, and whose expertise and familiarity with a city's fiscal and political situation is largely unknown.

These concerns have been confirmed through the experience to date of California's cities with forced arbitration. Six of California's 434 cities have requirements for arbitration in their charters, dating back as far as 1970. The experience of these six cities details the administrative and fiscal problems that can arise when control over a major portion of a city's budget is surrendered to a non-elected third party.

The overwhelming majority of California cities—more than 350—are incorporated under state law, instead of under charters. Ironically, the courts have held that the governments of these general law cities cannot require arbitration, because they would be il-

Reprinted with permission from the May 1983 issue of *Western City* magazine, the monthly publication of the League of California Cities.

legally delegating the responsibilities vested in them by the voters. The proposed state legislation to require arbitration would make that delegation legal but, cities argue, no less damaging to the interests of voters, taxpayers, and the local governments they support.

Oakland

The issue of forced binding arbitration in California is the latest chapter in the continuing process of modifying the original law that set up employee bargaining in the public sector, the Meyers-Milias-Brown Act, which became law (Section 3500 of the Government Code) in 1969.

Myers-Milias-Brown (MMB) determined that local government employees were to be represented by bargaining units, and that these recognized organizations were to "meet and confer" in good faith over "wages, hours, and other terms and conditions" of employment. While the merits, necessity, and organization of service provided by public agencies were to be excluded from employee bargaining under MMB, these aspects of management have also often become entangled in the arbitration process.

The city of Oakland recognized five bargaining groups following the implementation of MMB. Two of the more powerful groups, the International Association of Fire Fighters (IAFF) and the Oakland Police Officers Association (OPOA) went to the city council in 1972 to request that a charter amendment requiring arbitration for their collective bargaining disputes be submitted to the voters. Faced with the prospect of an even more destabilizing system of arbitration being enacted if the unions placed a measure on the ballot through the petition process, and with compulsory arbitration in the public sector still largely an unknown with little case history, the city participated in drafting an arbitration plan, which was approved in 1973.

The council soon discovered, however, that their intentions in drafting the charter amendment were not matched by the interpretations of the arbitrators, and because awards are legally binding and not subject to appeal, the city has been forced to accept decisions that have destroyed their budget planning and stymied management changes aimed at reducing overall costs of public services to taxpayers.

Faced with a budget deficit projected to increase in subsequent years, Oakland in 1974–75 required all departments to submit budgets designed to reduce services by 15 percent. For the fire department, that meant the elimination of 36 sworn positions. The IAFF protested, and took the issue to arbitration, where the city's policy of budget reductions was not only stopped, but reversed. Among the problems encountered:

Bargaining was negated   In negotiations prior to arbitration, all issues had been resolved except hours. However, under bargaining rules agreed to at the outset, agreements on issues were tentative pending final agreement on an entire package. When the union declared an impasse, all issues were submitted to the arbitrator.

Also, because the courts have been unwilling to determine the range of arbitrators' authority, nothing prevents them from involving themselves in management decisions, as occurred in two of Oakland's four arbitration cases to date. The effect of even a single decision on such management responsibilities as department manning can be long lasting: the question can be raised again in future negotiations and used as a bargaining chip that had not been available until a previous arbitrator's award created the issue.

City pay scales were upset   Under its charter, Oakland was required to grant all city employees a 5.88 percent pay increase, based on the changes in earnings of certain manufacturing workers in the area. The firefighters sought and won an additional 3 percent hike, putting them ahead of police officers in pay. Despite the obvious fiscal implications for the city in future negotiations with police officers, the arbitrator discounted comparisons with police pay in favor of a comparison with San Francisco firefighters, the highest paid in the state, noting that while Oakland's firefighters were the second highest paid, they would still earn less than San Francisco's.

Manning requirements were changed   Although manning is a management prerogative under MMB, and the issue had not surfaced during contract negotiations, the arbitrator effectively halted city plans to reduce the fire department by 36 positions by ordering five-man crews for all engine and truck companies, more than previously assigned, thus making Oakland the only city in California mandated to maintain five-man crews.

Other unusually generous terms   The arbitrator ordered Oakland's firefighters' workweek reduced by four hours over two years, making Oakland the only major city besides San Francisco where firefighters' workweek averages less than 56 hours. He also ordered the city to begin paying firefighters time and a half for overtime and granted the union an "agency shop," making union dues a condition of employment. He ordered the city to increase the annual uniform allowance and the city's contribution to the firefighters' health plan.

The city estimated the total cost of the award at $2.5 million annually. However, if the city's originally proposed reductions, nullified by the arbitrator's ruling, are included, total cost of the award exceeded $4 million. In addition, the city spent some $30,000 on the arbitrator's expenses, transcripts, and city staff time.

With a different arbitrator, the city was able to make some progress in controlling manning and total size of the department during the arbitration process two years later, in 1976–77. The city was forced to spend considerably more, some $150,000, in preparing for the case and its share of the arbitrator's costs, but the arbitrator held that issues such as company manning, daily on-duty manning, total authorized manpower, personnel reductions, and the closing of stations were management issues, with only the effect of these changes on wages, hours, and working conditions subject to meet and confer.

Again in 1978–79, firefighters demanded arbitration, claiming that staffing reductions had increased workload. The arbitrator granted an additional, retroactive 3 percent pay hike, costing Oakland another $2.9 million in a year when the city was forced to make budget reductions city-wide of over $6 million. Arbitration cost to the city: $25,000.

The results of the 1978–79 award, combined with other budget problems, forced the city to consider new cuts in the fire department in 1980–81, including changes in manning. Again the issue went to arbitration, and the award of a 7.75 percent pay hike paralleled what the city had budgeted. The city was also able to close four fire stations, but was ordered to maintain a certain ratio between engine and truck companies, effectively halting plans for a new, innovative approach to fire response. However, the process took almost an entire year, at a cost to the city of about $200,000, effectively negating the cost savings in the fiscal year for which they were planned, and causing new problems for the following year.

Alameda

A key argument against forced arbitration is the lack of accountability for the non-elected arbitrators, whose decisions vitally affect city budgets. In Alameda, the council need not take the heat for an arbitrator's award; instead, it can turn the issue over to the voters.

The city not only succeeded in amending the charter to require that excessive awards be ratified by referendum, but also managed to limit arbitration to economic issues. Although Alameda's arbitration requirement has been on the books almost three years, firefighters have not yet resorted to it.

Firefighters in Alameda garnered the 6,000 plus signatures necessary to place an initiative on the city ballot requiring binding arbitration for the fall 1980 election.

Alarmed at the prospect of losing control over firefighter personnel costs, the city council quickly added a charter amendment proposal of its own: if an arbitrator grants an award that exceeds what the council has budgeted, additional funds must be raised through a vote of the people!

Specifically, the Alameda city charter section 17-17 provides:

No additional financial burdens may be imposed on the taxpayers of the city as a result of binding fact finding, arbitration or parity without approval of the voters as set forth in this section. Any other provisions of this charter notwithstanding, no wages, benefits or employee related expenses shall be paid by the city that have not been approved by a resolution of the city council until additional revenues and appropriations therefor have been approved by a vote of the people pursuant to Proposition 13 (Cal. Const. Art. XIIIA, Sec. 4) and Proposition 4 (Cal. Const. Art. XIIIB, Sec. 4). The city council shall not be required to call such an election more than once a year and may consolidate said elections with elections held for other purposes.

While the amendment requiring arbitration narrowly passed, 10,872 to 10,363, the amendment requiring a vote of the people to finance any award beyond what the city council would approve passed overwhelmingly, 12,488 to 8,179.

With this amendment, the council has preserved some authority by empowering itself to vote against an award, effectively delegating the acceptance of the arbitrator's decision to the taxpaying public.

In November, 1982, the Alameda city council went a step further by proposing another charter amendment to limit the scope of arbitration for firefighters to economic issues only. Hoping to avoid situations where arbitrators' decisions would interfere with management responsibilities such as crew size and manning, the amendment defined economic issues as monthly salaries, all supplementary cash entitlements made directly to employees, and health insurance, retirement, vacation, holiday, and sick leave benefits.

The "economic issues" charter amendment was passed by a healthy majority of voters in Alameda.

Palo Alto

An initiative requiring binding arbitration of bargaining disputes for the local police and firefighter unions was placed on the ballot and passed by voters in Palo Alto in June of 1978. Arbitration has been invoked three times so far: for a dispute with firefighters in January, 1980; and for disputes with police officers in July, 1980, and again in July, 1982.

As a result of arbitration, Palo Alto has not only seen personnel costs for police and fire services rise beyond what the city felt was proper, given the other demands on the city budget in recent years, but arbitrators' awards have also forced the city to accept unseen, future costs that will pose a growing burden in years to come.

While cities across the state are looking at "two-tier" pension plans that would offer a lower, yet adequate level of benefits to new employees at a lower cost both to the employee and to the city, Palo Alto developed such a plan for its own system. The "two-tier" plan was one of the issues when the city's 102 non-management firefighters called for arbitration in 1980.

Under Palo Alto's charter, the arbitrator must choose either the final offer of the city or the final offer of the union on each issue in dispute. While the arbitrator chose the city's position on salary, allowing a 14.4 percent pay hike over 18 months, he sided with the union on two issues that will affect personnel costs in the future:

1. The arbitrator refused to allow the city to institute its proposed "two-tier" retirement system for new employees of the department
2. The arbitrator changed the formula by which an individual's pension benefits are determined at retirement. Instead of taking the average of the employee's three best earnings years as a base for determining benefits, as is common in most jurisdictions in California, the arbitrator ruled that the single year of highest earnings should be used.

The arbitrator, in effect, created a vested right extending far beyond the term of the agreement he was arbitrating. All firefighters, current and future, will be entitled to retirement benefits on the basis of this new, more generous and costly formula, estimated by the city to add another 1.4 percent, or approximately $50,000, to the annual payroll, which the city and its taxpayers must pay.

Later in 1981, the 88 non-management members of the Palo Alto Police Officers Association took the city to arbitration. The hefty salary increases of 9½ percent in 1980 and 10 percent in 1981 awarded by the arbitrator were actually based on the city's last best offers which tend to be forced higher to discourage an arbitrator from coming down on the opposing side. The arbitrator also apparently used the "single best year" benefit granted earlier to firefighters as a precedent and granted the same benefit to the police officers. The city estimated the cost of changing the formula for police retirements at about $36,000 per year.

This award for police officers again illustrates how one arbitrator's award can be used as a precedent and a bargaining chip in subsequent arbitration cases, particularly when different bargaining units can declare impasses at different times and demand arbitration independently of each other. There is little that a city can do to avoid a situation where new gains by one group become the starting point for the subsequent group.

Another arbitration process involving the Palo Alto Police Officers Association began when bargaining failed to produce an agreement, and the police officers contract expired June 30, 1982.

The arbitrator in March, 1983, granted officers a 9.8 percent raise, retroactive to July 1, 1982. He then went a step further and granted officers' demands to reduce their contributions to the Public Employees Retirement System from 9 percent of their salary to only 2 percent, forcing the city to pick up the difference.

This decision granted, in effect, another 7 percent pay hike, bringing police raises to 16.8 percent in the second year, far more than other city employees received. The city estimates the cost of the package at $540,601 over two years, funds that will have to be taken out of other city departments.

Forcing the city to pick up almost the entire tab for police pension payments causes other problems, too. Because this "hidden benefit" is not technically a salary increase—officers' salaries stay the same, but deductions are reduced—the city will have less bargaining leverage next time around. On the other hand, with less coming out of their own pockets for contributions to the pension system, there will be even less incentive for employees to support badly needed pension reform in the future.

Vallejo

Vallejo has logged more experience with binding arbitration than any other California city, with its charter amendment requiring arbitration taking effect in 1970. The amendment was proposed by a charter review committee reacting to a disastrous strike by police officers and firefighters in 1969.

The following decade of bargaining was plagued by confusion and hampered by a complicated arbitration process that included a lengthy mediation period, fact-finding, and finally a binding decision by an arbitrator. The entire process frequently took more than two and a half years, with awards made at the end of contract periods being paid retroactively.

Vallejo's system was also unique in that it included not only police and firefighter bargaining units, but also miscellaneous employees, represented in Vallejo by the International Brotherhood of Electrical Workers.

The chronic delays and confusion of the Vallejo system finally led the city's charter review committee to propose an amended process, which was ratified by voters in the fall of 1980 and took effect January 1, 1981. The new arbitration amendment was intended to give the process a fixed structure, and set forth a timetable designed to produce a contract before the current agreement expires:

1. The process begins 180 days before contract expiration, usually around December 12 of the preceding year, with the sub-

mission of names and selection of the arbitrator—even before any bargaining has taken place.

2. Offer demands by the union and the city's management are exchanged 150 days before contract expiration, in early January.

3. Negotiations based on the exchanged demands begin 120 days before contract expiration, in early February.

4. By April 1, mediation under the guidance of the agreed upon arbitrator begins.

5. After 14 more days, actual arbitration, with witnesses, transcripts, and all the trappings of a formal legal process, begins.

6. Fourteen more days are allowed to pass before employees and management are required to submit their "last best offers." The arbitrator is then required to choose between the last best offers on each of the issues submitted for arbitration.

The purpose of the change to "last best offer" arbitration was to provide an incentive for the two sides to develop positions closer to each other in the bargaining preceding arbitration. In theory, each side will compromise its own demands to present a more reasonable alternative for the arbitrator's consideration.

In practice, experience has shown little evidence that "last best offer" produces more acceptable proposals. In 1982, for example, in arbitration with miscellaneous employees, Vallejo, like other cities, was coping with a budget severely strained by inflation and lagging revenues. At the same time, federal employees were being held to 4 percent pay hikes, and state workers were scheduled to receive raises from 0 to 3 percent.

Under the pressure of the "last best offer" rule, the city raised its offer to a pay increase of 7.5 percent, yet still found itself saddled with an arbitrated raise of 10.5 percent when the arbitrator came down on the side of the union.

In effect, Vallejo's bargaining process has largely been replaced by arbitration. Instead of agreeing to automatic cost of living raises, the city negotiates contracts that include salary reopeners each year. Arbitration on salary alone is now pending with police and firefighters, and the city faces the grim prospect of arbitrating three entire, new contracts as the current two-year agreement with the police, three-year agreement with miscellaneous employees, and four-year contract with firefighters all expire simultaneously.

Hayward

Hayward's firefighters succeeded in winning voter approval in 1976 for their initiative requiring arbitration for their disputes with the city when negotiations over wages and working conditions reach an impasse.

Later in that same year, the firefighters made use of the new charter provision, and the city found its last best offer of a 7.25 percent pay increase raised to 9 percent by the arbitrator, with an additional 7 percent granted for the second year of the agreement. The city's offer of 7.25 percent, rejected by the arbitrator, was comparable to the raise granted the city's other bargaining units. Similarly, the arbitrator's 7 percent award for the second year exceeded the 5.5 percent negotiated by the city with other unions.

Not only did the arbitrator's award cost the city more money, but it also distorted salary negotiations with other city employees, particularly police. Police in Hayward traditionally received a slightly higher salary than firefighters because the city believed police work required more expertise over a greater range. Yet the arbitrator's award put firefighter pay ahead of police pay, creating strong pressure on the city to voluntarily reopen the police agreement three months early and grant additional pay increases.

Arbitration was invoked again two years later, despite the fact that city negotiators three times reached tentative agreements with firefighter representatives, only to have them rejected by the membership who thought they could do better under arbitration. Rather than bargain with the city, the firefighters presented a shopping list of 120 different proposals for changes to fire department practices, while the city raised only eight issues.

Among the firefighter demands granted by the arbitrator were elimination of "quality of service" as a factor in layoff decisions, leaving only seniority to determine who is laid off within a classification; the probationary period for firefighters was reduced from two years to one; firefighters were permitted to print reports by hand instead of typing them; and the use of fire engines for daily grocery shopping was permitted!

Many other union proposals were rejected, yet the city remains concerned because they can surface again in future negotiations, even though many clearly affect management's responsibilities. For example, the firefighters wanted a twice per month payroll system that would have forced the city to run a separate computer payroll program, complete with extra staff and processing, just for this one group of employees. They also sought to prohibit assigning firefighters to maintenance tasks during the long periods between alarms and fire-related duties, and they wanted minimum manning raised from 31 to 41 employees per shift, which would have forced the city to hire another 25 firefighters. The arbitrator turned down their proposal for the "single highest year" in determining pension benefits, which would have added another 1.9 percent to the total firefighter payroll. And the arbitrator turned down their proposal to require the city to reopen negotiations with the firefighters if any other city bargaining unit received a better settlement.

For the two years 1979 and 1980 covered by the agreement, the firefighters were actually granted a pay increase exceeding the last best offer of the city *and* the union itself. The city's best offer amounted to 13.2 percent for two years; the union's offer was 17.5 percent; the arbitrator's award amounted to 19.35 percent.

San Jose

The most recent California city to add provisions requiring arbitration for police and fire disputes, San Jose voters approved a ballot measure in the fall of 1980. Originally proposed as an initiative with petitions circulated by the police and firefighter unions, questions about whether the initiative actually had enough valid signatures by the official deadline caused the city council to place the measure on the ballot through a council action.

Since the charter amendment was adopted, negotiations with police and firefighters have occurred only once, in July 1981, and two-year agreements were negotiated without resorting to arbitration.

While San Jose does not yet have any experience with arbitrated contract awards, officials have observed that the threat of arbitration so far has tended to force more protracted discussions on lesser issues, and has forced the city to alter its bargaining mode from the more traditional reaction to union proposals to a more comprehensive set of city positions.

The Police Problem Employee

Hillary M. Robinette

Police supervisors at all levels are concerned with the marginal and unsatisfactory police employee. They analyze causes and symptoms in an effort to understand and to solve the complex problems of job disaffection, dissatisfaction, contraorganizational behavior, and reduced performance.

With steady increases of cost-push inflation[1] and the attendant effects on the costs of recruiting, selection, and training, police managers are looking more closely at ways to improve the performance of current employees. Those officers and police employees who are judged marginal or unsatisfactory are coming under closer scrutiny by police managers for several reasons. Efforts are being directed at finding the causes of marginal performance and determining solutions to the problem.

This article explores the issue of the marginal performer in the police department and the changing environments in today's society that have created different employee expectations, and therefore, disaffection and marginal performance. As part of this examination, the article also considers the results of a 1981 survey of police managers' perceptions of employee performance and offers some suggestions for dealing with marginal performance.

The Clay–Yates study

The results of a research study conducted by Special Agents Reginald R. Clay and Robert E. Yates of the FBI Academy indicated the scope of the problem of marginal police performers. The researchers set out to identify and profile the police marginal and unsatisfac-

Reprinted with permission of the *FBI Law Enforcement Bulletin,* January 1981.

tory employee by using a questionnaire survey given to a nationwide sample of police supervisors and managers.[2]

The Clay-Yates study was completed in early 1981. One hundred and eighty-three randomly selected participants of the 117th session of the FBI National Academy responded to an initial survey instrument. The instrument was modified for validation and then given to an additional 1,200 law enforcement supervisors. Five hundred and fifty-three of these were used to derive a significant sample of data for consideration.[3]

The study respondents were all supervisors of law enforcement personnel. Ninety-seven percent of the respondents had been police supervisors for over 2 years; 93 percent had been in police work for 7 or more years. The respondent group represented a variety of departments and agencies: 16 percent were from departments of 1,000 or more sworn personnel; 54 percent were from departments of intermediate size; and 30 percent were from small departments (50 or fewer sworn personnel). (See figure 1.)

The researchers set out to identify employee problem areas by frequency of occurrence and severity of the problem. Those surveyed were given 16 choices of problem behavior and asked to select the most frequently occurring and the most serious. The responses indicated that the most frequent employee problem area is often viewed as the most serious; 38.5 percent cited the most frequently occurring problem as the police officer who did "just enough to get by." The data also indicated that the supervisors regarded this employee as their most serious problem. The second most frequently occurring problem was absenteeism and tardiness (19.9 percent) followed by resistance to change (11.2 percent). (See figures 2 and 3.)

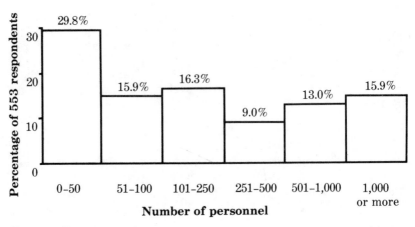

Figure 1. Department size.

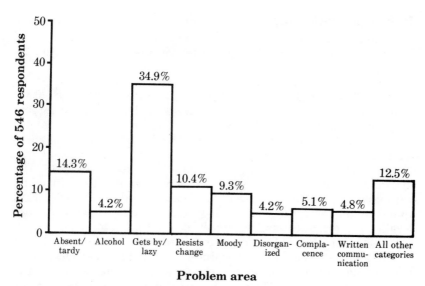

Figure 2. Most serious employee problem area.

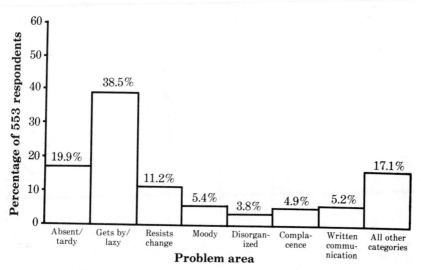

Note: Alcohol tends to be a serious
problem but not a frequent one.

Figure 3. Most frequent problem area.

Police problem employee profile

An examination of the Clay-Yates data produces a profile of the police problem employee in the United States today. The problem employee is a male officer assigned to patrol or investigation who has some college education and is between 25 and 39 years of age. As stated before, the most frequent and most serious difficulty is that he does only enough work to get by. The study shows that the largest single group of these employees (28 percent) were 30 to 34 years of age and had 6 to 10 years' service with the department. (See figures 4 and 5.)

Implied in the study is a definition of problem employees. The marginal performer is one who has demonstrated the ability and willingness to perform well, but who is actually doing only "enough to get by on the job."[4] The unsatisfactory employee is one whose level of performance is consistently below that established as acceptable by the law enforcement organization.

In addition, the Clay-Yates study asked police supervisors who were managing problem employees to identify the causes of the problems. Although complex by nature, these causes of poor performance can be broadly assigned as follows: (1) External influences, i.e., factors away from the job environment, (2) the personal and unique weaknesses of the individual, (3) departmental mismanagement, i.e., organizational forces other than the immediate supervisor, and finally (4) the immediate supervisor. Of the Clay-Yates study respondents, 39.9 percent laid the blame of poor performance on the individual employee; 26.9 percent located the cause in outside

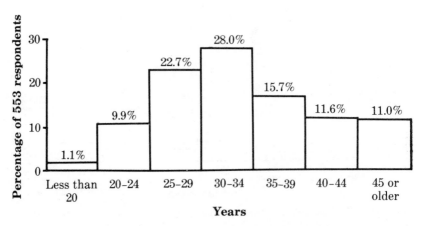

Figure 4.   Age of employees with most serious problem area.

influences; 26.6 percent accused departmental mismanagement; only 6.6 percent fixed responsibility on the immediate supervisor. (See figure 6.) In 60 percent of the cases, the duration of marginal performance had extended over a year.[5]

A clear understanding of marginal performance necessitates a closer examination of some of these causes.

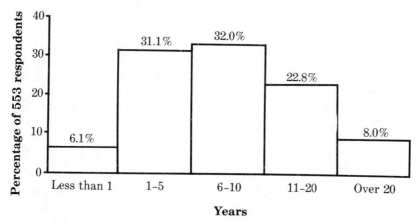

Figure 5. Tenure of employees with most serious problem area.

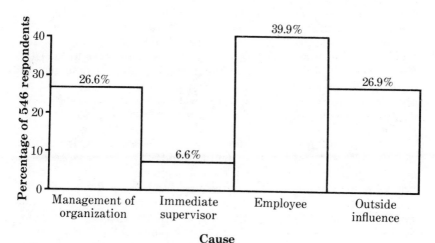

Figure 6. Primary cause of employee problem area.

External factors

Today's young police employee grew up in the 1950's and 1960's when a personalistic philosophy began to permeate American society and the national mood focused on material abundance, GNP growth, and technological advancement. American workers began to change the kind of jobs they performed. In the 1950's, 65 percent of the work force was engaged in industrial occupations and only about 17 percent was employed in information (personal service) occupations. In the following 30 years, the number of Americans in industry dropped to 27 percent while the ranks of the "white-collar" information worker rose to 58 percent in 1980.[6]

During the 1970's, a "self-fulfillment" movement started to spread throughout the United States. By the late 1970's, national surveys showed more than 7 out of 10 Americans (72 percent) spent a great deal of time thinking about themselves and their inner lives.[7] Traditional values were completely reversed, and the self-denial ethic which once fueled the faltering engines of industry was lost in the search for self-fulfillment.

The rising expectations of an expanding middle class and the higher educational levels of those entering the work force combined to produce a perception of needed self-fulfillment. Police departments were not excepted. During this time, the U.S. President's Commission on Law Enforcement and Administration of Justice called for the professionalization of police. The U.S. Congress voted large federal appropriations to increase police officer education and management training.[8] With subsequent liberal LEAA educational funds, law enforcement and criminal justice programs proliferated in newly created junior colleges and technical schools, as well as on traditional campuses. Previously, such programs were not available to the police aspirant. Education raises personal expectations. Those entering the police profession during the 1960's and 1970's brought expectations of advancement and personal income growth which traditional police departments can scarcely meet. Such a reality is bound to cause individual frustration and other discontent manifested in "burn out" and other forms of counterproductive behavior.

The police "problem employee" of the 1980's comes from that social, economic, and psychological turmoil. The pervading cultural psychology of affluence has reversed the self-denial ethic; the tradition of police service to the community is, in some instances, also reversed. Those who entered police service seeking affluence and self-fulfillment become bored with routines and cynical toward the public after the excitement of mastering police skills is gone.

Traditional police organization structures leave very little room at the top for large numbers of educated recruits. In 1977, 42 percent of the officers of departments surveyed by the Police Executive Research Forum had associate or higher degrees.[9]

The officers came to police work with expectations of promotion, pay increases, and enlarging job responsibilities. Not all of the expectations can be met. Frustration occurs, enthusiasm for the job diminishes, and behavior changes, often for the worse. Moreover, many of the young recruits joining departments today bring with them a psychology of affluence which moves them to seek increasing salary levels. This attitude flies in the harsh face of economics. Cost-push inflation and antitax movements, such as Proposition 13 in California and Proposition 2½ in Massachusetts, combine to strain public revenue. Cutback federal and state budget management requires police to share smaller and smaller portions of public revenues. Budget cuts affect salary levels. Consequently, there is less to go around at a time when individual expectations of affluence are rising. Such countervailing forces are another source of frustration for the individual officer.

Time-psych zones and the expectation curve

Coupled with social change are the individual, physical, and mental developments of each person's life. These circumstances of personal change can be described as "time-psych zones." Daniel L. Levinson published the results of a study of basic importance in his book, *The Seasons of a Man's Life.*[10] It is the first such study which explains adult development according to an age-linked timetable. He relates each stage of development to a man's job as the primary base for his life in society. The findings indicate that as we grow older, motivation patterns change. Personal, physical, and environmental circumstances change. Needs change; therefore, behavior changes.

Time-psych zones are the zones of personal expectations which change with age. In early adulthood, during one's first major job responsibility, achievement expectations run strong and high. These are modified by experience and reality during the midlife transition and become settled only through the turbulence of the transition. Often, this transition is marked by confusion of needs and desires. The desire to acquire additional possessions, to taste life in the fast lane, to travel to new places, and to meet new and important people engaged in exciting activities are all seen as needs. Personal goals are shaped by the marketing media which also raises these expectations in order to increase product sales. The individual needs more money, more leisure, and more freedom from commitment to job and home. As Yankelovich claims, " . . . desires are infinite. Anyone trapped in the fallacy that the self is a failure to the extent that all one's desires are not satisfied has set herself or himself up for frustration."[11] Stability is regained during the middle-adult era and carries over through a less turbulent transition into late adulthood. The significance and effect of the stages and transition on a police officer's career and worklife are important.

The early stages of a police officer's career are usually characterized by high expectations of service achievement. He often daydreams of exciting successes in his assignment. He views the successes as necessary coin with which to buy preferment and career-enhancing assignments of increased responsibility. Persons riding the expectation curve in their 20's and early 30's are adaptive to change. They view change as challenging, presenting new opportunities for achievement. They have a high tolerance for negative hygiene factors in the work environment and conditions.[12] They are future-oriented, seldom reflective, and have a high readiness for training. They have a low tolerance for perceived opportunity restriction. Often, they equate self-fulfillment with career advancement and will consider any real or imagined attempt to restrict their advancement with animosity and resistance.

As officers peak on the expectation curve (usually during or just after Levinson's midlife transition), they adjust their expectations. Motivation patterns and other job performance characteristics change. Those on this flat downside of the expectation curve are resistant to change. They often view a change in tactics, procedures, or policy as a threat to their new-found stability and will actively resist change, or worse, try to subvert it. The old saying about not being able to teach an old dog new tricks applies some folk wisdom to the reality. These officers also have a low tolerance for hygiene negatives and can take personal offense at minor adjustments in their work environments. They respond negatively to any deterioration in perks or seniority and working conditions. They are present-oriented and think of success in terms of completing today's task and not in terms of tomorrow's assignment. They have a high tolerance for stable policies, rules, and procedures, and a low readiness for training, new job-learning experiences, and additional career-related formal education. (See figure 7.)

The results of the Clay-Yates study support this expectation curve phenomenon. The large majority of marginal police performers fall in this age group. As reflected in the data, the average marginal performer has between 8 and 16 years' police service.

Change comes to the police department

Changes in the social environment, values, demographics, technology, and economy have all combined to create a managerial atmosphere of turbulence. Once the most stable of municipal organiza-

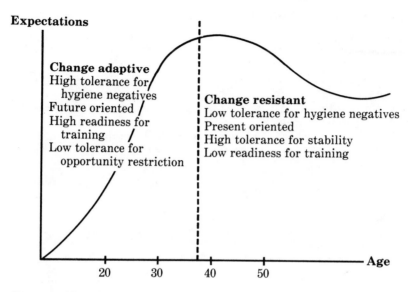

Expectations

Change adaptive
High tolerance for
   hygiene negatives
Future oriented
High readiness for
   training
Low tolerance for
   opportunity restriction

Change resistant
Low tolerance for hygiene negatives
Present oriented
High tolerance for stability
Low readiness for training

Age

20   30   40   50

Figure 7. The expectation curve.

tions, police departments now struggle through strikes, reorganizations, new public policy, and vastly increased operating costs. Between 1967 and 1977, the per capita cost of policing in a large city had risen from $27.31 to over $91, an increase of over 257 percent.[13]

Police work is labor-intensive. The human resources are the most effective of the resources applied in policing and also the most costly. Any cost-reduction analysis or efficiency-improvement effort must focus on improving human resource management. The intuitive perception of this reality has generated concerned interest in the management and salvage of the marginal performer.

The marginal or unsatisfactory performer is costly to police organizations. The difficult work of solving the problem of the marginal employee is discomforting to police managers. Some say it is impossible to take effective action because of legal restraints or union policies. Others cite lack of training in managerial skills for shift supervisors and first-line commanders. All are uncomfortable when confronted with the problem employee. Uncomfortable or not, police managers must seek solutions.

The management challenge

If these data and the trends they suggest are accurately understood, they raise new challenges for police managers. The first is to analyze carefully the factors which contribute to marginal police performance; the second is to find ways to keep the job alive for those who once did it well and with enthusiasm but who have now lost their motivation. Finally, police managers must develop and use effective coaching and documentation skills.

The first challenge, which is analytical in nature, is the most difficult. The police manager is action-oriented. He thrives in an atmosphere of activity. He has little time, inclination, or training for thoughtful reflection. George Odiorne identifies this predisposition as an "activity trap." He writes:

The activity trap is a self-feeding mechanism if you do not turn it around. Everybody becomes attached to some irrelevancy and does his or her job too well. Its ultimate stage is when the [chief] himself loses sight of why the [department] exists, and demands more and more activity rather than results. . . .

Meanwhile, all this activity eats up resources, money, space, budgets, savings, and human energy like a mammoth tape worm.

While it is apparent that the activity trap . . . fails to achieve missions, it has an equally dangerous side-effect on people; they *shrink* personally and professionally.[14]

Without constant attention to the results and contributions that a police manager expects of his subordinates, the manager falls into the activity trap. Some of his subordinates will shrink into the rote process of a job and lose sight of its goals and objectives. With the sure knowledge that activity without goals is wasteful, it is no surprise that these officers become bored or dissatisfied.

As Odiorne points out, however, the trap is not inevitable. It can be resisted and circumvented by enlightened and analytical leadership. The challenge of supervisory analysis calls for the police manager to focus on results in directing his subordinates, then clarify and communicate the results to the people doing the work. Only then will the work itself produce the satisfaction and enthusiasm that keeps the police employee productive. This is not an easy task, but it is specifically managerial and executive in nature. Where the symptoms of marginal performance are unenthusiastic and dissatisfied officers, the manager would do well to find out whether looking busy has become safer than being productive.

The next challenge is finding ways to energize employees. With clear goals and objectives identified, how does the police manager secure employee commitment and enthusiasm for task accomplishment?

The answer here lies in the manager's own commitment and enthusiasm. He must avoid the danger of transparent management, which is the depersonalized processing of organizational directives. If he becomes an executive rubber stamp, he will be viewed as an empty suit, not an effective police manager.

The third challenge is that of developing one's own perception, understanding, and communication skills. To meet this challenge, the police manager must examine his own assumptions about the marginal performer. He must test those assumptions against his wider and probably more objective nonorganizational experiences. He must learn to be sensitive to the expectations of his subordinates. He must also keep in touch with his own time-psych zones. More attention is now directed at officers and employees who are not meeting standards.

Daniel J. Bell, writing in *The Police Chief*, verbalizes the interest when he says: " . . . there needs to be a concentration of effort to move the 'drone' type police officer into other careers outside the police profession."[15] Who is the "drone-type police officer" Bell refers to? Can causes of poor performance be identified? How can they be remedied?

A decision for dismissal or a decision for salvage with the required coaching and counseling must be made. Salvage and renewal are practical, cost-effective ways to meet the challenge. Six out of 10 police managers (65.2 percent) surveyed recommend that the marginal police employee be salvaged.[16]

Dismissal is difficult and impossible without documentation. Changes in the legal environment, especially those brought on by affirmative action, equal employment opportunity, and the women's movement, require job analyses and validated performance standards. Job analysis and validation were activities that were formerly not required of the police. Standards are determined and stated. Formal defense of standards and associated personnel actions are now required, if not in a court of law then in an appeals commission or grievance board.

Strangely, the procedures to support either a dismissal or salvage decision are similar. Effective coaching *and* a permanent, legal termination begin with documentation. The manager must begin with a clear concept of the unit's goals and objectives. These must be communicated to the employee clearly. The work the employee is expected to do must relate directly to the goals and objectives and be so explained to the employee. The manager is required to plan carefully the marginal subordinate's work, just as the subordinate is required to perform the work. Some measurement of progress must be agreed upon. Performance must be documented on a timely basis; appraisal must be regular, realistic, and frequent.

Performance appraisal is just that—an evaluation of actual performance. The police manager needs to pay personal and honest attention to the work the marginal performer does and the work he fails to do. Only then can both understand when the work is done and the objectives are achieved. The manager has the opportunity to reinforce behavior in a nondestructive and objective way. The manager's feedback is the employee's guide to improving performance.

Significantly, almost half of the supervisors polled in the Clay-Yates study (44.5 percent) claimed success in dealing with their problem employees. The probability of success is good, but success is the result of difficult managerial work.

In these times of shrinking resources, police managers are looking for ways to do more with less—ways to meet the rising public demand to reduce violent crime, restore peace and tranquility, and spend fewer public dollars. There is no room for continued marginal performance in police work. Success can be obtained by a recommitment to excellence by the police manager, by a sensitive and attentive concern for the officers under his leadership, and by the acquisition and development of managerial skills.

1. The term "cost-push inflation" is used to describe the inflationary spiral in which increasing costs act to push up prices and wages in a cyclical effect.

2. *Problem Employee Survey: An Analysis of Employee Problem Areas in Law Enforcement*, Reginald R. Clay and Robert E. Yates, (Quantico, Va.: FBI Academy, 1981), p. 3.

3. "Of the 1,200 law enforcement supervisors surveyed, questionnaire responses from 535 were selected. The screening factors for selecting questionnaires for gathering meaningful data were gleaned from the following questions: (1) Does the respondent currently supervise employees? and (2) Does he have a problem employee?" Clay-Yates, p. 23.

4. Clay-Yates, p. 6.

5. Clay-Yates, p. 67.

6. John Naisbitt, "The Bottom-Up Society: America Between Eras" *Public Opinion*, April-May 1981, p. 19.

7. "In the nineteen-seventies, all national surveys showed an increase in preoccupation with self. By the late seventies, my firm's studies showed more than seven out of ten Americans [72%] spent a great deal of time thinking about themselves and their inner lives—this in a nation once notorious for its impatience with inwardness. The rage for self-fulfillment, our surveys indicated, had now spread to virtually the entire U.S. population." Daniel Yankelovich, *New Rules: Searching for Self-Fulfillment in a World Turned Upside Down* (New York: Random House, 1981), p. 5.

8. *The Challenge of Crime in a Free Society*, A Report by the U.S. President's Commission on Law Enforcement and Administration of Justice (Washington, D.C.: U.S. Government Printing Office), p. 109. The Commission recommends: The ultimate aim of all police departments should be that all personnel with general enforcement powers have baccalaureate degrees."

9. Michael T. Farmer, ed., *Survey of Police Operational and Administrative Practices—1977* (Washington, D.C.: Police Executive Research Forum, 1978), p. 63.

10. Daniel J. Levinson, *The Seasons of a Man's Life* (New York: Alfred A. Knopf, 1978).

11. Yankelovich, p. 238.

12. Frederick Herzberg says there are two elements which create employee motivation—the job itself and the hygiene factors. He de-

scribes hygiene factors as those things and circumstances incidental to work itself, such as salary, fringe benefits, working conditions, supervision, policies, procedures, rules, and regulations. These can be viewed either as positive or negative and can cause dissatisfaction or satisfaction but cannot be viewed as motivators because true motivation, according to Herzberg, comes from the job itself, its scope, its value,

and the sense of accomplishment it provides.

13. U.S. President's Commission, 1967, p. 91; Farmer, p. 13.

14. George S. Odiorne, *The Change Resisters* (Englewood Cliffs, N.J.: Prentice-Hall, Inc., 1981), p. 16.

15. Daniel J. Bell, "The Police-Personnel Upgrading for Professionalism," *The Police Chief* 45, no. 1, January 1978, p. 32.

16. Clay-Yates, p. 65.

Permanent Shifts vs. Rotation Shifts: Sick Time Use Among Police Officers

Paul G. Graupmann

Absenteeism, whether in the private or public sector, is costly. While the private sector reflects this cost in higher prices for goods and services, ultimately, the public sector passes the cost of employee absenteeism along to the taxpayer. The question arises, how does an institution combat this problem? In this era of strict labor contracts, it is difficult to assess disciplinary sanctions against an employee if he decides to "call in sick." Consequently, employers have sometimes resorted to creative means to cut down on the use of sick time in the work place. This article will examine how a small police department attempted to decrease absenteeism, and show how that plan both succeeded and failed.

The police department for the Charter Township of Shelby is located in Macomb County, Michigan, approximately 12 miles north of Detroit. The department consists of 39 sworn personnel, 26 of whom are patrol officers. The administrative personnel noticed that in the calendar years from 1978 forward, the use of sick time began to rise significantly among patrol officers. This condition persisted in spite of the fact that the patrol personnel were accruing additional vacation time each year. Not surprisingly, the majority of sick time was used during the winter months and the least during the summer months. In 1980, this problem was addressed during labor negotiations for the working contract between the municipality and the patrolmen's association. An agreement was reached between the two bargaining units whereby the officers were allowed to pick the shift they wanted to work,[1] and were allowed to work that shift

"Permanent Shifts as Opposed to Rotation Shifts: An Evaluation of Sick Time Use Among Police Officers," reproduced from *Journal of Police Science and Administration*, volume 11, no. 2 (1983), with permission of the International Association of Chiefs of Police, P.O. Box 6010, 13 Firstfield Road, Gaithersburg, Maryland 20878.

as long as they wished. The selection was done on a seniority basis, and the process was repeated every 12 weeks (roughly four times a year). This policy was put into effect in January 1981. The municipality believed that the officers would feel better, and therefore become ill less, if they were allowed to select what shift they would be working. It is medically recognized that improper sleeping and eating habits will contribute to stress and strain on the individual's system, and foster all manner of ailments including influenza, colds, and other minor illnesses. The municipality and the patrolmen's association both reasoned that if an individual were working a shift that was most compatible to that person's metabolism, it would follow that the individual would function better, feel better, become less run down and therefore use less sick time.

Literature review

While little work has been done in the area of the effects of shift work on police personnel, there are several medical studies in this area. Aschoff maintains that every body organ has its own "rhythm," and that the body is at the mercy of this rhythmic cycle, which Aschoff calls the "circadian rhythm."[2] Most humans are active in the daytime and sleep when it is dark. Aschoff tried to illustrate in his studies that other involuntary bodily functions, such as body temperature and endocrine excretions, are in a rhythm with this predominant sleep pattern. When the sleep pattern is disrupted, or changed, the other rhythms take time to catch up. The length of catch up time will vary with the individual. Aschoff found that changes in the rhythms do not seem to adversely affect workers who are assigned to a particular shift on a more or less permanent basis because their internal rhythms adjust to the new schedule over time, and their systems are not called upon to readapt periodically. The worker on a rotational work shifting program, however, must adapt each time that his schedule changes. Unfortunately, the internal rhythms, once disturbed, do not adapt readily to the new schedule, nor do they readapt with ease when the worker is returned to his former schedule. In rotation work shifting, just as the individual's rhythms are beginning to adjust to the new routine, he is switched to a different schedule. This repeated shifting is very debilitating, and organizations that employ it can be faced with the problem of workers whose health, work performance, safety awareness and emotional states are at a low ebb.[3]

Weitzman et al. found in their observations among shift workers that the reversal of the sleeping and waking periods caused fatigue for two reasons: (1) added stress due to disrupted social, personal and familial function; and (2) shorter, more disturbed sleeping periods. The Weitzman group also found that workers can adapt to this reversal, but that the adaptation takes time.[4]

Taylor found much the same in his study of factory workers.[5] Those on a fixed shift suffered fewer illnesses than those working on rotation shift systems. Wyatt and Marriott found that among factory workers, the longer an individual remained on a shift the higher the productivity and the lower the absenteeism rate.[6] DeLaMare and Walker discovered that most workers were not concerned so much about which shift they served on as long as they were assigned to that shift on a more or less permanent basis.[7]

Telkey did probably the most detailed medical study of shift work during the Second World War.[8] Prior to that time, there was little shift work as we know it today. With the onset of the war, however, production levels were forced upward, which forced around-the-clock work. Telkey found that frequent shift changes can cause:

1. Impairment of physical health
2. Emotional and behavior problems
3. Sleeping difficulties
4. Altered response to medication
5. A decrease in work performance and safety awareness.

The combination of these factors can result in absenteeism, decreased productivity, social disorganization and poor safety records. Also, as in the later studies, Telkey found that the longer an individual remained on a shift, the lower the incidence of the above mentioned dysfunctions.

It seems clear in reviewing the literature on this matter, from a health standpoint, that rotation shift scheduling imposes physiological and emotional stresses on the individual that are frequently debilitating. It logically follows then that an elimination of these stressors would allow the individual to remain more healthy, and therefore cut down on absenteeism.

The study

In order to show the success or failure of the permanent shift program, the author first made a careful study of the use of sick time by patrol officers in 1978 and 1981. In both years the total manpower of the department remained exactly the same. The year 1978 was chosen because it was the last year the department scheduled manpower on a strict shift rotation. The year 1981 was chosen by virtue of the fact that it was the first year the officer shift selection process was used. The officers were then asked to complete a questionnaire regarding their personal sick time use.

Sick time use   Each officer is allocated 12 sick days per year. These days are accrued at the rate of one per month and an officer may accrue an unlimited number of days. When an officer retires, he is reimbursed for his unused sick days at the pay rate he retires at. This alone is a powerful incentive to conserve days, as the days one "banks" in sick time actually grow in monetary value as time passes. The policy agreement on the use of sick time between the Charter Township of Shelby and the Shelby Township Police Patrol-men's Association for the period June 1, 1980, through June 30, 1982, is as follows (section 19.2):

Sick leave shall be granted for absence from duty because of personal illness or legal quarantine and for personal emergencies involving illness in an employee's immediate family or the immediate family of the current spouse, requiring the officer's presence. Immediate family is limited to spouse, children, step-children, mother, father, brothers, sisters, mother-in-law, father-in-law, and grandparents of the employee. The Township may require proof of illness, in the event of repeated absences or in the event of an absence of three (3) days or longer. Under normal circumstances, should an officer call in sick, he shall not return to duty for any part of that shift. This condition, however, may be waived with the permission of the command officer.

This policy is adhered to very loosely by management. It could be said that the "honor system" applies, and each officer follows his conscience in the use of sick time.

In 1978, the department used a 4-week rotation system for shift management. An officer would work 4 weeks on each shift, and then switch. The officer would work the midnight shift first (12 a.m.–8 a.m.), then the afternoon shift (4 p.m.–12 a.m.), then midnight again. This would be followed by a day shift (8 a.m.–4 p.m.). The cycle would then begin again, except that the midnight and afternoon shifts would be reversed. It is easy to see how this constant changing of work hours would be very hard on an individual's constitution. In 1981, this policy was changed, and each officer was allowed to select his own shift. Although this was done on a seniority basis, it should be noted that everyone received his first choice, except for the final man on the list.

A study of the 1978 annual sick day report for patrol officers showed that 204 days and one hour were used.[9] This total was adjusted down to 192 days, one hour. The adjustment was made by subtracting 12 days that were used by two officers for injuries they sustained while either on or off duty. The author believes that a true measure of the effectiveness of the program could only be ascertained if this study directed itself to sick time used on a daily basis, presumably as a result of some minor ailment. Over the long haul, severe injuries have little cumulative effect on the sick bank and are unavoidable in the most part. The adjusted total of 192 days translates into 7.3 days per man for the year.

By way of comparison, in 1981 the adjusted total sick time used for patrol officers consisted of 243 days, one hour, for an average of

9.3 days per man.[10] The totals show an increase of approximately 20 percent in the use of sick time by officers between the years 1978 and 1981. This increase is even more significant when one considers that each officer had, on the average, an additional week of vacation time in 1981 as compared to 1978. The use of an additional 51 days by the patrol division would seem to indicate that the officer shift selection program was unsuccessful in the lowering of sick time use.

Sick time questionnaire   To determine why the patrol officers used the sick time, a questionnaire was distributed to each of the 26 men (see accompanying box).

Questions 1 and 2 were used to determine whether or not the officer selected the shift he *enjoyed* working the most. Question 3 clarifies any discrepancy which may appear if numbers 1 and 2 were different. Question 4 addressed itself to the main precept behind the shift selection program. Questions 5 and 6 ask the officer how he perceived his use of sick time before and after permanent shifts

---

Patrolman's questionnaire

(All answers are strictly confidential)

1. Above all other shifts, which shift do you *enjoy* working the most?
2. Over the last year, which shift have you worked the most?
3. Stated briefly (1 or 2 sentences), why did you decide to work the shift or shifts you have worked over the past year (for example, spouse working, more interesting calls, etc.)?
4. From the standpoint of health, or just "feeling good," have you noticed any differences in the way you feel since we changed over to permanent shifts? If so, what?
5. Did you use more, less, or about the same amount of sick time in the last year (since permanent shifts), as in the year previous to permanent shifts?
6. Do you feel that working in the rotating shift manner (before permanent shifts) caused you to use more sick time?
7. When you use sick time is it usually because you are sick, or is it because you need the day for another purpose (child or spouse is sick, to babysit, etc.)?
8. When you use sick time, about what percent of the time is used strictly because you are too sick to work? (Circle one.)
    10–30%
    30–50%
    50–70%
    70–100%
9. Do you like the way shift selection is made, or do you prefer the old rotation? Why?

Thank you for your cooperation in this matter.

---

were instituted. Question 7 asks *why* and *how* an officer uses sick time. Question 8 is directly linked to question 7 in that it clarifies that answer by forcing the respondent to place a numerical value on his answer in question 7. Question 9 is self-explanatory.

The data   Initially, one could assume that the shift selection program was a failure in lowering the absenteeism rate. From a strictly utilitarian approach, that is, of course, true—the figures do not lie, and an increase of 20 percent is indeed a significant rise. The hypothesis, then, that allowing a patrol officer to pick the shift he works will cause less sick time to be used, is not true. The questionnaire illuminates, to an extent, the reasons for this. Of the 26 questionnaires administered (every officer received one), 18 were returned. All but four indicated that they picked the shift they liked working the best (questions 1 and 2). There were a variety of responses to question 3, with answers including problems concerning the spouse's working, to a more regular love life. Without an exception, in question 4, all the respondents indicated that they felt much better *physically* working a regular shift. In regard to question number 5, 15 of the respondents stated they used the same (8) or less (7) amount of sick time while working the permanent shift, as opposed to 3 who stated they used more than on the rotation method. Question 6 clearly shows that a majority (11 of 18) felt they used more sick time on the rotating shift schedule. This apparent contradiction between actual and perceived sick time use has two possible explanations. Either a few of the officers are using a great deal more sick time, or the officers' perception of their use of sick time is inaccurate. The statistics show exactly 13 men used less sick time between the 2 years. In only one case (16.6 days) was the discrepancy large. The second supposition then appears to be correct. Probably the two most revealing pieces of data are the responses to questions 7 and 8. Only two respondents stated they usually use their sick time for a personal sickness. When asked to put a percentage value on their use of sick time for purposes of actual sickness, 13 stated they were actually sick 10 to 30 percent of the time, 3 stated they were actually sick between 30 to 50 percent, and only 2 said they were actually sick most of the time or 70 to 100 percent. Finally, only one respondent indicated he did not like the shift selection process more than the old rotation method.

Conclusions
While the shift selection process failed to reduce the use of sick time at the police department in question, several salient points should be considered. The underlying assumption on this project was the premise that if an officer worked the same hours on a regular basis, he would get less run down, feel better, and therefore would use less

sick time. In respect to physically feeling better, it would seem the shift selection process was successful. All respondents stated they felt better as a result of working a permanent shift, and, in fact, most perceived themselves as using less sick time as a result of working regular hours (it has been shown, however, that this perception is inaccurate). The reasons for the excessive use of sick time appear to be a result of other than actual illness. This is evidenced in the response to question number 8. Roughly 70 percent of the respondents stated that almost all the time they call in sick, they are not sick.

It is the author's opinion as a member of the permanent shift program that the department's use of the permanent shifts was successful. The officers state they feel significantly better under this system. The fact that sick time use was not decreased is obviously due to other factors, and should be addressed in the appropriate manner. It should also be noted that 1981 was the first year that the permanent shift program was used. Perhaps in years to come, the use of sick time will be decreased—it could conceivably be that the program has simply not been given ample time to work as planned. In any case, the increased use of sick time is clearly not the result of the permanent shift policy, and if nothing else that policy is a good starting point in continued efforts to reduce absenteeism.

1. Section 24.15 of the agreement between the Charter Township of Shelby and the Shelby Township Police Patrolmen's Association for the period July 1, 1980, through June 30, 1982.
2. J. Aschoff, "Circadian Rhythms in Man," *Science* 148 (1965): 1427–32.
3. Charles M. Wingst, et al., "Physiological Effects of Rotational Work Shifting," *Journal of Occupational Medicine* 3 (1961): 204–11.
4. Ed Weitzman et al., "Reversal of Sleep Walking Cycle: Effect on Sleepstage Pattern and Certain Neuroendocrine Rhythms," *Trans. American Neurological Association* 93 (1968): 153–57.
5. P. J. Taylor, "Shift and Day Work: A Comparison of Sickness, Absence, Lateness, and Other Absence Behavior at an Oil Refinery from 1962–1965," *British Journal of Industrial Medicine* 24 (1967): 93–102.
6. S. Wyatt and R. Marriot, "Night Work and Night Shift Changes," *British Journal of Industrial Medicine* 10 (1963): 164–72.
7. G. DeLaMare and J. Walker, "Shift Working: The Arrangement of Hours on Night Work," *Nature* 208 (1965): 1127–28.
8. L. Telkey, "Problems of Nightwork: Influences on Health and Efficiency," *Industrial Medicine and Surgery* 12 (1943): 758–79.
9. Shelby Township Police Department, *Annual Report* (Macomb County, Mich.: Shelby Township Police Department, 1978).
10. Shelby Township Police Department, *Annual Report*, 1981.

Healthy
Police Officers
Are Cost-Effective
Police Officers

──────────── Terrence L. Ellis and Ralph A. Bailey

The city of Monterey has instituted a mandatory physical fitness program in its police department as a result of an unacceptably high injury and disability rate among Monterey police officers.

Many cities have developed entry-level fitness or "agility" tests, but few have addressed the matter of physical fitness maintenance after hiring. Monterey's decision to develop a comprehensive and mandatory physical fitness program was based upon two assumptions: that an officer who is out of shape has a greater probability of injury or illness than one who is in reasonably good shape; and that the stronger an officer is physiologically, the better the chances that an injury or illness may be less serious or easier to recover from. Cities have an enormous financial investment in a police officer, both in terms of training and liability for work related illness or injury. In increasing numbers, Monterey's officers were falling prey to a wide assortment of on-the-job and presumptive illnesses and injuries, ranging from lower back and knee problems to vascular disease. Workers' compensation claims reached an all-time high, and departmental overtime costs soared. In the wake of excessive overtime demands, some officers began to experience high levels of fatigue and stress, and department morale began to show signs of deterioration.

Clear standards

An approach was adopted which provided for a medical evaluation system, pre-employment and annual incumbent fitness testing based on validated performance standards, and professional physi-

Reprinted with permission from the January 1983 issue of *Western City* magazine, the monthly publication of the League of California Cities.

cal fitness counseling for incumbents to help improve and maintain physical fitness levels.

When the physical fitness problem was first identified early in 1980, a technical committee was appointed to investigate the problem and explore possible solutions. From the beginning, rank-and-file officers of the police department were actively involved in the development of the new fitness program. Without their input, the program could be perceived as some lofty scheme of city management, thereby leading to resistance and resentment by those very employees the program was designed to help. Implementation was also planned in such a way that "ownership" would be vested with the police department from the start.

The philosophy of the Monterey program recognizes that different people prefer to exercise and maintain physical fitness in different ways, and that any particular facility, set of equipment, or routine will typically only appeal to a subgroup of employees. The emphasis has been placed upon clearly defining job-related physical fitness standards, and then holding each officer individually responsible for maintaining these standards.

The possibility of establishing an on-duty exercise program was dismissed early in the process in favor of individual employee responsibility in accordance with clearly defined standards. The city was concerned about logistical problems and substantial costs associated with the on-duty physical training concept or a group exercise program.

The first step was to identify the physical skills and abilities necessary to perform the job of a police officer in Monterey. A test development specialist was retained to help develop a pre-employment physical fitness test, valid physical fitness standards, and a test for incumbent police officers.

The consultant developed an easily administered, four-event test, based on written and interview input from the 50 incumbent police officers of the department. Each event was designed to test critical physical abilities and to simulate typical physical tasks an officer could expect to encounter on the job. For recruitment testing purposes, minimum pass/fail test scores were established for each event, based on the average adjusted scores attained in an incumbent pilot test. These minimum standards were also set as the pass/fail points for incumbents. However, improving incumbent fitness beyond the minimum became the next concern.

Signed statement

The new physical fitness program was not only intended to maintain minimum requirements for incumbents, but also to improve their level of physical fitness where possible. "Target" scores established on a sliding scale based upon age served as the goals for the physical fitness maintenance program for incumbent employees.

In other words, even if an incumbent is capable of achieving the absolute minimum qualifying score in a given test event, this level of performance may still be less than desirable for an officer in an excellent state of health and fitness. A distinction was made between "normal" fitness levels and "normal/healthy" fitness levels. "Normal" was defined as the bare minimum needed to accomplish the job, and "normal/healthy" as that higher level of physical fitness where risk of injury or disease is reduced, and recovery capability improved.

All Monterey police department sworn personnel will take the physical fitness maintenance test once each year. The only exception to this mandatory rule is the chief of police, for whom participation in the program is optional.

Prior to employment, new police officers are now required to sign a statement acknowledging that maintaining the city's physical fitness standards is a bona fide condition of employment. Comprehensive medical testing begins with preemployment and continues on a periodic basis throughout the individual's employment career.

The next issue was the inevitable and delicate question of how to treat incumbent officers who fail to meet standards. Failure to pass the pre-employment test obviously results in disqualification of a candidate; however, such a black-and-white approach is not reasonable for incumbent officers.

Fitness counselor

The technical committee decided that officers who could not meet the target score for their age group in any test event would be required to work with a "fitness counselor" to correct the problem.

The fitness counselor is an expert in the field of physical training and testing, retained by the city to work with police officers in the development of individualized physical fitness programs that may include elements relating to exercise, diet, stress management and personal habits such as smoking. Any incumbent officer not able to attain the appropriate target score is required to meet and work with the fitness counselor as often as necessary. "Make-up" tests are scheduled on a periodic basis when the counselor believes the individual officer is ready to meet the target scores.

The difficult question of how to deal with incumbent officers not meeting the target standards was clearly on everyone's mind from the start. While special consideration for these officers is reasonable and necessary, somewhere down the line a form of potential penalty for non-compliance must be evident if the program is to be taken seriously by everyone.

As a result, the basic rule was established that failure to meet minimum standards within a reasonable period of time may result in disciplinary action up to and including termination; but, for incumbents employed prior to adoption of the program, disciplinary action will not be employed where "substantial effort and reasonable progress have been demonstrated by the officer." This criterion is defined subjectively by the chief of police, with the technical aid of the fitness counselor.

For officers successfully passing all events, the services of the fitness counselor are optional. The city will pay for up to two hours per year of counseling time to encourage further improvement of physical fitness and general health.

Sample program

One of the interesting sidelights of the program's development was the selection of the physical fitness counselor. Three highly qualified experts were interviewed from the local community, and each candidate was required to submit an individualized program for a fictitious police officer named "Bumper Morgan," based on a fabricated set of conditions and characteristics (see box).

The individual selected by the city stressed a combination of individual health education, weight control, a calorie intake program, and a physical conditioning routine.

Where applicable, the spouse is brought into the discussion of such important factors as meal preparation and "moral support." Careful records and regular monitoring are required on all aspects of the program, with regular and frequent personal contact between the counselor and the employee for the purposes of both monitoring and support.

Medical testing

Entry-level police officers have always been required to pass a comprehensive medical examination prior to employment with the city. However, no further medical testing was required from that point forward. Analysis showed this to be a false economy and that any new physical fitness program would also have to incorporate an incumbent medical testing component. With periodic and comprehensive medical testing, many types of health problems can be detected early and mitigated accordingly. A convincing argument for testing was the recognition that the costs of a single police officer disability would undoubtedly pay for the entire departmental medical examination program for a period of years. More police officers die each year of cardiovascular and similar conditions than of trauma result-

How would you advise "Bumper Morgan"?

Candidates for the position of fitness counselor for Monterey were given the fictitious case of "Bumper Morgan" to demonstrate the kind of counseling they would provide to enhance police officers' physical fitness.

1. **Name:** "Bumper Morgan"
2. **Age:** 42
3. **Height:** 6'0"
4. **Weight:** 230 Lbs.
5. **Blood pressure:** 135/90
6. **Pulse:** 88 (Resting)
7. **Physical performance test results:** *(Test taken 1 week ago)*
   Event 1: Balance Beam—Passed
   Event 2: Obstacle Course—Failed
           (Bumper's Time = 76 Seconds
           Passing Time = 46 Seconds)
   Event 3: Dummy Pull—Failed
           (Bumper's Time = 5.3 Seconds
           Passing Time = 5.2 Seconds)
   Event 4: 6' Wall—Failed
8. **Additional information:**
   a) Non-smoker
   b) Moderate-to-heavy drinker
   c) Never exercises
   d) Has high school football knee injury with occasional aggravation
   e) Has passed medical examination and his participation in a fitness program has been approved by a physician
9. **Attitude statement:** "I have been with the department for 15 years and can do my job. This is a waste of time, but I'll do what's necessary to keep my job."

The consultant should provide the following information after evaluating this profile:

1. Recommended program.
2. Expected time required before Bumper should be tested.
3. Estimate the number and the type of sessions you would require with Bumper. (Make assumptions where applicable.)
4. Explain how you would monitor and evaluate Bumper's progress and program.
5. Provide an estimate of what you would charge the city for the entire program for Bumper.

ing from police work. It therefore makes good sense to conduct comprehensive medical screening and testing for incumbents.

The city worked closely with the local hospital to develop a medical testing program which established a time-phased set of periodic physical exams based upon age. Initially, all incumbents received a complete medical examination to establish baseline medical histories for each officer, and to identify any health problems which might initially prevent an officer from participating in the physical fitness testing process. At least two potentially serious medical conditions were brought to light through this initial medical review. Once such a medical baseline is established, it is not economical or necessary to administer the full medical exam every year to each incumbent because the need for ongoing medical testing normally varies with age.

Nevertheless, the single largest ongoing expense of Monterey's program will be the medical testing component. The first year cost of the medical program is estimated at $17,000, and is expected to range from $4,000 to $8,000 per year thereafter. This cost is actually quite nominal, given the city's huge dollar investment and extensive financial responsibility associated with each police officer.

Cooperation with school

A secondary consideration for city management was the provision of exercise equipment and facilities. We found that physical fitness problems were not due to the unavailability of equipment or facilities, and that problems can normally be corrected and fitness maintained without the need for special equipment or facilities. However, to accommodate those situations where special equipment and facilities may prove helpful to an officer, an arrangement was worked out with the local high school (conveniently located next door to police headquarters) to make the school's weight and exercise facilities available to police officers on a 24-hour-per-day basis. But it was clear from the start that physical fitness is not a hardware problem, and that Monterey's problem would not be solved by putting a few thousand dollars worth of equipment in the basement and then proceeding with business as usual.

To date, reaction within the Monterey police department has been positive and supportive of the program. Although it will probably take a few years for all of the anticipated benefits of the new program to manifest themselves, confidence is high that the payoffs will come, and that they will prove to be well worth the trouble and expense. Departmental morale has already taken a turn for the better. It is expected that the next few years will show a marked reduction in city costs due to lost time and disability.

Quality Circles: The Shape of Things to Come?

Deborah D. Melancon

Today's young police officers have worklife aspirations that go well beyond efforts to improve pay and benefits. They are more individualistic, better educated, less fearful of economic insecurity, less automatically loyal and less responsive to authority. Employee opinion surveys reveal that officers today want more participation in the decisions affecting their work than their predecessors did.

Police administrators must address these changes in workforce attitudes. At the same time, however, economic conditions require doing more with less and the public demands greater productivity. Concurrently satisfying the better working condition demands of employees and the better service demands of the public at reasonable costs seems an impossible task. But while developing organizational processes that improve both productivity and the quality of worklife is difficult, it is not impossible. The Dallas Police Department is successfully meeting this challenge by using innovative management techniques, including one known as "quality circles."

In addition to creative problem-solving, quality circles offer perfect opportunities for managers to put such abstract motivational theories as McGregor's "Theory Y" and Maslow's "Hierarchy of Needs" into practical use. Both theories contend that employees, if allowed to influence job-related decisions, tend to take a more personal interest and pride in their work. Increased pride in workmanship results in increased productivity and a more effective organization. Through participation in a quality circle group, workers' job satisfaction increases because they are able to satisfy their psychological needs for personal achievement, recognition and increased self-esteem.

Reproduced from *The Police Chief* magazine, November, 1984, issue, with permission of the International Association of Chiefs of Police, P.O. Box 6010, 13 Firstfield Road, Gaithersburg, Maryland 20878.

Developing a concept

In the early 1960s, during a nationwide push for improved product quality, Japanese managers recognized this relationship between worker satisfaction and productivity. In 1962, the quality circle concept was developed and firms across Japan involved teams of workers in solving productivity and quality problems. Today there are approximately one million circles involving more than nine million Japanese workers. An estimated $25 billion in savings has been realized as a direct result of quality circles in Japan. The Toyota company alone reports an estimated $3 billion savings a year through its quality circles.

In 1974, two United States aerospace companies, Lockheed and Honeywell, began to experiment with quality circles. Both firms reported excellent success in their early efforts. Since then, many other organizations in the United States have started programs and report such benefits as a teamwork atmosphere, increased job satisfaction, quality improvement, productivity improvements, and better communication between management and labor.

During the 1980s, we are seeing the transition of this concept from its origin in private business to the public service sector, including several police departments across the country. The Dallas Police Department is included in the parent quality circle organization for the city of Dallas.

The city of Dallas began its program by orienting upper and middle management of departments wishing to participate in the quality circle program. This orientation included an introduction to quality circles, an explanation of the problem-identifying and solving techniques and a work session in which managers worked through a hypothetical problem.

After the orientation, the hierarchy of the program was formed by the selection of a steering committee, a facilitator, the team leaders, and the team members. The steering committee consists of various city department heads who have quality circles within their work areas. This committee, the governing board of the program, ensures management support and controls the expansion rate of the program. Although a facilitator handles the daily operations of the program, the steering committee meets quarterly for planning and evaluating the program's progress.

The facilitator is responsible for the orientation, implementation and overall operation of the quality circle program. He coordinates various teams' meeting dates, times and places. In addition, the facilitator trains the team leaders in methodology, group dynamic skills, and management presentation techniques. Currently, the city of Dallas has one full-time facilitator.

Team leaders are the supervisors of their respective work

groups. The Dallas Police Department generally fills this position with sergeants who have attended three-day seminars to learn quality circle philosophy, techniques and the fundamentals of operation.

The team members are workers drawn from specific work groups. Although extended participation is voluntary, the team members are required to attend at least three meetings before determining whether they wish to participate. Members may drop out at any time and others may be added. Members attend in both on-duty and off-duty status and receive overtime or compensatory time when applicable because quality circles are considered a part of the job.

Quality circles in Dallas

The first quality circle within the Dallas Police Department was organized at the Southwest Patrol Division in June of 1981 and consisted of 14 officers. Sergeant Tom F. Higgins was the circle leader. The team members received training in brainstorming techniques, cause-and-effect analysis, problem definition, data collection and sorting techniques. The team identified several problems and set up criteria to classify them. Two types of problems—readily solvable ones and complex ones—were then approached. The Southwest Circle favorably affected several of the problems identified and was subsequently used as a model to create other groups within the Dallas Police Department. At present, there are 14 quality circles operating among the various divisions of the department.

Many of the recommendations made by the department's quality circles have been implemented. An example of the productivity achievements being made is the ongoing implementation of a recommendation by the Central Patrol Division quality circle, which studied the police manpower and equipment hours wasted in handling prisoners arrested by Dallas Security Force officers, who have peace officer authority over city of Dallas properties. Although the security guards are considered arresting officers for courtroom testimony, they are required to call a police squad to do the report writing and prisoner transporting on all their arrests. Police officers resent having to do what they consider the arresting officers' jobs and the security guards do not like having their reports made through "second-hand" accounts.

The mutually agreed-upon solution offered by the Central Patrol quality circle was to train the Dallas Security Force officers in these areas and allow them to complete their prisoner and report handling through existing Dallas Police Department facilities and procedures. By circumventing police officer assistance, this plan will save at least 720 manhours yearly, which represents an approximate $11,500 savings in salaries alone.

Tangible and intangible benefits

An overall monetary evaluation of the city of Dallas quality circle program, which includes the Dallas Police Department groups, reveals the following:

Total direct cost savings as a result of quality circles	$771,600
Total cost of the program	$211,365
Net savings, 1981–1983	$560,235

Not all quality circle answers can be equated to a dollars-and-cents figure. Many circles spend weeks working out preventive measures that never show up as tangible savings. For example, how does one compute the price of a prevented accident?

Although difficult to calculate, cost savings are indirectly achieved through enhanced morale and "quality of worklife" improvements for the participating employees. A survey of team leaders of the pilot teams, taken in August 1982, indicated the quality circles were beneficial in solving problems in the work area and that management was supportive of the program. The survey showed officers felt that through the quality circle program, the city organization exhibited more openness, trust and support toward its employees.

To ensure similar quality circle program success, certain key ingredients should be included:

1. In-depth training, which includes orientation, quality circle philosophy, and operational techniques.
2. Management participation in and open support of the program. This includes a willingness to listen to suggestions and a commitment to encourage and use worker input in decisions.
3. Feedback through chain-of-command channels and proper follow-up on recommended changes or solutions.
4. Publication of quality circle team achievements in departmental newsletters, activity reports or graphic displays using bulletin boards or other posting.

These key ingredients, accompanied by management and employee cooperation, can solve the problem of low worker morale due to lack of job satisfaction. At the same time, the public's demands for increased productivity at lower costs can be met. However, police administrators must exhibit the willingness to listen to and act upon suggested solutions made by lower-echelon employees. They must also challenge their workers to offer creative and effective solutions to problems experienced in their work areas.

In Dallas, it has been found that if these things are done, quality circles can become effective tools in the management of police officers with expanded worklife expectations. At the same time, quality circles can help accomplish increased productivity goals. Quality circles just may be the shape of things to come for law enforcement agency administrators.

1. "Quality Circles—A Third Wave Intervention," *Training and Development Journal*, March 1981, p. 28.

Quality Circles:
Policy and
Procedures

Orlando Police Department

Policy
Each employee of the department is provided opportunities to voluntarily participate in the identification and resolution of operational or functional problems within their area of assignment. The quality circle program is a means of pursuing this policy.

Quality circles defined
A quality circle is a group of volunteer employees who meet to solve problems within their working environment. A circle should consist of 5 to 11 people who have a common interest and common work hours.

Bureau commander responsibilities
The bureau commander of each bureau shall establish and maintain facilitator committees for each bureau. The bureau commander shall ensure that the committee performs its appointed duties and shall ensure facilitators are replaced when vacancies occur.

Quality circle coordinator
The quality circle coordinator shall be responsible for establishing and monitoring the circle program. He will provide training for facilitators and provide materials for the circles as needed. The quality circle coordinator will provide a place for circle records.

Reproduced from *The Police Chief* magazine, November, 1984, issue, with permission of the International Association of Chiefs of Police, P.O. Box 6010, 13 Firstfield Road, Gaithersburg, Maryland 20878, submitted by John C. Bowden, Planning and Research Section, Orlando, (Florida) Police Department.

Facilitator committee

Structure   The facilitator committee shall consist of five to seven members appointed by the bureau commander, with a chairperson also appointed by the bureau commander. Although not mandatory, members should be of a supervisory level.

Duties   The committee:
1. Will maintain the circles under its control.
2. Shall facilitate no more circles than there are members on the committee.
3. Shall ensure a facilitator meets with the circles at each circle meeting.
4. Should provide guidance for the circles.
5. Should preview management presentations before they are presented for the final decision.
6. Will not direct the circles in the selection of their projects. However, the committee may offer projects for consideration by the circle.
7. Shall meet a minimum of once every two months or as called by the chairperson.
8. Shall be responsible for maintaining circle records.
9. Should encourage the circle in every way.

Facilitator

Following is a list of the facilitator's responsibilities:
1. The facilitator is the circle's representative to the facilitator committee.
2. The facilitator is to meet with the circle at every meeting.
3. The facilitator will use good meeting techniques to ensure a free flow of information and work.
4. The facilitator should take a neutral position in the meetings, acting only as a guide to ensure a smooth, productive meeting.
5. The facilitator will be primarily responsible for ensuring that the circle receives the proper training.
6. The facilitator should provide input to the circle by advising on organizational policy and direction.
7. The facilitator shall be the person primarily responsible for providing information to management on circle projects and progress.

Quality circle procedures

Meetings   The quality circle shall normally meet one hour each week to work on solutions to problems chosen by the circle. They may meet more or less often, as necessary, to work on their current projects. Circle members meet on department time or are compensated by paid time or compensatory time for the time spent in meetings. They are not compensated for time spent outside meetings.

Problem selection   The circle will choose a specific project or problem to address. This project is chosen solely by the circle. However, facilitators may make suggestions for the circle to consider in its problem selection process. When such a suggestion is made to the circle, the circle members will decide whether the problem will be worked on by their group. No pressure should be placed on the circle to work on any suggested projects.

Problem solution   After a problem has been chosen, circle members shall use the problem-solving techniques they have learned in training to solve the problem. This should include testing if necessary. After a final solution has been developed and field-tested, the circle will prepare a management presentation for the manager or the staff that will make the final decision.

Work group presentation
The first presentation made by the circle should be to the members of the work group represented by the quality circle. This practice presentation will give members of the work group a chance to review and critique the presentation and the proposal.

Committee presentation
The second presentation will be to the facilitator committee. The committee should ask questions and give constructive criticism. This is in preparation for the management presentation.

Management presentation
This final presentation is to the chief's staff/bureau commanders and/or the manager with the authority to make the final decision. The presentation should be prepared so that all questions can be answered on the spot. It is at this time that the chief and/or the manager should make his decision.

Circle records
Circle records shall be kept by the facilitator committee as follows:

1.   A record is to be kept of the circle minutes from each meeting.
2.   A record of each circle's projects will be kept with all the pertinent research data and information.
3.   The master record shall be kept in the quality circle coordinator's office, located in the Planning and Research Section.